LETHAL ENGAGEMENT

LETHAL ENGAGEMENT

Barack Hussein Obama,
the United Nations & Radical Islam

Joseph A. Klein

TATE PUBLISHING & Enterprises

Published by Tate Publishing & Enterprises, LLC
127 E. Trade Center Terrace | Mustang, Oklahoma 73064 USA
1.888.361.9473 | www.tatepublishing.com

Tate Publishing is committed to excellence in the publishing industry. The company reflects the philosophy established by the founders, based on Psalm 68:11,
"The Lord gave the word and great was the company of those who published it."

Book design copyright © 2010 by Tate Publishing, LLC. All rights reserved.
Cover design by Chris Webb
Interior design by Stephanie Woloszyn

Published in the United States of America

ISBN: 978-1-61739-225-2
1. Political Science / International Relations
2. Political Science / Political Freedom & Security / International Secur
10.09.08

Dedication

To my dear wife, Roberta, whose constant love and support have made this book possible.

Acknowledgments

I wish to acknowledge Dr. Richard Tate, founder and chairman of Tate Publishing, for his belief in my book and utmost integrity and responsiveness in all of our dealings. I also wish to acknowledge the editor who helped me polish the manuscript before I submitted it for publication, Kathy Shaidle. This book also required much work from people behind the scenes at Tate Publishing, to whom I extend my gratitude.

TABLE OF CONTENTS

CHAPTER ONE

The Trojan Horse

Soon it will be a crime to criticize Islam.

Leaders of terrorist organizations such as al Qaeda, Hamas and Hezbollah will be exempt from prosecution under the new international crime of "aggression." But our government leaders and soldiers trying to eliminate the terrorist threat will not escape prosecution.

Islamic finance, based on Islamic law (known as sharia), will assume a preeminent place in a new global economic order and help finance jihadist terror at home and abroad.

These are not doomsday forecasts. They are a few of the stated goals of international Islamic leaders, who have a clear strategy of how to achieve them.

These leaders are not the al Qaeda terrorists who reject all traditional trappings of law and politics, and who impose their will by brutal force. Rather, they are radical Muslim politicians, lawyers, scholars, and clerics who regard Islam as a universalistic, supremacist socioeconomic, and political ideology. They relentlessly seek to transform existing global institutions, including international law, so they comply with sharia—the Islamic laws rooted in the Koran, the holy book of Islam; the Sunna and Hadith, the religious actions, customs and sayings of the Prophet Muhammad; and the interpretations of the classic Muslim legal schools that were largely frozen in place by the twelfth century. Under sharia, women are inferior to men, infidels are inferior to Muslims, polygamy (and in some cases, child marriage) is encouraged, and a Muslim's conversion to a non-Islam religion, homosexuality, and adultery are capital crimes.

President Barack Hussein Obama is pursuing policies of engagement with the Muslim world, including the terrorist sponsoring Islamic Republic of Iran. At the same time, Obama is bent on engaging the United Nations as if it were the central part of his foreign policy, as well as the sole arbiter of international law—all while the UN itself is rapidly succumbing to the influence of radical Islam. We are witnessing a set of lethal engagements that play right into the Islamists' hands.

The Islamists' *UN-istan Intifada*

Robert Spencer, the author of *Stealth Jihad: How Radical Islam Is Subverting America without Guns or Bombs,* uses the term "stealth jihad" to describe the nonviolent but lethal tactics Islamists are using to undermine our democratic institutions from within.[1] Their strategy involves seizing power within the institutions of modern civil society—such as academia, the media, nonprofit charities, politics, and more—then wielding them as weapons against the West itself.

In particular, the United Nations has become the Islamists' version of the Trojan horse. By penetrating and transforming the secular norms of international law through the UN, Islamists aim to infect our political and economic systems with a sharia-friendly ideology, in which strict, draconian Islamic rules apply to all people, regardless of their faith or nationality.

Despite scandal after devastating scandal, the United Nations is still regarded by many nations—including the United States under President Obama—as the most legitimate arbiter of international legal norms. And since the United States and other democracies take international legal norms and world opinion into account when crafting their own policies and domestic laws, the Islamists have now found a potent means to use our own system of laws against us. Because of his aggressive outreach to the Muslim world and his obsession with currying international approval, President Obama is leading the United States directly into the Islamists' trap.

I call the Islamists' battle plans to lay this trap the "UN-istan Intifada."

Why "UN-istan?" The names of various Islamic countries often end in the suffix "-istan"—Pakistan and Afghanistan being the most prominent examples. Formed from an old Iranian root word meaning to stand or stay, "-istan" is Persian for "place of." And all evidence indicates that now the Islamists are making the UN their "special place." How? That is where the intifada comes in.

While the term "intifada" is popularly associated with the armed uprising of Palestinians against Israeli "occupation" of the West Bank and Gaza Strip, its literal translation from the Arabic is "the act of shaking off."[2] The Islamists are "shaking off" the secular Western democratic underpinnings of the United Nations and remaking that powerful world body into a more sharia-friendly institution.

And unless President Obama stops courting the Islamists and international opinion so assiduously, the United States is in danger of becoming another "special place" for sharia-friendly institutions.

Obama Plays into the Islamists' Hands

President Obama spoke to the Muslim world from Cairo University in June 2009 and delivered nothing short of a paean to Islam. He praised Islam as the precursor of the Renaissance and the Enlightenment, and called it a religion of peace and tolerance—a sentiment he repeated three months later during a White House banquet to celebrate Ramadan.[3]

None of Obama's paeans to Islam are based in historical fact. President Obama is complicit, along with the United Nations whose power he wants to enhance, in a propaganda campaign. They are using the irreproachable shield of "religion" to disguise a barbaric system of oppressive laws. The radical ideology built on this "religion of peace and tolerance" is really the enemy of modern civilization.

And President Obama didn't just heap undeserved praise on Islam in that Cairo speech. He also apologized for the supposed transgressions of the West against the Muslim people. All this obsequiousness accomplished was to feed the Islamists' narrative of victimhood at the hands of an imaginary "neo-colonialist" American-Zionist cabal. This false narrative, constructed mostly from bizarre conspiracy theories, helps fuel resentment and murderous fury throughout the (mostly illiterate) Muslim world.

Why did President Obama reinforce the Islamists' portrayal of the United States as a fundamentally flawed nation by emphasizing this country's alleged mistakes, rather than the immense good it has done in the world? Why didn't he mention instead that the United States protected Muslims in Bosnia, aided Muslims in post-tsunami Indonesia, and liberated millions of Muslims from the yoke of brutal dictatorships in Iraq and Afghanistan—all to the tune of billions of dollars and thousands of American lives? The answer is that Obama believes the United States is too powerful for its own good. Apologizing, in his mind, offers us a way to finally cleanse ourselves of our supposed wrongs. As an act of contrition for our past arrogance, America will then submit its foreign policies to the judgment of world opinion. This, in a nutshell, is how Obama plans for America to "re-engage" with the world. How fortunate Obama must feel that the United Nations provides a ready-made global forum for just that purpose.

In his Cairo speech, President Obama declared that "it is important for Western countries to avoid impeding Muslim citizens from practicing religion *as they see fit*" (emphasis added). He apologized to the Muslim world that his country's "rules on charitable giving have made it harder for Muslims to fulfill their religious obligation." Obama then promised to change all that: "I'm committed to work with American Muslims to ensure that they can fulfill *zakat* [the Islamic duty of charitable contributions]."

Interestingly, the Holy Land Foundation for Relief and Development, a large US Islamic "charity" set up expressly to accept *zakat,* was convicted in 2008 by a federal jury for giving more than $12 million to the Palestinian terrorist organization Hamas.[4] Perhaps Obama simply forgot that all those tough rules on charitable giving exist for a good reason—to prevent such front groups posing as "charities" from funneling donations to terrorists. Or perhaps, in his zeal to make "amends," and new "friends," he simply does not care how far Islamists will go in "practicing religion *as they see fit*"— no matter the consequences.

Obama's Top State Department Legal Advisor Believes That the US Constitution Must Conform with International Norms

As for Obama's obsession with international opinion, consider his choice of Harold Koh as the State Department's top legal adviser. Koh, a former dean of Yale Law School, believes American courts should apply international legal norms to their interpretations of the Constitution—even if such norms are embodied in treaties our elected officials have previously rejected. Although Koh's spokeswoman would not confirm or deny Koh's exact words, he reportedly told a 2007 meeting of the Yale Club of Greenwich that he did not see why sharia law could not be applied to decide a case in the United States.[5] And he has unequivocally endorsed a "transnational" approach to jurisprudence, which aims to bring the US into line with international norms. So much for the self-governing sovereign nation our Founding Fathers created more than two centuries ago.

The Islamist Assault on International Norms That the West Is Too Afraid to Stop

Islamists now have the power to rewrite international law because they dominate the United Nations General Assembly, the Human Rights Council (the UN's principal human rights body), and other global forums. This dominance comes thanks to their enormous voting bloc, consisting of 56 Muslim member states. These states usually vote in unison, and often bring with them their left-leaning allies in Latin America, Asia, and Africa who like nothing more than to stick it to the Western "imperialists."

Each UN member state's vote counts equally. The more votes there are in the 192-member General Assembly for the Islamists' sharia-friendly agenda, the easier it is for them to claim that they are simply reflecting international opinion. And Obama gives every indication of wanting to be in synch with world opinion.

The Europeans often acquiesce to the Islamic agenda because they are too afraid to offend the Islamists or too economically beholden to them to take a moral stand. Indeed, some European nations are in danger of being radically transformed by their own rapidly growing Muslim populations, which have been known to riot (and worse) if they believe their religion has been insulted or reduced to second-class status.

That leaves Israel and a handful of other member states, sometimes including the United States, as the small minority voting in futile opposition to the imposition of worldwide sharia.

And with President Obama busy placating world opinion in general and the Islamists in particular, expect the United States to increasingly join in Europe's appeasement. Actually, we do not have to wait. It is already happening. Just look at Obama's groveling "engagement" with the thugs in Iran.

International Islamic Networks and Their Agendas— The Organization of Islamic Conference and the Muslim Brotherhood

The National Intelligence Council predicts that over the next fifteen years, the "force of ideology is likely to be strongest in the Muslim world" and that "[R]eligion-based networks may be quintessential issue networks and overall may play a more powerful role on many transnational issues."[6]

The Organization of Islamic Conference (OIC), with its fifty-six Muslim nations (plus the Palestinian "government") is the principal transnational network among Muslim governments. It is the second largest intergovernmental group in the world after the United Nations, where it has official observer status on a reciprocal basis. According to its Web site, the OIC has "consultative and cooperative relations with the UN and other intergovernmental organizations to protect the vital interests of the Muslims ..."[7] That is an understatement. Just take a look at its *Ten-Year Programme of Action to Meet the Challenges Facing the Muslim Ummah in the 21st Century.*[8] The Programme of Action demonstrates OIC's ambition to pack UN and other international bodies with its member states' candidates and then steer the UN's agenda "to protect and promote the collective interests of the Muslim Ummah [the worldwide community of Muslim believers]."

As a group, OIC member states pay less then 3 percent of the UN's regular annual budget.[9] Yet by coordinating a single Islamic position on key issues, the OIC has ensured that it controls 30 percent of the total votes in the General Assembly and then garners the balance of votes it needs from its left-leaning allies in Latin America, Asia, and Africa. That's how they get to limit the freedom to criticize Islam, focus human rights investigations on Israel and the West rather than on their own atrocities, and redistribute wealth to Muslim countries from the West. And the OIC had an additional advantage during the 2009–2010 General Assembly session: two of its key members, Libya and Sudan, hold the two top General Assembly positions—president and vice president, respectively.

While the OIC is the Islamists' principal intergovernmental arm, it works in tandem with the Muslim Brotherhood, the largest Islamic "people's" movement in the world. The Muslim Brotherhood was founded in Egypt in 1928 and has grown into an interlocking network of more than seventy branches worldwide.[10] The Muslim Brotherhood's central creed is that Islamic sharia should be the basis for "controlling the affairs of state and society."[11] The Brotherhood has been described as having a "double identity"—a moderate façade that engages in economic, social, educational, and political initiatives, and a violent core that supports terrorism.[12]

In its manifesto entitled *Toward a Worldwide Strategy for Islamic Policy,* the Muslim Brotherhood outlined a 12-point strategy to "establish an Islamic Power on the earth."[13] Paralleling the OIC's strategy, the Muslim Brotherhood aims "to influence centers of power ... worldwide to the service of Islam."[14] At the United Nations, the Muslim Brotherhood works through accredited "charities," "Islamic youth groups" and other activist nongovernmental organizations (NGOs) such as the Muslim World League and World Assembly of Muslims. These NGOs have significant clout in shaping the UN's agenda in "the service of Islam."

The Muslim Brotherhood has also planted roots in the United States. According to the International Analysts' Network, which reports on counter-terrorism and the Middle East, the Muslim Brotherhood "either founded or is linked to most major US Muslim organizations such as the Council on American-Islamic Relations (CAIR), the Muslim Students Association (MSA), the Muslim American Society, and the Islamic Society of North America (ISNA)."[15]

Obama Pleases the Muslim Brotherhood and the Organization of Islamic Conference

The Muslim Brotherhood has a sympathetic ear in the Obama administration. At least ten Muslim Brotherhood members were invited to attend President Obama's Cairo University address. The Egyptian daily *Al-Masyroon* reported that the invitations were "extended at the request of US Ambassador to Egypt, Margaret Scobey."[16] More efforts at engagement, no doubt, even if they involve the courting of a radical Islam organization.

The Muslim Brotherhood's North American affiliate, the Islamic Society of North America, applauded "the President's recognition of the problems Muslim American charities have been having and the hardship that resulted from the 'rules on charitable giving' by federal agencies."[17] Why not, considering that loosening those rules would make it much easier for them to fund jihad against Israel and the West?

And the Obama administration has gone further than mere rhetoric in its efforts to please radical Islamists. Consider two of Obama's appointments. His pick for special envoy to the Organization of Islamic Conference was Rashad Hussain, who served in the Obama White House counsel's office and advised Obama on the content of his Cairo speech to the Muslim world. Hussain is one of those apologists for radical Islam who in 2004 had attacked the US government's case against terrorist enabler Sami Al-Arian at a conference sponsored by the Muslim Brotherhood affiliated group, the Muslim Students Association. Al-Arian pleaded guilty in 2006 to conspiracy to aid the Palestinian terrorist group Islamic Jihad. After denying what he had said until confronted with an audiotape of his terrorist-friendly remarks, Hussain said he now regrets the way he expressed his opinion. Obama also appointed Arif Alikhan as Assistant Secretary for Policy Development in the US Department of Homeland Security. Alikhan, a Sunni Muslim, had previously served as Deputy Mayor of Homeland Security and Public Safety for the City of Los Angeles, where he derailed the police department's plan to monitor the Los Angeles Muslim community, including numerous radical local mosques and madrassas.[18]

CAIR, one of the Muslim Brotherhood-linked groups, loved Obama's appointment of Alikhan.

"Congratulations to Mr. Ali Khan on this well-deserved appointment," said CAIR-LA Executive Director Hussam Ayloush. "Mr. Alikhan's new position reflects his and the community's dedication to helping preserve the security of our country. The American Muslim community can be proud of him."[19]

Is CAIR really "proud" that President Obama has hired an Islamist who is soft on counter-terrorism to work at the very federal agency tasked with combating terrorist plots against our homeland? Certainly. They could not have asked for a better partner in the Obama administration, alongside radical Islam apologist and OIC envoy Rashad Hussain.

This is Obama-style engagement in action, enhanced by his love affair with the United Nations that the Islamists are playing like puppet masters.

CHAPTER TWO

What Are Islamists Doing with Their UN Power (And How Obama Is Helping Them)

Limits on Free Speech

David Littman, an historian and the Association for World Education's UN representative, has described how Muslim states demand, and often receive, special treatment at the United Nations when it comes to protecting Islam from criticism. He wrote that

> non-diplomatic terms such as "blasphemy" and "defamation of Islam" have seeped into the United Nations system, leading to a situation in which non-Muslim governments accept certain rules of conduct in conformity with Islamic law (the Shari`a) and acquiesce to a self-imposed silence regarding topics touching on Islam.[20]

Littman experienced this censorship firsthand when he tried to deliver a speech to the UN Human Rights Council that criticized the stoning to death of women accused of adultery, and the marriage of girls as young as nine years old, in countries where sharia law applies. He was interrupted by no fewer than sixteen points of order. The proceedings of the Council were finally suspended entirely when the Egyptian delegate proclaimed that "Islam will not be *crucified* in this Council" (emphasis added).[21]

"Intellectual freedom can't be cited in matters related to beliefs"

The Muslim Brotherhood states on its Web site that "intellectual freedom can't be cited in matters related to beliefs."[22] During a sermon in response to the Danish Muhammad cartoons that so infuriated the Islamic world, the spiritual leader of the Muslim Brotherhood, Sheikh Yusuf al-Qaradawi, demanded action from the United Nations in accordance with sharia-based conceptions of blasphemy.

Al-Qaradawi said that "the governments [of the world] must be pressured to demand that the U.N. adopt a clear resolution or law that categorically prohibits affronts to prophets—to the prophets of the Lord and his Messengers, to His holy books, and to the religious holy places."[23]

This has also been a longstanding cause of the Organization of Islamic Conference. Its ten-year plan includes the following plank: "Endeavor to have the United Nations adopt an international resolution to counter Islamophobia, and call upon all States to enact laws to counter it, including deterrent punishments."[24]

UN Resolutions Against Free Speech

The Organization of Islamic Conference is well on its way to achieving this objective. It used its power in the UN Human Rights Council and General Assembly to pass a series of resolutions defining "defamation of religions" as a violation of international law, overriding any right of free expression.[25] The OIC Secretary General Ekmeleddin Ihsanoglu, has the West in the Islamists' cross-hairs. Said Ihsanoglu with unabashed arrogance, "confronting the Danish cartoons and the Dutch film *Fitna* [which showed Muslims acting on violent passages in the Koran], we sent a clear message to the West regarding the red lines that should not be crossed."[26]

These UN resolutions codify the Islamists' core belief that "freedoms have limits, what is sacred should be respected."[27] That core belief conflicts with that of our Founding Fathers: that the sacred is best respected by maximizing individual freedom of expression and conscience. This is the essence of the First Amendment's protections for freedom of religion, freedom of speech, and the prohibition against establishment of religion by the state. America is a religious nation, but the separation of church (or mosque) and state ensures that all religious believers and nonbelievers receive equal treatment under the law and that the government will never establish an official state religion. The Islamists, on the other hand, demand that limits be placed on these freedoms under international law. In effect, they wish to establish an official *international* religion: Islam. And they are trying to accomplish this by passing Islamist resolutions by way of their United Nations Trojan horse—a model of UN-istan at work.

Saudi Hate Speech Is Exempt

The OIC dresses up its attempts to curb freedom of expression by claiming to be concerned about hate speech directed at *any* religion. OIC Secretary General Ihsanoglu made this very point at a press conference I attended at UN headquarters on September 28, 2009. He said that while "Islamophobia" was a very dangerous trend, the OIC was equally concerned about "Christian-phobia" and anti-Semitism. But the real truth was laid bare when I asked him if the OIC intended to press Saudi Arabia (where the OIC is headquartered and from which it receives much of its funding), to abolish that Islamic country's blatant discrimination against non-Muslims.

I reminded him that Christians, Jews, and other non-Muslims cannot worship in public or visit Mecca or Medina. (And, as we shall see, Saudi Arabian children are provided with hate-filled textbooks describing Christians and Jews in the vilest terms.)

Ihsanoglu replied that Saudi Arabia was a special case because it was the home of Islam's holiest cities. He added that the OIC was not responsible for Saudi Arabia's behavior. So much for the Organization of Islamic Conference's professions against religious hate *wherever* it appears.

How Is the Obama Administration Making It Easier for Islamists to Trash the First Amendment?

Any weakening of laws ensuring freedom of speech and a free press by the Obama administration or Congress helps the Islamists spread their model of UN-istan from the United Nations to the United States. So it is alarming, to say the least, that the Obama administration not only decided to join the Islamist-dominated UN Human Rights Council (which regularly produces free speech suppression resolutions) but cosponsored its own resolution with Egypt that would have the same effect. Although this resolution purports to protect freedom of expression, it feeds right into the Islamists' agenda. It condemns "the promotion by certain media of false images and negative stereotypes" and calls for action against anything that smacks of "negative racial and religious stereotyping."[28]

President Obama's choice to head the White House Office of Information and Regulatory Affairs, Cass Sunstein, supports suppression of free speech on the Internet. Sunstein believes the Internet should be regulated to ensure that "falsehoods" are not disseminated. He said that "[A] 'chilling effect' on those who would spread destructive falsehoods can be an excellent idea." To that end, he proposed a "notice and take down" law that would require bloggers and service providers to "take down falsehoods upon notice."[29] Falsehoods as defined by whom? The government no doubt.

What's more, a bill introduced in the Senate by Sen. Jay Rocke-feller, a West Virginia Democrat and chairman of the Senate Commerce Committee, would permit the president to seize temporary control of private-sector networks during a so-called "cybersecurity emergency." And in the House of Representatives, Representative Linda Sanchez from California—one of President Obama's strongest supporters—introduced a bill making it a federal felony to use the Internet, e-mails, or even the telephone to cause "substantial emotional distress" through "severe, repeated, and hostile" speech. [30]

The Federal Communications Commission, which regulates radio and television broadcasting, has named the left-wing Obama appointee Mark Lloyd as its Chief Diversity Officer.[31] Lloyd throws around innocent sounding terms like "local control," "diversity," and "accountability rules" as a subterfuge to suppress the free speech of broadcasters—especially the conservative voices with whom Lloyd and other leftists disagree. In fact, Obama's choice to enforce "diversity" in broadcasting believes that freedom of speech and press are "all too often an exaggeration" and that "blind references to freedom of speech or the press serve as a *distraction from the critical examination of other communications policies*" (emphasis added).[32]

The Obama administration has its own political reasons for trying to undermine freedom of speech and press in favor of "other communications policies." It wants to push conservative voices to the periphery of public debate—and perhaps off the air altogether. But the Islamists don't care about Obama's partisan tactics. They just like the result, which limits the First Amendment. The Muslim Brotherhood-linked Council on American-Islamic Relations (CAIR) has already intimidated certain radio stations that have broadcast criticisms of Islam or depicted Muslims in what they consider to be a negative light.[33] CAIR regularly monitors conservative broadcasts and distributed guidelines to broadcasters about what they should and should not say about Islam.[34] And consistent with the Islamists' strategy to leverage the UN norm against "defamation of religions," CAIR has used the American legal system to bring, in its words, "a defamation lawsuit against those who make false claims against the Muslim community."[35]

The Obama administration's regulations of the Internet and broadcasting, as well as proposed legislation in both houses of the Democratic Congress, would arm Islamists with powerful legal tools to stop Internet users and broadcasters from "defaming" Islam or face punitive consequences. And they have found a new ally on the UN Human Rights Council that supports the erosion of free expression—the United States of America under President Obama.

Letting Terrorists off the Hook

There's No Such Thing as Islamic Terror

In addition to its campaign to punish defamers of Islam, the OIC blocked the United Nations from even defining the terms "terror" or "terrorism." The Islamists do not want groups like Hamas and Hezbollah to be defined as terrorists, for example, irrespective of how many innocent women and children they deliberately target for death. Instead, the Islamists want these murderers classified as heroic resistance fighters.[36]

For his part, until he realized that he had no choice but to respond forcefully to the al Qaeda-directed Christmas Day 2009 plot that nearly succeeded in taking down a passenger flight over Detroit, President Obama would not even use the phrase "war on terror," and his administration has banned the term "jihad" to describe Islamic-inspired violence against nonbelievers. He is playing games with words, just as the Islamists are doing—blurring the truth in the process.

New International Crime Exempts Terrorists

In another victory for the terrorists, a new universal crime of "aggression" is being considered for adoption by the International Criminal Court (ICC). "Aggression" committed by *individual* leaders of member states will henceforth be subject to prosecution—but, conveniently for Islamists—the likes of Hamas, Hezbollah, and al Qaeda murderers would be exempt from prosecution. By sleight of hand, an intergovernmental working group is resurrecting an old 1974 UN General Assembly resolution defining "aggression" as an invasion or similar military action by one member state against another. This Special Working Group on the Crime of Aggression is an arm of the Assembly of States Parties to the Rome Statute of the International Criminal Court. Working closely with UN officials, it intends to use that older General Assembly resolution to establish a new universal crime of aggression committed by *individual leaders of member state governments.* [37]

In response to my question at a press briefing at United Nations headquarters in February 2009, the chairman of the Special Working Group on the Crime of Aggression finally admitted what had been buried in all of the UN-speak—that the individuals subject to prosecution for the new "universal" crime of aggression "would *not include acts of terrorism performed by non–State actors, such as leaders of Al-Qaida*" (emphasis added).[38]

This means that if a democratic nation's leaders were to order military attacks on terrorist strongholds in another state or territory in response to a terrorist attack, they could be prosecuted by the International Criminal Court under the Working Group's definition of the crime of aggression. However, the Islamic terrorists whose aggressive acts initiated the conflict in the first place would escape prosecution. This is another example of the perverse makeover of international law—this time, in the Alice-in-Wonderland world of the UN-affiliated International Criminal Court.

The United States is not a signatory to the Rome Statute, which is the treaty establishing the International Criminal Court. Yet its chief prosecutor, Luis Moreno Ocampo, told me during a press briefing at UN headquarters on December 4, 2009, that he still has jurisdiction to prosecute anyone whom he alleges to be war criminals operating in Afghanistan, for example, because Afghanistan is a signatory to the treaty. This means that American soldiers are in his sights. So are our government leaders who ordered strikes by unmanned drones that killed terrorist leaders in Afghanistan but also resulted in limited unintended civilian casualties.

You would think these consequences might worry the Obama administration. But you would be wrong. The administration regrets not being a part of the International Criminal Court, according to Secretary of State Hillary Clinton.[39] In a telling sign of what is to come, the Obama administration has decided to take the interim step of participating as an observing non-State Party during the first Review Conference of the Rome Statute of the International Criminal Court involving negotiations of key issues such as the proposed addition of the crime of aggression to the jurisdiction of the Court. It may just be a matter of time before the United States officially joins the International Criminal Court, in yet another demonstration of President Obama's zeal to win favor in the court of international opinion.

Economic War against Capitalism

In the economic sphere, rising oil revenue and the global economic crisis have provided Islamists with a valuable opportunity to promote sharia-based finance, which adheres to the laws of the Koran (including its prohibition against charging interest). The Islamic system is presented as a fairer system than Western-style free market capitalism. The Islamists' pitch is that the 2008–2009 economic meltdown would not have occurred had global banking been based on Islamic practices.

What are those practices? Islamic banking "is governed by strict religious laws and principles, it has a clear implementation strategy, and importantly, is non-debt based."[40] We will examine Islamic finance and the hypocrisy that underlies it in a later chapter. But hypocrisy does not stop many opportunists in the West from taking it seriously.

French Finance Minister Christine Lagarde said in late 2008, for example, that "Islamic finance is calling out to us" as global leaders try to establish "new principles for the international financial system."[41]

The UN's Push for a Global Currency

To help broadcast the Islamists' siren call to the world, an interlocking network has developed between Muslim institutions promoting global Islamic finance within the United Nations. This network wants to replace the US dollar as the world's recognized reserve currency, and substitute an as-yet-to-be-concocted global reserve currency, under UN auspices.

For example, the International Centre for Education in Islamic Finance (ICEIF) was established in 2006 "to support the global development of the Islamic financial industry."[42] The chairperson of the ICEIF is the governor of Malaysia's central bank, Dr. Zeti Akhtar Aziz. In speeches delivered to various Islamic finance forums, she has touted the success of Malaysia's Islamic-based economy and laid out a broader mission: "positioning Islamic finance as an integrated component of the International Financial System."[43] She has also noted that "Shariah is the key pillar of Islamic finance from which Islamic finance derives its unique characteristics."[44]

Dr. Aziz believes that "a global reserve currency" is "a viable proposal that should be considered."[45] Her government is pushing to replace the US dollar with the Islamic gold dinar as the new alternative international reserve currency.[46]

Guess where Dr. Aziz has been working lately? She has been contributing her expertise on Islamic finance as a key member of the *United Nations Commission of Experts on Reforms of the International Monetary and Financial System.*[47]

Another UN Global Conference
and Task Force of Experts

This high-level task force was tasked by the UN General Assembly with recommending radical reforms to the global economic system. The task force's recommendations were discussed during the June 2009 UN Conference on the World Financial and Economic Crisis and its Impact on Development.

The initiator and organizer of this bloviation session was Miguel d'Escoto Brockmann of Nicaragua, the president of the UN General Assembly for the 2008–2009 term. D'Escoto also was responsible for appointing the members of the UN Commission of Experts. [48]

When you meet d'Escoto Brockmann in person as I did, he seems like a gentle soul. But this former priest's low-key manner belies his radical message. When you listen to *what* he has to say in his muted tone, you understand why he was suspended from his priestly duties by the Vatican two decades ago and reprimanded by the late Pope John Paul II for his involvement with the left-wing Nicaraguan Sandinistas.[49] He quickly steered the conference agenda to reflect his redistributionist ideology. And he started the redistribution ball rolling by putting two of his own relatives on his staff— paid out of UN funds—to help him organize the conference.[50]

This anti-American Marxist counts among his friends Iranian president Mahmoud Ahmadinejad, whom he claims has been unfairly "demonized" by the United States. Needless to say, d'Escoto Brockmann's effusive praise of Ahmadinejad got a lot of play in the Islamic press.[51]

The alliance between the radical left and the Islamists is alive and well.

In addition to appointing Dr. Aziz to his twenty-two-member UN Commission of Experts, d'Escoto Brockmann brought in Malaysian economist Jomo Kwame Sundaram, who is also the Assistant Secretary-General for Economic Development in the

United Nations Department of Economic and Social Affairs. Sundaram is the UN's own resident expert on Islamic finance.[52]

"The international financial system needs urgent overhaul as the current infrastructure is a mess...To call the current global financial system an architecture is an insult to architects," claimed this UN economist.[53]

A Nobel Prize Laureate Joins Forces with the UN to Undermine Western Capitalism

So in preparation for his June 2009 economic and financial conference of world leaders, d'Escoto stacked the deck with his own picks on the Commission of Experts and with his own relatives on his staff. But he cleverly made sure the chairman of the Commission was a world-recognized economist whose credentials alone would legitimize the Commission's conclusions and recommendations. For this role, d'Escoto Brockmann selected Dr. Joseph Stiglitz, the winner of the Nobel Prize for economics in 2001 and former senior vice president and chief economist of the World Bank.

But Dr. Stiglitz is not a neutral academic who could be expected to provide an objective, rigorous analysis of the economic crisis. He has his own policy biases, which are not necessarily friendly to Western free market capitalism. He has called, in one of his articles, for "another world," while attacking the United States.[54] In another article he praised the "Malaysian miracle."[55]

When I asked Dr. Stiglitz during a press briefing at United Nations headquarters whether Islamic finance contained any lessons for a new global economic order, he praised the sharia-based system for focusing on "non-exploitative lending" and as an antithesis of American-style financing. "One of the characteristics of the American financial market is that they discovered that there was money at the bottom of the pyramid and worked hard to ensure it didn't remain there," he quipped. "There has been a shortage of...ethics guiding lending practices."[56]

So it is little surprise that, under Dr. Stiglitz's leadership, d'Escoto Brockmann's handpicked UN Commission of Experts recommended a massive reordering of the world economy involving trillions of dollars of wealth transfers, global regulation, and global taxes, all under the supervision of the United Nations.[57]

Predictably, the Commission of Experts also recommended dumping the dollar as the standard international reserve currency, and the instrument for international payments for products traded on the global market, such as oil. In its place would be a new "Global Reserve System," created and controlled by an international financial governance institution under UN oversight.[58]

In a separate but overlapping report, the UN Conference on Trade and Development, in conjunction with the United Nations Department of Economic and Social Affairs and several regional UN commissions, reached essentially the same conclusion. Their interagency report was entitled *World Economic Situation and Prospects 2009—Global Outlook 2009.*[59]

In a pre-release of their report during the three-day UN-organized International Conference on Financing for Development held in the Muslim country of Qatar, the UN agencies said that "use of the dollar as the global reserve currency is an intrinsic source of instability." The agencies recommended "a multilaterally backed multi-currency system which, perhaps, over time could evolve into a single, world currency-backed system."[60]

There is a good explanation for some of the overlap between the UN Commission of Experts and the UN interagency reports. Recall that the Malaysian economist Jomo Kwame Sundaram, who is a member of the UN Commission of Experts, is also the Assistant Secretary-General of the UN Department of Economic and Social Affairs, the department that co-authored the interagency report.

In an interview he held at the UN's Qatar conference (at which President Mahmud Amadinijad of Iran and President Robert Mugabe of Zimbabwe were among the "distinguished" speakers), Sundaram told reporters that the United States was responsible for the economic crisis. This UN Assistant Secretary-General and member of the UN Commission of Experts went on to say that "[L]eadership by exclusive groups such as the G7 and the G20 have been found wanting, they've certainly not been inclusive, and certainly lack legitimacy ... It is very important that the redesign of the international financial system involves a process of inclusiveness and multilateralism."[61]

The Impact of the UN's Conference on the World Financial and Economic Crisis

I observed portions of the UN conference from the press gallery of the General Assembly hall. The hall was half-empty, and many of those in attendance were not paying much attention. No wonder, since speech after speech repeated the same tired charges against capitalism. The Iranian representative, for instance, threw out the standard anti-US verbal fusillades about "unjust income distribution," "system injustices," and the "greedy attitudes of a few." He lambasted what he called the "self-authorized" bodies such as G-8 and G-20, which he said must be replaced by the entire United Nations membership. He even managed to bring the wars in Afghanistan and Iraq into his address.

I'm sure that President Ahmadinejad would have liked to attend the UN economic and finance conference personally and make another anti-American, anti-Israel General Assembly speech. But he was too busy at home trying to cling to power, in the wake of mass protests against his rigged re-election. This included the arrest of seventy professors from universities across Iran, after they met with the opposition leader Mir Hossein Mousavi.[62] Arrests, torture, and executions were Ahmadinejad's responses to his critics.

Because of the radical direction the conference was taking, the United States and other Western countries declined to send their top leaders to the conference. Nor did the conference get much attention in the press. But what makes it potentially significant is not what was said in the speeches, but rather what was memorialized in the Commission of Experts Report and in the final outcome document.[63] These documents put a marker in the ground, with the active participation and endorsement of the renowned economist Dr. Stiglitz, for a global reserve currency in place of the dollar and new global governance institutions under the auspices of the United Nations. Dr. Stiglitz repeated these recommendations in his oral remarks at the conference with a tone of moral indignation against the present global order.

One wonders why Dr. Stiglitz did not speak out with equal moral indignation (or, for that matter, at all) against the arrest of his fellow academics in Iran, instead of bolstering Ahmadinejad's pal Brockmann's radical and destructive plans to change the entire economic and financial global architecture.

The United States government gave mixed signals regarding the conference. That's a polite way of saying that the Obama administration, as usual, spoke out of both sides of its mouth. On the one hand, the United States Mission to the UN declared that "the UN does not have the expertise or mandate to serve as a suitable forum or provide direction for meaningful dialogue on a number of issues addressed … such as reserve systems." But at the same time, the US ambassador to the UN, Susan Rice, said the "UN's universal membership and its well-institutionalized intergovernmental process gives it a unique advantage in responding to many dimensions of the crisis."[64] Guess which side of the Obama administration's mouth will ultimately have the last word?

In any event, the concerted drive for these radical changes will not fade with the end of the conference. Creating a crisis mentality and assembling panels of "experts" to address these "crises," and then pressuring world leaders to adopt game-changing reforms under its auspices—this is simply the way the UN operates. And Obama is bowing in the UN's direction.

There is already talk of establishing a permanent panel of economic experts to keep pushing for the radical changes recommended by the Commission. The UN's scare-mongering Intergovernmental Panel on Climate Change is the most famous precedent for this sort of thing. That environmental panel produced a report by 2,500 scientists from 130 countries that was meant to "shock people, governments into taking more serious action" to avert "global warming," in the words of the panel's chairman.[65] And that is precisely what is happening, despite serious questions being raised about the integrity of the data underlying the report, as a new (and extremely costly) global climate treaty, with the Obama administration's buy-in, is being pushed forward aggressively by the United Nations.

Similarly, the UN uses American taxpayers' hard-earned dollars to set in motion the crisis mentality, rationales, and mechanisms which in turn undermine the value of the dollar as the de facto global reserve currency. Sooner or later, as the dollar's value continues to deteriorate, the Obama administration will cave and hand the UN the key leadership role in steering economic and financial global governance.

CHAPTER THREE

Why Care What the United Nations Does? (Because Obama Does, and So Do Our Courts)

Why should Americans care what happens at the UN? After all, it is largely ineffectual and has no real enforcement powers. And laws are only binding if made by governmental entities with duly constituted powers to enforce them. Thankfully, the United Nations has no such formal authority (with the possible exception of Security Council resolutions passed pursuant to its enforcement powers under Article VII of the UN Charter). As long experience has borne out, the Security Council's enforcement powers are only as robust as the willingness of member states to abide by them. So long as the United States maintains its veto power in the Security Council, the theory goes, the UN is unable to do much harm.

So what difference does it make what the United Nations' 192 member states decide to do? Well, for one thing, the United States provides the UN with nearly 25 percent of its total budget. Hardworking American taxpayers subsidize the UN to the tune of over $1 billion each year, including activities that are actually hostile to our national interests and values.

Wasting money on this dysfunctional organization is bad enough. As we shall see in chapter six, we are being robbed blind by mismanaged and corrupt UN agencies—and the beneficiaries in this "Robin Hood" scheme are often anti-American Islamists.

The UN was kept at arm's length during George Bush's administration. The UN was treated as an annoying but meaningless outlet for mostly powerless nations to release their frustrations, while occasionally performing some good humanitarian deeds, albeit inefficiently. The US formed multilateral coalitions to accomplish its foreign policy objectives, rather than rely on the United Nations.

But that changed drastically for the worse under the Obama administration. The UN was granted pride of place at the very center of American foreign policy. UN ambassador Susan Rice even has a cabinet rank, to show the world how important the Obama administration believes the United Nations is to the US government. The Obama administration bows to the UN's pronouncements of international consensus, regardless of the consequences to our national interests or values. Gone is the blunt condemnation of immoral UN actions that former UN ambassadors Daniel Patrick Moynihan, Jeane Kirkpatrick, and John Bolton expressed.

Obama's "Partnership with the Muslim World"

Obama's Mea Culpas

While fawning over the United Nations, President Obama is making amends to the Muslim world for what he claims are past mistakes by the United States.

In his speech on Islamic-American relations in Cairo on June 4, 2009, Obama declared that

> tension has been fed by colonialism that denied rights and opportunities to many Muslims and a Cold War in which Muslim majority countries were too often treated as proxies without regard to their own aspirations. Moreover, the sweeping change

brought by modernity and globalization led many Muslims to view the West as hostile to the traditions of Islam.[66]

In a speech he delivered several months earlier to the Turkish Parliament, Obama intoned: "Let me say this as clearly as I can. The United States is not and will never be at war with Islam. In fact, our partnership with the Muslim world is critical."[67]

News Flash to President Obama— Islamists Have Been at War with the United States Since the Days of the Founding Fathers

We may not be at war with Islam, but the Islamists are at war with the United States and the free world. And they hate us because of who we are, not for any alleged harm that we've ever caused them. Only three years after the United States won its independence, when there was no Jewish state for Muslims to resent, and no American troops on Muslim soil, Thomas Jefferson, then US ambassador to France, and John Adams, then US ambassador to Britain, learned from a Muslim ambassador to Britain why the Muslims were so hostile toward Americans, even then.

Jefferson and Adams were attempting to negotiate a peace treaty with the Muslim "Barbary pirates," an exercise that ultimately proved to be futile.[68]

As Jefferson and Adams later reported to Congress, the Muslim ambassador explained to them that Islam

> was founded on the Laws of their Prophet, that it was written in their Koran, that all nations who should not have acknowledged their authority were sinners, that it was their right and duty to make war upon them wherever they could be found, and to make slaves of all they could take as Prisoners, and that every Musselman [Muslim] who should be slain in Battle was sure to go to Paradise.[69]

This hostility, so intense then, has not abated more than two hundred years later. But the Islamists' methods have come a long way from those far-off attacks by pirates (although lately we have witnessed a resurgence in that tactic, too.). Violent Islamic terrorism and nonviolent "stealth" jihadism are the new dual threat. But sadly, President Obama fails to grasp that the supremist, sharia-inspired ideology underlying both threats is one and the same. So is the Islamists' end-game, even if their methods may vary amongst them.

Eventually, Obama's "partnership with the Muslim world" will lead to paralysis, lest we "offend" our newfound "friends." Changes in the language we use reflect this. As far as the Obama administration is concerned, the global war against Islamic terrorism is an "Overseas Contingency Operation."[70] Don't you feel much safer now?

Obama Legitimizes the Anti-Free Speech, Anti-Semitic UN Human Rights Council

And, in a troubling demonstration of his desired partnership with the Muslim world, President Obama has lent legitimacy to the worst body in the United Nations, by joining the UN Human Rights Council. Even the hopelessly liberal *New York Times* called the Human Rights Council "dysfunctional."[71] Despite its Orwellian name, the Human Rights Council is run by the world's worst human rights abusers and dominated by the Islamic bloc of member states. Remember, it was the Human Rights Council that initiated the Islamists' infamous "defamation of religions" resolutions and then pressured the General Assembly to pass them. As Anne Bayefsky, editor of EYEontheUN, put it, "the United States is joining a fundamentally flawed body in order to make it something that it isn't."[72]

As the UN's biggest financial supporter, the United States should insist on scrapping the Human Rights Council rather than becoming a member. Otherwise, we will be cooperating with its unconstitutional resolutions that make criticism of Islam an international crime, and will be unable to prevent other threats to our democratic values. As we have seen in chapter two, this has already begun to happen. Recall that the United States cosponsored a Human Rights Council resolution with Egypt that condemned "the promotion by certain media of false images and negative stereotypes" and called for action against anything that smacks of "negative racial and religious stereotyping."

We know from his extensive outreach efforts that President Obama will not risk offending his partners in the Muslim world. He is unlikely to stand against the UN Human Rights Council that is so beloved by the Islamists, even though it produces atrocious resolutions that strike at the heart of our core beliefs.

If the potential consequences flowing from such resolutions never reached beyond the halls of the Human Rights Council and General Assembly where the Islamists hold sway, they would not matter much. However, international human rights norms are now influencing decisions made in US courts.[73] The legal protections and entitlements that have been swept under the rubric of "human rights" have grown exponentially over the years. And the most prolific source of international human rights norms happens to be the United Nations.

Transnationalizing the US Constitution

Our activist courts are increasingly bent on internationalizing the US Constitution and US law, particularly in the realm of human rights. This trend in the judiciary is an example of "transnationalism," the global movement to merge the economic, social, and legal systems of countries without regard to national sovereignty.[74]

As we have seen, the Islamists have captured the UN General Assembly and Human Rights Council, in which international legal norms are created and given legitimacy. The Islamists' power to influence those norms will lead to laws with a decidedly sharia-friendly bias. Transnational judges rely upon these very norms to interpret our constitutional provisions in ways that best conform to international law. As American constitutional law morphs into international law, international law morphs into sharia law—until eventually, sharia law may well be declared "constitutional." After all, as President Obama said in his Cairo speech, we must not do anything to impede the Islamists "from practicing religion *as they see fit*."

Constitutional Rights for Terrorists

Most Supreme Court justices already use international norms and foreign laws to interpret the United States Constitution.[75] For example, by invalidating the special military tribunals set up by the Bush Administration to try enemy combatants held at Guantánamo Bay, the Court inexplicably granted civilian protection (under Common Article 3 of the Geneva Conventions) to suspected terrorists, including al Qaeda. The Court reasoned that the detainees were entitled to "protections recognized by customary international law."[76]

However, Common Article 3—like the rest of the Geneva Conventions—was written before the advent of organized but stateless global terrorism, which targets innocent civilians worldwide in violation of the most elementary laws of war. These terrorists set off bombs, impersonate civilians or police to infiltrate and then assassinate their enemy, hide among the civilian population, and use mosques as terrorist sanctuaries. When captured, these are not uniformed soldiers who have peacefully surrendered, nor are they innocent bystanders caught in the crossfire of a civil war—the sorts of hapless individuals that Common Article 3 was intended to protect. They are dangerous killers who hate America and will plot to kill American civilians the first chance they get if they are ever released.

After the Supreme Court handed down this disastrous decision, it determined that terror suspects designated as "enemy combatants" are also entitled to have their habeas corpus petitions heard in federal civil court. In so doing, the Supreme Court struck down an earlier congressional statute that created an alternative process of military and civil review. Rather than defer to the judgments of elected legislative and executive branches of government, the Court ruled in favor of terrorist suspects. This was the course of action recommended by the then UN High Commissioner for Human Rights, Louise Arbour, who had filed a Friend of the Court brief in the case. [77]

As long as incarceration in offshore US detention facilities triggers full judicial involvement, and the courts continue to apply criminal law procedures to military detention, dangerous terrorists will be released to wreak more harm on US citizens. With President Obama's plans to close Guantánamo in 2010, and his Attorney General Eric Holder's intention to try some al Qaeda ringleaders (including possibly the 9/11 mastermind Khaleid Sheikh Mohammed) in federal civil court with full constitutional protections, the possibility becomes a probability.

Internationalizing the Constitution

Transnationalist justices also give international human rights norms priority above the domestic policy judgments made by our elected officials. Justice Breyer (whom President Obama considers his ideal Supreme Court justice) described the process in terms of "cross-country results that resemble each other more and more, exhibiting common, if not universal, principles in a variety of legal areas." Obama signaled his desire to move the Supreme Court more in Justice Breyer's internationalist direction with the nomination of Solicitor General Elana Kagan for the Supreme Court. Kagan is a transnationalist. Perhaps recalling that when Kagan was Harvard Law School's dean the law school had opened an Islamic Finance Project, Obama invited the Director of the Washington, DC office of the radical Muslim Public Affairs Council to join the President and cabinet officials at the White House as he announced Kagan's nomination. As Harvard Law School's dean, she also oversaw the introduction into the *mandatory* first-year law curriculum a class "that looks at law in a comparative or international framework." Constitutional law, however, is no longer a required course. During her confirmation hearings for the position of Solicitor General, Kagan said that she supported using foreign law in the office's legal arguments, noting the Justices who were receptive to such arguments particularly in cases applying the so-called "evolving standards of decency." It is no surprise that Kagan has received the active support for her Supreme Court nomination from progressive human rights organizations that favor US submission to UN human rights law, such as the Leadership Conference on Civil and Human Rights. [78]

Recall that the single most prolific source of "universal principles" of international human rights law is the United Nations. And the forces in control of the UN's Human Rights Council and General Assembly are the Islamists who believe that anyone disparaging their religion is violating Muslims' "universal" human rights and deserves to be punished.

Libya was elected president of the UN General Assembly for the 2009–2010 session. *Sudan, whose president is currently evading an international arrest warrant on war crimes and crimes against humanity, serves as the General Assembly's vice-president.* What's more, Algeria was elected chairperson of the UN's Legal Committee, the primary forum for the consideration of legal questions in the General Assembly, and Iran was elected a vice-chair.

With this dynamic quartet of Islamic countries running the world's "most representative" chamber and its primary legal forum, more sharia-friendly resolutions can be expected. President Obama, in turn, is nominating more transnational judges to the Supreme Court and lower courts. And these judges will most certainly listen very carefully to what the Islamic-led General Assembly has to say.

Destroying the Dollar

On the economic front, as we have seen, the UN is exploiting the economic meltdown to try to replace the US dollar as the global reserve currency.

President Obama has already inflicted significant damage on the US economy through reckless spending and tax programs, and statist encroachments on the free market. However, he will wreck our economy altogether if, as appears to be the case, he goes along with the UN's radical proposals for re-engineering the entire international economic order.

How Islamists Will Capitalize on the Economic Crisis

Here is how the plan is supposed to play out.

Islamists will rally their ideological troops around the idea that free market capitalism is the sole cause of the global economic crisis. They will reach out to non-Muslim countries that also resent the US dollar's unique status as the world's de facto global reserve currency.

At the Fifth World Islamic Economic Forum hosted by Indonesia in March 2009, for example, Bank Indonesia Governor Boediono boasted that "sharia-based banking and economy were virtually at 'no risk' of succumbing to a crisis if implemented correctly, because unlike the conventional capital system, they rejected speculative practices without underline transactions—the culprit behind the ongoing global crisis."[79]

Malaysian Prime Minister Abdullah Ahmad Badawi opened that forum with the declaration that the Western financial system had collapsed because of "unbridled greed" and that Islamic finance was an alternative to a failed Wall Street model.[80]

And Sheikh Yusuf al-Qaradawi, spiritual leader of the Muslim Brotherhood, told an international conference hosted by the Al-Quds (Jerusalem) International Institution that "[T]he collapse of the capitalist system, which is based on usury and securities rather than commodities in markets, shows us that it is undergoing a crisis and that our integrated Islamic philosophy—if properly understood and applied—can replace the Western capitalism."[81] The conference was attended by Muslim and non-Muslim organizations.

Don't Trust the Dollar, Say the Oil Bandits

Since the economic crisis began in the United States, Islamists argue, the dollar can no longer be trusted as the global reserve currency. "We really need a system where a national issuer of currency does not have the added responsibility of providing global currency," declared the UN's Islamic economics expert Jomo Kwame Sundaram whom, as we have seen, is also UN Assistant Secretary-General for Economic Development, and a member of the UN Commission of Experts on Reforms of the International Monetary and Financial System.[82]

Oddly enough, these critics never mention the unbridled greed of OPEC members, whose extortionate prices per barrel of oil burdened oil consuming countries in the months leading up to the economic meltdown. In fact, the use of oil as an economic weapon against the West was the brainchild of the Muslim Brotherhood's Sheikh Yusuf al-Qaradawi himself.[83]

Islamists contend that since the price of oil is pegged to the dollar, a volatile dollar leads to volatile oil prices. The theory goes that an increase in the price of oil in dollars equals precisely the decrease in the value of the dollar (because more devalued dollars are needed to pay for a barrel of oil, to match the target price the OPEC cartel have established.) However, while there is a correlation between the exchange value of the dollar and the price of oil pegged to the dollar, the fact is that between 1999 and 2008 the dollar has depreciated by 30 percent, while the price of oil today is ten times what it was in 1999.[84] Moreover, according to an energy infrastructure counterterrorism specialist with the US Department of the Interior the price of oil shot skyward between March and June 2008, even though the value of the dollar held relatively steady.[85]

Not to exonerate Wall Street, the banks, and the US government for helping bring about the economic crisis, but surely something else must have pushed our economy over the cliff. There was indeed, and the Muslim Brotherhood's Sheikh Yusuf al-Qaradawi has given us the answer. The sharp increase in the price of oil set by the OPEC cartel was the economic weapon the Sheikh knew would set the West's economic decline in motion. This put downward pressure on the dollar and supposedly showed the world how inferior Western capitalism is to the Islamic economic system.

"All riches are ours," said the Muslim Brotherhood's spiritual leader. "The Islamic nation has all or nearly all the oil, and we have an economic philosophy no one else has."[86]

Unsurprisingly, oil-exporting countries such as Russia and members of OPEC also question the dollar's continued viability as the global reserve currency. So does China, which holds the largest reserve of dollars in the world. And the European Union has its "Euro" waiting in the wings to push the dollar aside—assuming it survives its own crisis of confidence. Sooner or later, particularly if the dollar deteriorates further thanks to massive stimulus spending (financed by the Federal Reserve's newly printed money), the world's major holders of dollars will revolt.

Islamists see all these developments leading to "a rapid international abandonment of the dollar as the international currency, which would in turn 'bring down the towers' of the heavily debt-ridden US economy."[87] (That's an interesting turn of phrase following al Qaeda's physical destruction of the World Trade Center towers in 2001, which had symbolized the strength of America's economy!)

The UN Is Supposed to Rescue the World Economy by Bringing Down the Evil Dollar

If enough major holders of the US dollars as their reserve currency switch to an alternative, the value of the dollar will crash. *That is where the United Nations comes in.* Under control of America's adversaries, the UN will lead the stampede of nations no longer willing to trade in US dollars.

While Islamists prefer the gold dinar as the alternative reserve currency of choice, some acknowledge that switch will be a hard sell because of its potential negative impact on non-gold producing countries. The adoption of the gold dinar could also result in the emergence of a few powerful, newly dominant gold-producing countries.[88] China and Russia have talked about a "basket of currencies" approach to a new global reserve currency. Thus, the most likely candidate will be the new synthetic global reserve currency recommended by the United Nations Commission of Experts on Reforms of the International Monetary and Financial System. This new global reserve currency's value will most likely be established by a UN body, assigning relative weights to an assortment of member state currencies, to reduce American purchasing power in relation to that of oil exporting and developing countries.

While denying any desire to embrace a new global reserve currency, President Obama went along with provocative reforms at 2009 Group of 20 summit meetings, presumably to show undeveloped countries how much he wants to get along with the rest of the world. Specifically, he signed on to International Monetary Fund's (IMF) surveillance of the US economy, the creation of a global "Financial Stability Board," and use of the IMF-created international reserve asset called Special Drawing Rights to provide funding to undeveloped countries.[89]

These reforms will eventually lead to the death of the US dollar as the world's reserve currency. According to an October 2009 report,

Gulf Arabs are planning—along with China, Russia, Japan and France—to end dollar dealings for oil, moving instead to a basket of currencies including the Japanese yen and Chinese yuan, the euro, gold and a new, unified currency planned for nations in the Gulf Co-operation Council, including Saudi Arabia, Abu Dhabi, Kuwait and Qatar.[90]

President Obama's response to date has been passive at best, complicit at worst, in agreeing to subject our economy to this new UN-centric global regimen.

If and when the conversion away from the dollar begins in earnest—which the chairman of the UN Commission of Experts, Dr. Stiglitz, hopes will happen as early as 2010[91]—we may well find ourselves giving away dollar devalued hard assets at ridiculously low prices to countries in the Middle East that are hostile to our democratic values. The United States will be forced to accumulate enough of this new currency to pay our debts and purchase oil and other commodities.

Moreover, the US government will no longer be able to borrow money at a comparatively cheap rate, since there will no longer be a significantly larger market for the dollar than for other currencies. This will have a ripple effect throughout our economy. Americans will end up paying much higher interest rates on their credit purchases, including automobiles and houses. [92]

With consumer demand drying up, our economy could then sink into a catastrophic depression from which we may not recover for many years—the Islamist dream come true. And the United Nations, with our money, will have sold us the rope we used to hang ourselves.

CHAPTER FOUR

What Do the Islamists Want?

No Need to Obey the "Kaffars"

President Obama has praised Islam for its "proud tradition of toler-ance."[93] What he does not seem to understand is that the Islamists' notion of tolerance is very different from ours.

Except for the most fanatical jihadists, it is true that the Islamists are not obsessed with having to convert every last human being on earth into a devout Muslim. In fact, they pride themselves on their "tolerance" of non-Muslims living in Muslim society—so long as those non-Muslims do or say nothing to offend Muslims, of course. Islamists really want the West to adapt its democratic political, eco-nomic, and social systems to accommodate Muslim supremacism.[94]

Islamists also want the West to pay the equivalent of the Islamic *jizya* tax, which was the special tax required of non-Muslims living amidst Muslims.[95] Such non-Muslims are called *dhimmis* because, rather than become Muslims themselves, they agree to pay the *jizya* with "willing submission."[96] The Koran commands Muslims to

[F]ight those who believe not in Allah nor the Last Day, nor hold that forbidden which hath been forbidden by Allah and

His Messenger, nor acknowledge the religion of Truth, (even if they are) of the People of the Book [Christians and Jews], until they pay the *Jizya* with willing submission, and feel themselves subdued.[97]

Now think of all those petrodollars flowing from the West to OPEC members, most of which are Islamic countries. They are, quite simply, today's version of the *jizya*.[98] Islamists also use sharia-based finance in the West to exact charity or tithing known as *zakat*, which the Islamists spend to support their supremacist causes.[99] We will examine these tools used by the Islamists to finance jihad in a later chapter.

Islamic Definition of Tolerance: We Accommodate Whatever They Want, and They (Might) Leave Us Alone

As long as the laws and customs of our own country accommodate Islamists' requirements, no matter how alien they are to our way of life, and we continue to replenish the Islamists' coffers, most Islamists do not care whether we kaffars [unbelievers] bow to Mecca five times a day, wear long beards or face coverings for women, or fast for Ramadan. For now.

As Robert Spencer observes in *Stealth Jihad* (with numerous citations to Islamic sources to back up his observation), "[T]he object of both the classical and the contemporary jihad is not the mass conversion of Westerners to Islam ... but the chastened subservience of non-Muslim states, groups and individuals, and their recognition of the superiority and hegemony of Islam."[100]

Spencer cites an internationally renowned Iraqi scholar of Islamic law, who explained in his 1955 book *War and Peace in the Law of Islam* that Islamic law refuses to recognize the peaceful co-existence of non-Muslim and Muslim communities "except perhaps as subordinate entities, because by its very nature a universal state tolerates the existence of no other state than itself."[101]

Another twentieth century Muslim scholar put the Islamists' objective this way: " ... the objective of Islamic jihad is to eliminate the rule of an un-Islamic system ... Islam does not intend to confine this revolution to a single state or a few countries; the aim of Islam is to bring about a universal revolution."[102]

Accordingly, Islamists don't believe they have to submit to any laws except the divine laws of Allah (sharia). They reject the notion that any "kaffar" could wield authority over them, based on such Koran tenets as the following:

The rule is to none but Allah. [6:57]

If anyone rules by other than what Allah has revealed they are kafiroon (unbelievers). [5:44]

Clearly, a pluralistic society—in which Islam is one of many beliefs, with no more and no less legal recognition than any other belief (or nonbelief)—is incompatible with this worldview. Islamists believe that laws passed in Western democracies are invalid if they impose "barriers which prevent the people from having access to the call of Islam."[103] So if Allah required the segregation of men and women, then laws in our secular democratic society that protect the equal civil rights of men and women are seen to interfere with *Muslims' freedom* to practice *their* religion as they see fit. If freedom of expression, as defined and protected in Western law, leads to the publication of cartoons or writings in non-Muslim countries that Muslims believe are insulting to their religion or prophet, then Muslims feel that it is their religious duty to demand the creation of special laws that outlaw "defamation of religions."

In his outreach to the Muslim world, President Obama promised to do all that he can to ensure that there is nothing in *our* laws to impede "Muslim citizens practicing religion *as they see fit.*"

The Islamists' nonviolent "stealth" strategy to undermine American laws, financial systems, and democratic secular values that get in the way of Islamic sensibilities includes manipulating our own institutions against us. This is part of the Muslim Brotherhood's long-term plan to use Western legal instruments as part of a grand jihad to destroy Western civilization from within.[104]

As the Muslim Brotherhood puts it: "Allah is our objective. The Prophet is our leader. The Koran is our law. Jihad is our way."[105]

President Obama's unconditional engagement with the Muslim world—on their terms—is helping to make their way, our way.

The Secular United Nations had to change to accommodate sharia

So what role does the United Nations play in this plan for Islamic supremacy? At first, it seems an unlikely "marriage."

Islamists detest the UN's secular foundation. They recoil at its founding premise of durable peaceful coexistence among equal sovereign nation-states who enter into universally applicable, man-made treaties with each other, such as human rights covenants. This defies the Islamists' ideal of the unified global community of believers (*Ummah*) ruled by the divine law of the sharia.

With its headquarters in two infidel Western cities—New York and Geneva—the UN was founded and run by *kaffars* on secular principles. Indeed, the Islamic Thinkers Society, a radical Muslim group based in New York City with ties to Muslim Brotherhood organizations, described the UN's origins in sinister terms. They say its roots can be traced back to a

> Christian league Raabitat Al Usar Al Massahiyyah established in the 18th century which was set up by certain European countries in order to protect themselves from the Muslims and the expanding Othmani Khilafah...re-named in time (1911–1920) as the League of Nations Usbaat Ul Umam which became the United Nations Al Umam Al Mutahida after World War II.[106]

Not a very good pedigree, as far as Islamists are concerned.

The idea of Muslim countries belonging to any organization in which they subject themselves to secular rules and norms, heavily influenced by Western values, offends Islamists to the core.

The Muslim Brotherhood's spiritual leader Yusuf al-Qaradawi explains what it means for Muslims to embrace secularism:

> Secularism may be accepted in a Christian society but it can never enjoy a general acceptance in an Islamic society. Christianity is devoid of a shari`ah or a comprehensive system of life to which its adherents should be committed ... For Muslim societies, the acceptance of secularism means something totally different; i.e. as Islam is a comprehensive system of worship (`ibadah) and legislation (Shari`ah), the acceptance of secularism means abandonment of Shari`ah, a denial of the divine guidance and a rejection of Allah's injunctions; It is indeed a false claim that shariah is not proper to the requirements of the present age. The acceptance of a legislation formulated by humans means a preference of the humans' limited knowledge and experiences to the divine guidance: 'Say! Do you know better than Allah?' (2:140)
>
> For this reason, the call for secularism among Muslims is atheism and a rejection of Islam. Its acceptance as a basis for rule in place of Shari`ah is downright riddah [apostasy]. The silence of the masses in the Muslim world about this deviation has been a major transgression and a clear-cut instance of disobedience which have produces a sense of guilt, remorse, and inward resentment, all of which have generated discontent, insecurity, and hatred among committed Muslims because such deviation lacks legality.[107]

If the UN Won't Disappear, Then It Must Be Changed to Accommodate Islam

As long as the United Nations welcomes Muslim nations as member states who have been willing to join but can still create international norms that conflict with sharia, the Islamists knew they had to change the UN itself. The kaffars had to be beaten at their own game. The Islamists' best strategy to change the UN from within came out of the Muslim Brotherhood's 1982 manifesto, *Toward a Worldwide Strategy for Islamic Policy,* also referred to as "The Project."[108]

The Project recommended manipulating existing Western institutions until they can be put into service of Islam.[109] The goal is to steer the UN away from its secular roots until the Western-created institution "can be put into service of Islam."

As the largest intergovernmental group other than the UN itself, the Organization of Islamic Conference (OIC) speaks for the global Muslim community at the United Nations, where it has had official observer status since 1975. From that perch, and with the combined voting power of its member states and its allies in the undeveloped world, the OIC has created its own power centers within the UN structure, such as the General Assembly and Human Rights Council, in order to ensure that the UN helps advance sharia principles.

Islamicizing Human Rights

The OIC's number one priority was to control the direction of the UN's human rights agenda. That was tricky because the United Nations Universal Declaration of Human Rights (Universal Declaration or UDHR)[110], adopted by the UN in 1948, and the OIC's Cairo Declaration on Human Rights in Islam (Islamic Declaration),[111] adopted by the OIC in 1990, reflected diametrically opposed worldviews.

The Universal Declaration's organizing principle is that "[A]ll human beings are born free and equal in dignity and rights. They are endowed with reason and conscience and should act toward one another in a spirit of brotherhood."[112]

The Universal Declaration promotes the ideal that self-governing human beings all have certain inalienable rights such as the right to life and liberty, freedom of expression, and equality before the law. These universal rights apply to all human beings equally, whichever geographical location, country, race, culture, or religion they belong to.

The Universal Declaration was adopted in response to the atrocities of World War II, and drafted by members of the Human Rights Commission, with former First Lady Eleanor Roosevelt serving as its chairperson. Although technically it is not a legally binding treaty, the Declaration is part of "customary international law," which is often invoked by courts. The Declaration also gave rise to legally enforceable UN human rights treaties that embodied its core principles, such as the International Covenant on Civil and Political Rights (ICCPR) and the International Covenant on Economic, Social, and Cultural Rights (ICESCR).

Virtually all Muslim member states of the United Nations, with the notable exception of Saudi Arabia, signed the Universal Declaration, the ICCPR and the ICESR.[113] But as Islamic revivalism came into its own after the formation of the OIC in 1972, and after the Islamic revolution in Iran in 1979, Islamists refused to be ruled by any human rights document that deviated from God-given Islamic law (sharia).

For example, in 1981, the Iranian representative to the United Nations, Said Rajaie-Khorassani, asserted that the Universal Declaration was merely "a secular understanding of the Judeo-Christian tradition," which could not be implemented by Muslims without violating Islamic law.[114]

The Cairo Declaration on Human Rights in Islam

As the Islamic response to the United Nations Universal Declaration of Human Rights, the Organization of Islamic Conference foreign ministers adopted *The Cairo Declaration on Human Rights in Islam* in 1990.

The Cairo Declaration reaffirmed "the civilizing and historical role of the Islamic *Ummah* which God made the best nation that has given mankind a universal and well-balanced civilization in which harmony is established between this life and the hereafter and knowledge is combined with faith." After reciting a litany of human rights that it pledged to protect, the Cairo Declaration subjected all of its protections to the requirements of Islamic law:[115]

Article 22 (a)
"Everyone shall have the right to express his opinion freely in such manner as would not be contrary to the principles of the Shari'ah."

Article 24
"All the rights and freedoms stipulated in this Declaration are subject to the Islamic Shari'ah."

Article 25
"The Islamic Shari'ah is the only source of reference for the explanation or clarification to any of the articles of this Declaration."

By making Islamic law the sole authority for defining the scope of human rights, the OIC's Cairo Declaration sanctioned limits on freedom of expression, discrimination against non-Muslims and women, and a prohibition against a Muslim's conversion from Islam.[116] Such restrictions are completely at odds with the fundamental human freedoms spelled out in the Universal Declaration.

Ironically, in the very same Egyptian city that gave its name to the OIC's antihuman rights declaration, President Obama later told the world that "Islam has demonstrated through words and deeds the possibilities of religious tolerance and racial equality."[117]

Many of the member states of the OIC were still signatories to the Universal Declaration, the ICCPR and the ICESR, but the

West was certainly not about to replace the Universal Declaration with the Cairo Declaration. Thus, the OIC has worked hard to expand its influence at the United Nations so it can nevertheless incorporate key sharia concepts into universal human rights obligations agreed to by the Muslim member states. To paraphrase the "Muhammad comes to the mountain" parable[118], if the Universal Declaration will not embrace sharia, then sharia will have to wrap its venomous tentacles around the Universal Declaration.

The UN-OIC Partnership

By the mid-1990s, the OIC had partnered with the UN Secretariat and UN specialized agencies such as UNESCO and UNICEF on a whole range of issues. Each year, the General Assembly passed a resolution recognizing this partnership and encouraging as much cooperation as possible in priority areas that included human rights.[119]

In keeping with this collaborative spirit, twenty Islamic experts from the OIC countries—including representatives from Iran, Saudi Arabia, and Sudan—presented their papers on "Islamic Perspectives on the UDHR" to a specially convened UN conference in November of 1998, organized by the UN's Office of the High Commissioner for Human Rights, Mary Robinson.[120]

In her invitation to the event, Ms. Robinson wrote:

> The seminar is being organized during this 50th Anniversary year of the UDHR as part of the process of providing Islamic perspectives on the UDHR. I accept responsibility for the process in response to the invitation made by the Minister of Foreign Affairs of the Islamic Republic of Iran, during his address to the fifty-fourth session of the Commission on Human Rights (1998). I believe this process will help promote understanding and respect among peoples.[121]

While no changes to the Universal Declaration were made as a result of this conference, it made the UN establishment more receptive to altered interpretations of the Universal Declaration. As David Littman put it, "[T]he problem is that these efforts to undercut international paradigms, which are at the core of the world order since 1945, are henceforth guaranteed an institutionalized forum and legitimacy within the United Nations system."[122]

And that is precisely what happened.

A Mockery of Human Rights

In 2006, the General Assembly replaced the Commission on Human Rights with the Human Rights Council. The old Commission's credibility had declined over the years as some of the worst human rights violators in the world (such as Sudan) assumed the prestigious chair originally held by Eleanor Roosevelt. But from the outset, it was clear that this new Council would remain "a table for tyrants," in the words of former president of the Czech Republic and human rights activist Vaclav Havel.[123] Hopes that membership in the forty-seven-member Human Rights Council would be based on a country's human rights record were dashed from the start. Only twenty-two of the forty-seven members of the Council are considered free nations by the human rights watchdog Freedom House.[124] After all, the United Nations itself is a club of 192 member states that any nation—no matter how brutal, autocratic, or warmongering—can join and then enjoy the same voting privileges in the General Assembly as the most law-abiding democratic member state.

Council members are elected by the General Assembly, with each of five regional groupings allocated a certain number to sit on the Council.[125] OIC members dominate the representatives from the African and Asian regions, which in turn have the most members serving on the Council.[126] Since the Council's inaugural year of 2006, the OIC's percentage of the total Council membership has hovered between around 30 to 35 percent.[127] OIC members vote as a bloc and have formed voting majorities with their non-democratic friends like Cuba, Russia, and China. Thus, they are assured of enough votes to define key elements of the UN's human rights norms in a manner that is compatible with Islamic law.[128]

The Islamists accomplished their goal by manipulating the Western rhetoric of multiculturalism, calling for "sensitivity" to religious and cultural "identities" and "specificity." This moral equivalence argument seems rather ironic considering the fact that Islamists believe in the absolutism of Islamic law as the only valid universal truth.[129] But as long as playing on "the desire of some Western liberals to accommodate the cultural sensitivity of Islamic nations" is working according to plan, the Islamists consider it a tactic worth pursuing.[130]

We shall return in more detail to the subject of moral equivalence and multiculturalism in chapter ten and see how these two trends have ensnared the West to the benefit of the Islamists. We shall also see how President Obama has accelerated the Islamists' ability to exploit these dangerous trends.

But for the present purposes, just to show how perverse the canard of "respect of cultural, legal, and religious diversities" can become, take the case of Pakistan. Speaking on behalf of the Organization of the Islamic Conference, that country denounced the appointment of a new UN Human Rights Special Rapporteur to monitor laws that discriminate against women.[131] Among those "cultural, legal and religious diversities" are legal systems that do not criminalize rape or violence against women, usually found in nations like ... Pakistan.[132]

The Islamists also play on Western guilt about "racism," which they have successfully equated with "Islamophobia." And thanks to their efforts, "hate speech" is now broad enough to include speech which criticizes Islam.[133]

So, with a straight face, the Ambassador of Pakistan marked the 2007 observance of United Nations Human Rights Day (that is, the anniversary of the Universal Declaration of Human Rights) by proclaiming that the Cairo Declaration of Human Rights in

Islam "is not an alternative, competing worldview on human rights. It complements the Universal Declaration as it addresses religious and cultural specificity of the Muslim countries."[134]

By making criticism of Islam a human rights violation, the OIC worked a fundamental sharia principle into the Universal Declaration by the back door. No longer was the Universal Declaration of Human Rights a secular abomination to Islamists. They had successfully transformed its original meaning to serve their purposes.

The OIC's Propaganda Campaign Pays Off

In 2007, the UN's Special Rapporteur on racism, Doudou Diene, endorsed restrictions on freedom of expression, and linked defamation of religions to racism—that is, a violation of Muslims' human rights.[135] This followed his 2006 report criticizing the Danish government for failing to clamp down on the newspaper that published controversial cartoons mocking Islamic fanaticism:

> The dominating message of the caricatures was ... to associate Islam with terrorism. The caricature relating to the sexual gratification of suicide bombers with virgin women suggests the return of a age-old historical islamophobic Western imagery: the association of Islam and its prophet with sexual depravity. The way in which these caricatures defames Islam has now been defined.... Their [the Danish publishers] defense of a Freedom of Expression without limits or restrictions does not conform with international standards ... There is a great need to establish a balance between freedom of speech and freedom of faith. This publication explicitly shows a lack of understanding and emotion for believers." [136]

Doudou Diene is from the predominantly Muslim country of Senegal but studied extensively in France. Evidently, whatever Diene might have learned in France about Voltaire and other Age of Enlightenment thinkers did not stick.

In fact, enlightenment about the true meaning of human rights has become a rare commodity at the United Nations itself.

Just eight days after that 2008 celebration of the sixtieth anniversary of the Universal Declaration of Human Rights the UN General Assembly passed another OIC "religious defamation" resolution.[137] The resolution called for all member states to "provide adequate protection against acts of hatred, discrimination, intimidation and coercion resulting from defamation of religions."[138] The only religion named in this resolution was Islam.

An Ad Hoc Committee on Complementary Standards, chaired by Idriss Jazairy, Algeria's Permanent Representative to the United Nations' Human Rights Council, was established in December 2008. It discussed the need to fill in "substantial protection gaps" in human rights standards against "defamation of religious symbols; and incitement to racial hatred and dissemination of hate speech and xenophobic and caricature pictures, through traditional mass media and information technology, including the Internet."[139] Jazairy duly drafted a protocol to amend the UN's International Covenant on the Elimination of Racial Discrimination.

Although Jazairy cleverly used existing legal terminology of this UN treaty, the explanatory notes to the amendments made clear that the true purpose of this new protocol was to ban "defamation of religions."[140] As the UN Watch Web site explained,

> [I]f successful, it would be the first time in history that one of the world's core human rights treaties were rewritten according to the Islamic states' decade-long U.N. campaign against free speech, a move that would have dramatic consequences for the legal systems of countries around the world. The adoption of the changes would mark a dramatic setback for the cause of free speech and free exercise of religion worldwide.[141]

Who will be the arbiter of what constitutes defamation of religions, or which religious beliefs would be protected from criticism? Who will decide the punishment for infractions? We know how Islamic courts and religious leaders treat those whom they consider "blasphemers." The sentence is death.[142] Just ask Salman Rushdie.[143]

Strengthening International Norms against Free Speech

In 2009, the OIC issued its strongest resolution yet, calling for new laws criminalizing attacks on religious beliefs, organizations, and symbols. It was promptly adopted by the Human Rights Council on March 26.[144] Only time will tell whether such resolutions will successfully ban critiques of Islamic supremacism tenets in the West. The world has already watched the United Kingdom bend over backwards to accommodate Islamic sensibilities.[145] Soon, restrictions on free speech, renamed "hate" speech by the Obama administration, could increase in the United States as well.

All these UN resolutions are a direct assault on the First Amendment. As constitutional lawyer Floyd Abrams said, "What they would do would be to make it illegal to put out a movie or write a book or a poem that somebody could say was defamatory of Islam."[146]

Recall the Islamists' strategy to contaminate international norms with sharia principles, using the United Nations as their Trojan horse. They achieved this using the Human Rights Council and General Assembly to make "defamation of religions" an accepted part of international human rights law. Then the Islamists will be better able to work within Western democratic institutions, especially the courts, to inject these contaminated norms into Western nations' own laws.

Will our courts stay true to the Constitution, or will they make the Islamists' goal easy to achieve, by incorporating international norms into future decisions? With more Obama judicial nominations on the way for all federal courts, I fear the worst.

Obama's Stamp of Approval

President Obama further legitimized the sharia-boosting work of the UN Human Rights Council by deciding that the United States should finally join it. The US is now serving on the Council along with such human rights luminaries as Saudi Arabia, Libya, Cuba, and China. Predictably, the United States issued a groveling statement expressing its "gratitude" and "humility" when it became a member of this notorious club in June 2009.[147]

Anne Bayesfsky, the editor of EYEontheUN.com and a watchdog on UN human rights activities, observed that when the US joined the Human Rights Council, it

> became part of the problem and not the solution. By being elected to pretend to protect human rights along with the likes of China, Cuba and Saudi Arabia, the United States gave the election and the council a stamp of approval it didn't deserve. Promoting the tool of human rights abusers promotes human rights abuse - now courtesy of the president of the United States.[148]

Whether or not we oppose future "defamation of religions" resolutions, we are now an active participant in the Islamic-dominated agenda of the UN's chief human rights organization.

The increasing number of judges who will integrate sharia-friendly international human rights norms into their decisions will cite our participation in the UN Human Rights Council as yet another justification for doing so. Such is the twisted "logic" of "transnational jurisprudence." With Obama's expected nomination of more transnational judges to the federal bench, this sort of jurisprudence will mushroom.

But the Islamists' battle to have the UN's human rights norms adapt to sharia was not won overnight. The Islamists first needed an issue they could exploit to prove that the UN's very own formative secular Western values were hypocritical and corrupt. They needed to put the United States in particular on the defensive, and rally the UN majority to their side. The Islamists found their wedge issue in the Israeli-Palestinian conflict embroiling the Holy Land.

CHAPTER FIVE

The Islamists' Wedge Issue— Palestine

The Islamists' key issue, which they have used to acquire their position of influence at the United Nations, dates back to 1947, with one of the earliest decisions by the UN itself: General Assembly Resolution No. 181, which divided the Palestine Mandate in two, thus creating the hated Zionist state of Israel.

The Muslim Brotherhood manifesto declares that one of the Islamists' key strategies was to "adopt the Palestinian cause as part of a worldwide Islamic plan."[149]

This plan also involved the formation of the Organization of Islamic Conference, the intergovernmental organization of Muslim states that operates in parallel with these states' membership in the United Nations. For nearly four decades, these parallel lines have been converging as the Islamists use the Palestine issue to increase their collective power within the UN.

The Organization of Islamic Conference was established in 1972, three years after an intergovernmental Islamic summit meeting, prompted by the burning of Jerusalem's al-Aqsa mosque by an

Australian Christian. A supporter of the OIC described the events that led to its founding, falsely blaming the incident on the Jews:

> The OIC was established in the wake of the criminal arson per- petrated on 21 August 1969 by Zionist elements against Al-Aqsa Mosque, in occupied Jerusalem. It was to defend the honor; dignity and faith of the Muslims, to face this bitter challenge launched in the holy city of Al-Quds [Jerusalem], against the Mosque of Al-Aqsa, the first Qibla and third holiest Shrine of Islam. At that time, the OIC was able to muster unanimous worldwide condemnation of this heinous act. OIC also provided a forum for the Islamic states to think together of their common cause and overcome the differences, unite and lay the foundations of this large grouping of States. The OIC was also entrusted, in absolute priority, to work toward liberating Jerusalem and Al-Aqsa.[150]

The Early Secularization of the Palestinian Issue

Before the OIC's founding, the Palestinian-Israeli conflict was usu- ally presented as a secular territorial dispute between Arabs and Jews, which Arabs cloaked in the fashionable language of national liberation. In those days, the protection of Islamic holy land was never the rallying cry. In fact, the Palestine Liberation Organiza- tion Charter of 1968 (PLO Charter) makes no reference to Islam or Muslims.[151] Article 1 of the PLO Charter states that "Palestine is the homeland of the Arab Palestinian people; it is an indivisible part of the Arab homeland, and the Palestinian people are an inte- gral part of the *Arab nation*" (emphasis added).

In 1974, the UN General Assembly invited Yaser Arafat to address the body, which he did on November 13. He dressed in revolutionary garb with a holster attached to his hip (although he did not carry his gun into the hall). His rhetoric echoed that of anticolonialist, nationalist movements all over the world.[152] Barely a year later, the UN General Assembly passed its infamous Resolution 3379, equating Zionism with racism. (This Resolution was repealed in 1991.)[153]

During his infamous address, Arafat made only one reference to "Islamic countries":

> Here I must also warmly convey the gratitude of our revolution-ary fighters and that of our people to the non-aligned countries, the socialist countries, the Islamic countries, the African coun-tries and friendly European countries, as well as ail our other friends in Asia, Africa, and Latin America.[154]

(Note that "socialist" countries are mentioned before "Islamic" ones.) Arafat pointedly did not present the Palestinian cause as part of a broader Islamic jihad.

"Palestine Does Not Belong Only to the Palestinians but to All Muslims"

Today, of course, Islamists do see the Palestinian cause solely in terms of a broader pan-Islamic cause. In the words of the Muslim Brotherhood's spiritual leader, Yusef al-Qaradawi, "Muslims must carry out jihad to liberate all the land of Islam. Palestine does not belong only to the Palestinians but to all Muslims."[155]

The Hamas Charter, adopted nearly twenty years after the PLO Charter, is cast entirely in Islamic terms, sometimes referred to as "The Charter Of Allah: The Platform of the Islamic Resis-tance Movement."[156]

The Hamas Charter says that Palestine is

> an Islamic *Waqf* [possession] throughout all generations and to the Day of Resurrection. Who can presume to speak for all Islamic Generations to the Day of Resurrection? This is the sta-tus [of the land] in Islamic Shari'a, and it is similar to all lands conquered by Islam by force, and made thereby *Waqf* lands upon

their conquest, for all generations of Muslims until the Day of Resurrection.[157]

But even before 1987, when Hamas emerged as the Muslim Brotherhood's underground armed wing in the Gaza Strip (and as the Islamic Palestinian rival to the secular Palestinian leadership), the Islamists worked assiduously to make the Palestinian issue their own. Following the Muslim Brotherhood 1982 manifesto's directive to use secular nationalist movements to achieve their objectives through more peaceful means they accepted "the principle of temporary cooperation between Islamic movements and nationalist movements in the broad sphere and on common ground such as the struggle against colonialism, preaching and the Jewish state."[158]

While recognizing the PLO as the sole representative of the Palestinian people (at least up to Hamas' founding in 1987), the OIC purported to speak for Muslims worldwide at the United Nations and at its own forums. The OIC fused the revolutionary antiracist, anticolonialism rhetoric used with some success by the Arab secular nation states and by the PLO, with the language of universalistic Islam preferred by the Muslim Brotherhood.

In its 1974 Declaration of Lahore, for example, the OIC called for all OIC members "which still have relations with Israel to sever these relations in all fields thus supporting *Islamic solidarity*" (emphasis added).[159]

The Declaration of Lahore made the Palestinian issue an Islamic issue. A localized territorial fight between Arabs and Jews was transformed into a test of world-wide Islamic solidarity.

Significantly, the Declaration linked Israel's "flagrant violation of international law" with the "feelings" of the "members of the Islamic Conference, and of the Islamic World":

> Al-Quds [Jerusalem] is a unique symbol of the confluence of Islam with the sacred divine religions. For more than 1300 years, Muslims have held Jerusalem as a trust for all who venerate it. Muslims alone could be its loving and impartial custodians for

the simple reason that Muslims alone believe in all the three prophetic religions rooted in Jerusalem. *No agreement, protocol or understanding which postulates the continuance of Israeli occupation of the Holy City of Jerusalem or its transfer to any non-Arab sovereignty or makes it the subject of bargaining or concessions will be acceptable to the Islamic countries.* Israeli withdrawal from Jerusalem is a paramount and unchangeable prerequisite for lasting peace in the Middle East...Any measure taken by Israel to change the character of the occupied Arab territories and in particular of the Holy City of Jerusalem is *a flagrant violation of international law and is repugnant to the feelings of the States, members of the Islamic Conference, and of the Islamic World.*" (emphasis added)[160]

In 1977, the OIC sent UN Secretary General (and former Nazi) Kurt Waldheim a communiqué adopted by the Eighth Islamic Conference of Foreign Ministers. The OIC asked Waldheim to circulate the communiqué to all UN member states, as an official document of the General Assembly.[161]

This communiqué was the Islamic organization's blueprint for increasing its influence within the United Nations, a marketing tool to sell the Islamic worldview to the entire UN membership. That membership was increasingly made up of the so-called non-aligned countries of the third world, and this Islamic worldview was presented as an alternative to the Western worldview on which the UN itself was founded.[162] Palestine was now the OIC's wedge issue, having wrenched it away from the secularist Arafat and his PLO.

The OIC's communiqué cleverly bound together Palestine, Islam, and the struggle against racism and imperialism in the third world, especially Africa. It "reaffirmed the close links which binds Muslims to the Holy City of Jerusalem and the responsibility of the Islamic States to secure its liberation and restoration to Arab Rule."[163]

After calling for the expulsion of Israel from the UN and all other international organizations, the communiqué "reiterated the commitment of the Islamic countries to the struggle against racism in Southern Africa, Namibia, Zimbabwe and occupied Palestine."[164] The communiqué introduced the Islamist's narrative of moral equivalence between Israel and the apartheid South African regime, and the theme of Islamic solidarity with oppressed people everywhere.

The communiqué "invited all member States to co-operate with the Secretary General of the Islamic Conference in convening the International Conference for Combating Racism and Racial Discrimination, in compliance with the relevant United Nations General Assembly Resolution."[165]

The Racist UN Conferences

The first World Conference to Combat Racism and Racial Discrimination was held in Geneva in 1978. In its Declaration and Programmes of Action, this conference concluded that "[A]partheid, the extreme form of institutionalized racism, is a crime against humanity and an affront to the dignity of mankind and is a threat to peace and security in the world." While it focused attention on the apartheid regime of South Africa, this document specifically linked Israel to that regime and condemned "the insidious propaganda by the Government of Israel and its Zionist and other supporters against the United Nations organs and against Governments which had advocated firm action against apartheid."[166] One paragraph accused Israel of practicing "diverse forms of racial discrimination against Palestinians affecting all aspects of their daily lives in a manner which prevents their enjoyment of their elementary human rights on a basis of equality."[167]

The second World Conference to Combat Racism and Racial Discrimination, also held in Geneva, took place in August 1983 and repeated the same rhetoric.[168]

In 1997, the UN General Assembly called for a World Conference against Racism, Racial Discrimination, Xenophobia, and Related Intolerance, to take place no later than 2001.[169] Also in

1997, nearly two decades after the revolution, the Islamic Republic of Iran hosted the Organization of Islamic Conference summit meeting, and assumed the presidency of the OIC for a three-year term.

"Holding the OIC Summit Conference in Tehran successfully demonstrated the potential of the Islamic Republic of Iran for carrying out titanic tasks and presence in international arena as a strong Islamic country with high potentials," remarked Iran's then-president Mohammad Khatami.[170] Indeed, Iran played an important role in the subsequent 2001 and 2009 World Conferences against Racism, Racial Discrimination, Xenophobia and Related Intolerance. These conferences are now commonly referred to as Durban I and Durban II.

Iran became co-leader of the OIC along with Saudi Arabia when both countries forced Qatar, the host of the 2000 OIC summit, to sever ties with Israel. Iran and Saudi Arabia threatened to boycott the conference if Qatar did not relent. Both countries also demanded that the question of Palestine be the summit's top priority.[171]

Khatami led by example at the 2000 OIC summit, calling Israel a "terrorist racist Zionist regime'" and urged "resolute action" to punish it.[172] He urged formation of an international war crimes tribunal for Israel, and declared that the

> Sanction Committee of the OIC should seriously explore ways and means of economic embargo of Israel. It is essential for those member states that have not yet severed their diplomatic relations with Israel; relations that should not have ever been established, to break at the shortest possible time their ties with this regime in response to the volition of the Islamic Ummah and the public opinion of the nations.[173]

And don't forget that Khatami was supposed to be the moderate in Iranian political circles, at least when compared to Ahmadinejad and his call for the destruction of Israel![174] Both presidents were in fact simply following the declaration of the founder of the Islamic Republic of Iran, Ayatollah Ruhollah Khomeini, that "Every Muslim has a duty to prepare himself for battle against Israel."[175]

So it was no surprise when Iran led the planning for the United Nations' 2001 Durban I Conference. There, the OIC and its allies in the non-aligned movement held sway and the Palestinians were singled out as victims of racism. In fact, the "antiracist" Durban I conference turned into a racist hate fest against the Jewish state.[176]

Iran also headed up preparations for the equally biased follow-up Durban II Review Conference in 2009. Iranian President Ahmadinejad opened the conference with an attack on Israel, which he called the most racist country in the world. Several delegates, mostly from the European Union, walked out during his speech. Most delegates, however, not only remained for the speech but applauded at its conclusion. Fortunately, the United States, along with Australia, Canada, Germany, Israel, Italy, the Netherlands, New Zealand, and Poland, had boycotted the whole conference, rightly sensing in advance that something like this would happen.[177]

As a reward for its president's speech, Iran was elected one of three vice-chairs of the committee which adopted the 2009 Durban II conference's final declaration. This official UN document, as described by EYEontheUN editor Anne Bayefsky, "reaffirms the 2001 Durban Declaration which alleges Palestinians are victims of Israeli racism and mentions only Israel among all 192 UN member states. It also multiplies the anti-Israel provisions, using the usual UN code, by adding yet another rant about racist foreign occupation."[178]

True, Secretary General Ban Ki-moon publicly condemned Ahmadinijad's speech, calling it "unacceptable," a "very disturbing experience," and "destructive."[179] However, he remained seated during the entire speech, rather than walk out and thereby salvage whatever shred of dignity the UN had left. Although later admitting Iran had given him false assurances that its remarks at the Durban II conference would be "moderate," the Secretary General stayed put while Israel and the UN itself were verbally attacked.

The reason Ban Ki-moon provided for his inaction, during a private meeting with high-level Israeli officials (and which was later described to me by Israel's UN ambassador) was that, as the presiding UN officer of the conference, he was obliged to stay.[180] That flimsy rationale illustrates the moral rot the Islamists have fostered within the UN system.

Stretching back to that 1977 communiqué which the OIC sent UN Secretary General (and former Nazi) Kurt Waldheim, Israel has been increasingly isolated by the "international community" for committing "racist crimes" against the "oppressed" Palestinian victims. At the same time, the United States and other Western democracies were pilloried for their support of the "neo-colonialist" Zionist regime. These attacks undermined the moral standing of Western democracies and enhanced solidarity between the Islamists and their non-aligned ally countries, whom now have enough votes to guarantee the Islamists a solid majority in the General Assembly.

Although UN organizers—from the Office of Secretary General on down—were warned what to expect by the time Durban II rolled around, they didn't lay down any ground rules regarding acceptable behavior at a UN-sponsored conference. They didn't threaten to withdraw from Durban II if the conference began to resemble the disgraceful Durban I. Instead, the UN never wavered from its decision to host Durban II at its Geneva headquarters, even as conference planners pushed their racist agenda.

In short, the Islamists, backed by their non-aligned friends, successfully used the Palestinian wedge issue to turn another "anti-racism" conference into one demonizing Israel and the West, with the tacit approval of the UN.

The UN's Idea of Standards—Double or Nothing?

Double Standards

Between the OIC-dominated UN Human Rights Council, the Division for Palestinian Rights, the Special Committee to Investigate Israeli Human Rights Practices Affecting the Palestinian People and Other Arabs of the Occupied Territories, the Committee on the Exercise of the Inalienable Rights of the Palestinian People, and the United Nations Relief and Works Agency for Palestine Refugees, more UN resources and time are devoted to the advocacy of the Palestinian cause than to any other issue.

When the Human Rights Council is not busy dutifully passing the Organization of Islamic Conference's resolutions restricting freedom of speech, it goes after Israel while conveniently whitewashing the records of the real serial human rights violators the world over, some of whom sit on the Council.[181]

To quote EYEontheUN editor Anne Bayefsky, the Human Rights Council

> has adopted more resolutions and decisions condemning the state of Israel than all other 191 U.N. member states combined. At the same time, it has abolished human rights investigations into the abysmal human rights conditions in Belarus, Cuba, the Democratic Republic of the Congo, Liberia, Iran, Kyrgyzstan, Turkmenistan and Uzbekistan.[182]

In 2008, for example, Israel was subjected to a record 120 UN condemnations for alleged human rights violations.[183] This was more than twice as many as its nearest "competitor," Sudan, where the black population is being systematically wiped out by the Arab government and militia.[184] Israel was subjected to seven times as many UN condemnations as Iran, where stoning of women, executions of political dissidents and homosexuals, and rampant discrimination against non-Muslims are a way of life.[185]

By the way, the United States was fifth on this list (tied with Iraq), with twenty-six condemnations for its human rights record. That's nine more than Iran, which came in twelfth. Saudi Arabia—which forbids non-Islamic religious worship and strictly segregates men and women—received fourteen condemnations (tied with Pakistan and Malaysia). The United Kingdom fared worse than these three Islamic countries, receiving fifteen UN condemnations for its human rights record in 2008 (tied with Algeria and Bangladesh).[186]

This farcical exercise is a stark reminder of the double standards at work in the UN, where Islamic despots and their friends wield enormous power. In fact, the OIC Secretary-General has openly boasted about his organization's success in getting *five* of its anti-Israel resolutions through just one session.[187]

Obama Joins the Double-Standard Charade

Now that the United States is also a member of the Human Rights Council, we will be necessarily complicit in the continuation of this despicable track record. What's more, President Obama has signaled his intention to come down hard on Israel by initially demanding a complete freeze on settlements—including on any growth in existing settlements.[188] He has clearly bought into the leftist narrative of Palestinian victimhood.[189]

The UN Renounces Its Own Original Two-State Solution

But double standards may not be enough to describe what has become of the United Nations. In some ways it has no standards at all.

Beginning in 1977, the United Nations has sponsored the International Day of Solidarity with the Palestinian People on November 29th, the date in 1947 when the UN General Assembly approved its partition resolution. Former UN Secretary General Kofi Annan called November 29th a "day of mourning and a day of grief."[190] The event takes place every year at UN Headquarters in New York and at the UN Offices at Geneva and Vienna and elsewhere.

In other words, every November 29th, the United Nations publicly mourns the passage of its own peaceful solution to the Arab-Jewish dispute. The UN is effectively repudiating its own original two-state solution, spurned by all of the Arab countries back in

1947, which still lies at the heart of the solution that the UN claims to support as the basis for ending the Palestinian-Israeli conflict today.[191]

Into such a moral vacuum step the Islamists. Remember the so-called moderate former president of Iran, Mohammad Khatami, who represented Iran as president of the OIC and addressed one of its summit meetings? He called for one "democratic Palestinian state in the entire territory of Palestine with Al-Qods Al-Sharif as its capital."[192] We all know where that will lead. Just take a look at Lebanon. A pluralistic state with a thriving Christian population, called in its heyday "Switzerland of the East," has devolved into another Islamic-dominated wasteland.[193]

The one-state solution, cloaked in the high-sounding rhetoric of a democratic pluralistic society, is really a way to use Western democratic institutions against themselves. The "Kaffars" must be relegated to their proper place and "the heroic resistance of the children of the Muslim and Arab Ummah against suppression and bullying of the terrorist racist Zionist regime" must be rewarded.[194]

I have little doubt that the United Nations will help lead the way, abandoning for good the two-state solution of a Palestinian state and a Jewish state living side by side in peace.

The Larger Islamic Agenda

We must not forget, however, that Palestine is simply the Islamists' wedge issue, used to legitimize Islam as an ideology in solidarity with oppressed people everywhere. Such faux solidarity with the non-aligned countries of Africa, Asia, and Latin America helps the Islamists garner the votes of the majority of the General Assembly and thereby gain more influence at the UN to implement their own agenda. As Khatami said in his speech to the OIC, the

Islamic Ummah as a nation of balance, in order to be an example for all, must assume a central role in the issues of our time ... drawing from the great personality of the Prophet of Islam ... today, by drawing upon the teachings of Islam and the valuable historical experience of humanity, we can attend to the growing needs and demands of our present world from the vantage point of religion and lay down the foundations of a new civilization. (sic)[195]

Before such "a new civilization" can be built, the secular Western foundations of international finance and law must be replaced, in order to advance "the cause and the interest of the Islamic Ummah" and "enhance the role of the OIC at the international arena."[196] Islamists have concrete plans to accomplish this objective, and the UN and President Obama are helping them.

CHAPTER SIX

Thick as Thieves

The Islamists and the United Nations
Delight in Taking the West's Wealth

The Islamists' Grasping Hands

The Muslim Brotherhood's "Project" manifesto ("Toward a World-wide Strategy for Islamic Policy") outlines the Islamists' master plan to co-opt Western economic "foundations, capitalism and democracy."[197] It emphasizes the need for, among other things, "the necessary economic institutions to provide financial support" to spread fundamental Islam.[198]

The plan is to develop "a parallel 'Islamic' financial system to exploit and undermine Western economies and markets."[199] As is true with everything else that Islamists do, they are guided by the Koran's command to defeat all enemies of the Islamic Ummah.

Fundamentally, Islamists reject capitalism's primary focus on private property ownership, material wealth and the charging of interest in financial transactions. They believe that all property is created and owned by Allah, and that human beings hold property in trust for Allah and the Muslim community.[200]

Islamists claim that capitalism permits the exploitation of the poor by the rich and powerful.[201] They say Islamic law commands sharing all wealth with the poor through equitable distribution.[202]

That's what the Islamists say, but the reality is far different. The two oil-rich and most sharia-abiding countries—Iran and Saudi Arabia—fall far short when it comes to the equitable distribution of wealth, especially when compared to the center of Western secular capitalism, the United States.[203] And that is not likely to change any time soon.

We have seen how Islamists use the United Nations as a critical part of their plan to destroy the value of the dollar as the global reserve currency. Amidst the wreckage they anticipate this will cause to the dominant Western capitalist system, the Islamists will present sharia-based Islamic finance as "a genuine alternative global financial system."[204] At least, that's what they are planning to do.

But until that happens, the Islamists consider it their right and duty to take as much wealth from the greedy capitalist West as possible and redistribute it to the Muslim world's "oppressed" victims of foreign occupation. Possessions confiscated from non-believers are "a way of exacting revenge," explained an eleventh century Islamic jurist Abul Hasan al Mawardi.[205]

How else can the Islamists fund their notion of the "just" society if not by the redistribution of wealth confiscated from the kaffars (unbelievers)?

The Islamists' Accomplice

The United Nations establishment agrees that capitalist democracies should be punished for their supposed exploitation of the poor. We have already discussed the *UN Conference on the World Financial and Economic Crisis and its Impact on Development,* produced and directed by the Nicaraguan Sandinista president of the General Assembly, Miguel d'Escoto.

But a single conference does not compare to the mischief UN agencies do every day, particularly the United Nations Development Programme (UNDP) which is the largest of the UN bureaucracies.

The UNDP describes itself as "the UN's global development network."[206] Its broad mandate encompasses something called "gender and capacity development," achieving the UN's Millennium Development Goals and reducing poverty, fostering democratic governance, crisis prevention and recovery, energy and environment, and responding to HIV/AIDS.[207]

The UNDP is funded by voluntary contributions rather than mandatory assessments. Monies from donor countries such as the United States fund the UNDP's regular core budget, along with monies from other UN agencies (to which the United States also contributes), and local resources channeled through UNDP by countries in which UNDP is administering the UN's development projects. The UNDP's regular core budget for 2007 was approximately $1.1 billion. Including the funds from other UN agencies and those local resources the UNDP administers, it oversaw nearly $5 billion in 2007.[208]

As indicated, the United States is one of the biggest contributors to the UNDP's core budget.[209] Interestingly, out of the *top twenty-five donor* countries, there is only *one Muslim country:* Kuwait.[210] Other than China, the rest are functioning democracies: European nations, Australia, New Zealand, and India.[211]

Just like the Islamists, the United Nations Development Programme embraces anticapitalism and wealth redistribution as its guiding ideology. For example, in 2003, UNDP Administrator Mark Malloch-Brown proposed a *"guerrilla assault"* on the free market principles the IMF and the World Bank use to set their policies.[212]

In its 2005 annual report, the UNDP presented its simplistic diagnosis of the world's problems: "growth has been unequally distributed between countries and within countries."[213] The UNDP blamed "the failure of governments in wealthy countries to develop a pattern of globalization that incorporates redistributive mechanisms to correct fundamental imbalances in life chances."[214]

The UNDP also offered its cure-all remedy: "Aid policies should reflect a commitment to reduce inequalities in human capabilities and income."[215] The UNDP believes in what it calls "universal entitlements, not optional or discretionary allowances."[216] Sounds much the same as President Obama's big government "spread the wealth around" philosophy, doesn't it?

In addition to its other functions, the UNDP administers the world's all-time biggest give-away aid program to the developing countries, known as the Millennium Development Goals (MDGs).[217] These goals, scheduled to be achieved by 2015, focus on raising the standard of living around the globe through massive wealth redistribution programs that would supposedly enable poorer countries to develop their economies, health systems, education and infrastructures.

Although foreign aid programs in the past have turned out to be a colossal waste due to such problems as corruption, the United Nations wants us to pour much more money down the same sinkhole. The UNDP is pushing each developed country to give away 0.7 percent of its gross national income (GNI) to meet these goals: "0.7% of rich world GNI can provide enough resources to meet Millennium Development Goals, but developed countries must follow through on commitments and begin increasing ODA [Official Development Assistance] volumes today."[218]

The UNDP estimates that contributions of that magnitude would raise approximately $50 billion a year. Barack Obama demonstrated back in 2008, when he sponsored legislation in the Senate, that he was prepared to have the United States contribute hundreds of billions of dollars in additional aid from American taxpayers to this cause over a span of thirteen years or so. As a presidential candidate, Obama said that "I'll double our foreign assistance to $50 billion by 2012, and use it to support a stable future in failing states, and sustainable growth in Africa; to halve global poverty and to roll back disease."[219]

Naturally, the UNDP would like nothing better than help recipient countries spend all the money the United States and other "rich" donors are providing.

In commenting on the impact of the recent global economic crisis on development aid, the outgoing UNDP administrator expressed the same redistributionist, soak-the-rich philosophy when he remarked: "So for us at the U.N., it's going to be extremely important to hold those donors and countries to account to really make sure that the rich man's worry doesn't remain the poor man's plight."[220]

Unfortunately for the "rich man" and the "poor man," the UNDP lacks any transparency.[221] In a letter dated December 8, 2006, sent to a reporter requesting information about findings of UNDP mismanagement and corruption, the UNDP replied that "we do not release the reports of our internal audits and investigations."[222] As a matter of fact, the UNDP makes no reports available to the general public.[223] Only summaries are available, and only to 36 out of the UN's 192 member states.[224]

I wanted to see whether anything had changed since Helen Clark became UNDP Administrator in April 2009. So at a forum held by the UNDP and the government of the Netherlands on September 24, 2009, concerning the impact of the economic crisis and climate change on human development, I asked Ms. Clark to comment on transparency and accountability at the UNDP. She denied any problems, declaring that the UNDP ranked extremely well on its accountability and transparency. Ranked well compared with what? The UN's scandal-ridden Oil-for-Food program?

To make matters worse, the Islamic Republic of Iran is serving as the president of the UNDP's Executive Committee as this book is being written.[225] As we shall see, Iran has been tapping the UNDP's funding resources with no accountability for years. Ms. Clark did not respond to my follow-up question regarding the controls, if any, the UNDP has in place to ensure that the aid, technology, and resources transferred by the UNDP to Iran aren't used to support Iran's military programs.

In fact, the Islamists rip off the West to fund their jihads from a number of sources. Two major sources are oil revenues and forced tithing. In particular, the United Nations Development Programme and other UN agencies help Islamists channel monies from these sources through interlocking relationships with Islamic financial and charitable institutions, to fund nefarious causes.

And of course, the third source of the Islamist's funding is the United Nations itself.

The Oil Jizya

Oil remains the Islamists' main way to transfer a massive amount of wealth from the energy-dependent West to the Muslim world.[226] Muslim countries control a major chunk of the world's oil reserves. As of the end of 2006, for example, the Persian Gulf countries (Bahrain, Iran, Iraq, Kuwait, Qatar, Saudi Arabia, and the United Arab Emirates) held 55 percent of the world's crude oil reserves.[227] They also produced 28 percent of the world's oil supply.[228]

The United States alone, with 3 percent of proven reserves, consumes about 25 percent of the world's annual production.[229] The Islamists literally have us over a barrel so long as we remain dependent on their oil.

Muslim world economies garnered approximately $1.08 trillion in total revenues for 2006.[230] That same year, the United States spent about $260 billion on foreign crude oil and refined petroleum products.[231] With oil costing over $125 a barrel in 2008, it was estimated that US spending could double at that price level, translating to a tax of more than $1600 a year for every American man, woman, and child.[232]

These oil payments by industrialized countries are today's version of the old Muslim tax on non-Muslims, known as the *jizya*.[233]

What the Oil Jizya Pays For

Rising oil prices have kept that *jizya* pot overflowing, providing a veritable money machine for the Islamists to use as they wish.

Oil export revenues account for nearly 90 percent of Saudi Arabia's total export earnings. Saudi Arabia earned about $116 billion in net oil export revenues in 2004 alone.[234] In 2008, that figure rose to $236 billion.[235]

The Saudi government uses billions of dollars in oil revenues to promote Wahhabism, Saudi Arabia's extreme Islamic ideology, in America and across the globe.[236] David D. Aufhauser, a former Treasury Department general counsel, told a Senate committee in June 2004 that estimates of Saudi government spending went "north of $75 billion." The money financed thousands of mosques, schools, and Islamic centers; the employment of thousands of propagandists; and the printing of millions of religious teaching tracts.[237] As an article on jihad finance put it, the purpose of financing all these efforts, as well as Islamic studies programs in universities around the world, is to "undermine Western economic, political, cultural, educational, and legal structures and replace them with the shari'a."[238]

Saudi leaders have acknowledged providing financial support for Islamic causes, including Palestine, but claim that no official government funds finance terrorist organizations.[239]

As we have seen, Islamists define terrorists in such a way as to exclude groups they consider "freedom fighters," including Hezbollah and Hamas.[240] Thus, such Saudi government assurances are not worth the paper they are written.

Continuing with the Saudi example, official government revenues are only one source of money for radical Islamic causes. According to the US State Department 2007 International Narcotics Control Strategy Report, "Saudi donors and unregulated charities have been a major source of financing to extremist and terrorist groups over the past 25 years."[241]

The 9/11 Commission concluded that al Qaeda found "fertile fund-raising groups" in Saudi Arabia, "where extreme religious views are common and charitable giving was both essential to the culture and subject to very limited oversight."[242]

The UN Channel

Unregulated charities supported by wealthy Saudi donors and Islamic banks awash in oil money are channeling donations directly—and *through the United Nations' sprawling human development agency, the United Nations Development Programme*—to Palestinian families of suicide bombers.[243] One of these charities is the Al Quds Intifada Committee, whose stated purpose is to disburse donated funds "to the families of Palestinian martyrs fallen in the Intifadah."[244]

The Al Quds Intifada Committee's funds are administered by the Islamic Development Bank (IBD), a subsidiary organ of the Organization of Islamic Conference set up during the 1970s to foster economic and social development among Muslim communities in accordance with the principles of Islamic law.[245]

The IBD has official observer status at the United Nations, which entitles it to various diplomatic privileges. And the IBD and the UN have a close twenty-year-plus relationship, cooperating on various projects of mutual interest, including operations in the Palestinian territories.[246]

In 2001 alone, the IDB transferred more than a half billion dollars to support the Palestinian intifada and suicide bombers' families.[247] That same year, the Islamic Development Bank started supporting the United Nations Development Programme's "Assistance to the Palestinian People," resulting in multi-million dollar contributions.[248]

The United Nations Development Programme also signed a tri-partite agreement with the Islamic Development Bank and yet another charitable organization, known as the Qatar Charity, "to assist projects in Palestine."[249] Indeed, according to its Web site, Qatar Charity "has pursued cooperation and partnership with UN agencies as a global development agency since 1997. At this time QC was granted a special consultative status with UN ECOSOC. On the other hand QC has extensively supported relief and development operations of various UN agencies in different countries."[250]

The Qatar Charity has the same domain name as the one registered to the Qatar Charity Society, and thus appears to be one and the same organization.[251] This is significant because the Qatar Charity Society is part of a coalition of charities, called the Union of Good, which was founded by the Muslim Brotherhood spiritual leader so often quoted in this book, al Qaradawi.[252]

According to Palestinian intelligence (and quoted in a report by the Washington Institute for Near East Policy), "The Union [of Good] is considered—with regard to material support—one of the biggest Hamas supporters."[253]

To close the circle, then, the United Nations Development Programme has signed an agreement with what for all intents and purposes is a Muslim Brotherhood front organization that goes by two names. Whether it fully realizes it or not, the UN is more than likely helping to obscure the sources and nature of the 'charity' funds, in concert with the Islamic Development Bank, before they reach Hamas. It does so by facilitating the movement of funds from one account to another in order to obscure the original source—akin to a stage of money laundering known as layering.[254] The funds might also be disguised as over-payments for goods or services the UN is supposed to provide.

By the way, the United Nations Development Programme is not new to laundering money through its development programs. A report by the Permanent Subcommittee on Investigations of the US Senate Committee on Homeland Security and Governmental Affairs concluded that the North Korean government used its relationship with the United Nations Development Programme to execute deceptive financial transactions.[255] The UN agency also reportedly transferred UN funds to a company with ties to an entity involved in North Korean weapons activity.[256]

Not only does it appear that Islamic charity-sourced funds are being channeled through Islamic Development Bank accounts and, in some cases, through United Nations development programs before reaching the Islamists' beneficiaries. Sometimes it works the other way around. For example, bank records discovered in the West Bank and Gaza document the trail of UN money from the Islamic Development Bank to Hamas.[257]

Saudi Arabia Demands a Piece of the UN Funds to Help Countries Adapt to Climate Change

The Islamists are doing whatever they can to keep the oil *jizya* money rolling in to fund their jihads. They even want to be made whole by the United Nations for any loss of oil revenues resulting from their customers' reduced use of fossil fuels. The world's biggest oil exporter, Saudi Arabia, is complaining that its economy will suffer from any global "environmental" pact that curbs demand for its oil.[258] Therefore, it is demanding access to UN funds that are supposed to help countries adapt to climate changes from global warming, such as the supposed rise in sea levels and extreme weather.[259]

Saudi Arabia's lead climate negotiator complained that Saudi Arabia is "among the most vulnerable countries, economically" from any shift to alternative fuels.[260] "I'm surprised to see that developed countries expect they can get away with the things they want without giving equal treatment to what we want," he said.[261]

In short, Saudi Arabia wants the UN to steer more money its way to compensate it for the oil revenue it will lose due to the shift by industrialized countries to alternative fuels—money it will no doubt use to continue funding jihad. In the meantime, Saudi Arabia is working with the large "G-77 and China" bloc on finance proposals of common interest.[262]

I asked Rajendra Pachauri, chairman of the United Nations' Intergovernmental Panel on Climate Change, what he thought of Saudi Arabia's proposal to be compensated for lost revenues resulting from the global move toward renewable energy. He responded that the compensation idea "should work in both directions." When oil prices rise to above average levels, then the excess profits reaped by the oil-producing nations should be shared with the rest of the world. Aware of the political implications of his even-handed suggestion, Mr. Pachauri made it clear that he was speaking only for himself and not for the Intergovernmental Panel on Climate Change.

Of course, Mr. Pachauri's candid response is not likely to see the light of day in any official UN sponsored forum or recommendation. Remember: the Organization of Islamic Conference is the largest single voting bloc within the "Group of 77 plus China" bloc, which has 132 member states.[263] They share a common interest in demanding subsidies from the industrialized countries to help with the conversion to alternative fuels as the price for supporting a new UN treaty on climate change.

Rich countries are already being asked to accept a compulsory levy on international airline tickets and shipping fuel to raise billions of dollars for the UN kitty.[264] Developing countries also demand a separate assessment on rich countries based on the size of their economies, fossil gas usage, and population. This assessment would fill the coffers of yet another UN kitty, to be known as the "green fund."[265] President Obama's special envoy for climate change, Todd Stern, called this financing scheme "highly constructive."[266] Of course, the Obama administration would find any tax and redistribution scheme "highly constructive."

The OIC will block any new global warming treaty until it is sure that Saudi Arabia and its other oil-rich members are made whole. If it succeeds, money from the UN green fund will end up in Saudi Arabia's pocket, instead of helping countries that may truly need seed money to invest in green technologies. And you can be sure that Saudi Arabia and its OPEC allies will not be sharing any of their windfall profits from oil sales anytime soon.

Forced Tithing for Islamic "Charities"

Sharia commands charity payments or tithing, known as *zakat*.[267] The alms are only for the poor and the needy, and those who collect them, and those whose hearts are to be reconciled, and to free the captives and the debtors, and for the cause of Allah, and (for) the wayfarers; a duty imposed by Allah. Allah is knower, Wise.[268]

The Price of Sharia-Compliant Finance

Zakat is supposed to be charity paid exclusively by Muslims.[269] However, non-Muslim companies engaged in sharia-compliant financial transactions must also contribute a *zakat*-style tithe.[270]

It is estimated that more than 400 Islamic financial institutions currently operate in seventy-five countries.[271] Major Western financial institutions such as HSBC, UBS, J.P. Morgan Chase, Deutsche Bank, Lloyds TSB, and BNP Paribas offer Islamic banking and sharia-based products.[272] Sharia-compliant finance requires these financial institutions to tithe in accordance with *zakat* in order to be sharia-compliant.

And foreign companies doing business in Muslim countries pay a flat mandatory tax on foreign company profits.[273] In 2007 alone, Saudi Arabia collected $18 billion from the tithes, including its 20 percent flat tax.[274]

Western institutions handing over money don't control where it goes. More often than not, it funds Islamic charities that are fronts for jihad causes. As national security expert Alex Alexiev explained, "much of this huge financial windfall for Islamic extremism is now generated by sharia finance in the West, making us a key sponsor of those that want to destroy us."[275]

To make sure all tithing monies are spent on Islamic causes, the Organization of Islamic Conference set up a clerical International Commission for *zakat* in 2007.[276]

One of the most enthusiastic supporters of the International Commission for *zakat* is Muslim Brotherhood spiritual leader, Yusuf Al-Qaradawi.[277] He wants *zakat* spent on such causes as Islamic charities that support families of suicide bombers.[278] Helping truly needy poor people with the proceeds from oil money or *zakat* isn't on his agenda.

Yet, astonishingly, President Obama wants to make it easier for Islamists in the United States to set up and run phony charities. In his speech to the Muslim world at Cairo University, Obama said that "in the United States, rules on charitable giving have made it harder for Muslims to fulfill their religious obligation. That's why I'm committed to work with American Muslims to ensure that they can fulfill *zakat*."[279]

So is his beloved United Nations.

UNICEF's Link to an Islamic Front Group

We have already seen how the United Nations Development Programme has provided the Islamists cover for their dubious charitable activities. Here is another example, this time involving the famous United Nations Children's Fund (UNICEF) and an Islamic charity known as the International Islamic Relief Organization, which has been implicated in funding terrorist and propaganda operations.[280]

On June 9, 2008, UNICEF signed a memorandum of understanding with the International Islamic Relief Organization to provide support, supposedly to help children in Saudi Arabia and other countries.[281] "Building partnerships with leading organizations like the International Relief organization is the result of our trust in their continuous and effective efforts to protect and secure a better future for children," declared Dr. Ayman Abu Laban, UNICEF Representative in the Gulf.[282]

UNICEF's trust is misplaced. Here is what the US Treasury Department had to say about the International Islamic Relief Organization (IIRO) when it designated two of its branches as terrorist organizations. Note that the Treasury Department named the International Islamic Relief Organization's Executive Director of the Saudi Arabian office as a money man for al Qaeda and other terrorist groups:

> Abd Al Hamid Sulaiman Al-Mujil (Al-Mujil) is the Executive Director of the IIRO Eastern Province (IIRO-EP) branch office in the Kingdom of Saudi Arabia. Al-Mujil has been called the "million dollar man" for supporting Islamic militant groups. Al-Mujil provided donor funds directly to al Qaida and is identified as a major fundraiser for the Abu Sayyaf Group (ASG) and Jemaah Islamiyah (JI). Both ASG and JI are al Qaida-associated terrorist groups in Southeast Asia designated pursuant to the authorities of E.O. 13224. These terrorist groups are also on the United Nations 1267 Committee's consolidated list of individuals and entities associated with the Taliban, al Qaida and/or Usama Bin Ladin.[283]

If UNICEF prefers to take the International Islamic Relief Organization's word over the US Treasury's, then so be it. But UNICEF should have noticed that the same two branches of the International Islamic Relief Organization have been designated as terrorist groups by the UN itself![284]

UNICEF is helping fulfill one of the key recommendations of the Muslim Brotherhood Project: to collect sufficient funds from wherever possible, including so-called donations, to perpetuate and support jihad around the world.[285] As the Muslim Brotherhood's spiritual leader Yusuf Qaradawi put it, "I don't like this word 'donations.' I like to call it jihad with money, because God has ordered us to fight enemies with our lives and our money."[286]

The United Nations Aid Programs—
The Islamists' Cash Cow

As we shall see, the Islamists control UN money ostensibly intended to help impoverished Muslims, but much of that money goes to Islamic jihad causes instead.

In this regard, it is tempting to highlight the mother of all UN financial scandals: the United Nations' Oil-for-Food program. Corrupt, inattentive UN officials allowed Iraqi dictator Saddam Hussein to divert billions of UN administered dollars to his own personal accounts. That money was earmarked for critical humanitarian goods for suffering Iraqis. Instead, Hussein used some of it to bribe foreign business and government leaders—as well as some UN officials. The rest lined his pockets. And $8.4 billion of that plunder came from smuggling oil to the Islamic countries of Jordan, Syria, Egypt, and Turkey. [287]

Nevertheless, the Oil-for-Food scandal is only interesting for the purposes of this book because it illustrates UN corruption, and the UN's complicity with dictators like Saddam Hussein. But Saddam Hussein was a power-hungry secularist who happened to be an Arab Muslim, rather than a committed Islamist.[288] Thus, the Oil-for-Food theft is less useful as an example of how Islamists siphon off UN funds to finance their jihads.

However, we do not need the Oil-for-Food scandal to show how Islamists plunder UN resources. Below are some examples of how UN money flowed to Islamists with little, if any, accountability for how the money was spent.

Don't forget that as taxpayers contributing billions of dollars to the UN's budget every year, we are paying much of the tab—and will be paying even more if President Obama has his way.

UN Humanitarian and Relief Aid

The Organization of Islamic Conference member states should adopt a new motto—"It is better to receive than to give."

Forty percent of all donations to UN humanitarian and relief agencies since 1992 have found their way to Organization of Islamic Conference member states.[289] That money originated mostly from the West, on top of all the oil money the West is already sending the Islamists' way—a compounded *jizya*, if you will.

Conversely, little money flows in the other direction—from OIC member states to UN humanitarian relief agencies. According to records of global humanitarian contributions, compiled by the United Nations through mid-September 2009, the United States is the largest contributor—approximately $2.197 billion dollars or 28.6 percent. Norway contributed approximately $316.2 million dollars or 4.1 percent. By contrast, Saudi Arabia, Kuwait and the United Arab Emeritates combined totaled approximately $100.25 million dollars or only 1.3 percent. [290]

Iran's ATM Machine—
The United Nations Development Programme

The Islamic Republic of Iran is a major beneficiary of United Nations developmental funding. Between 2005 and 2009, this Islamic theocracy raked in $177 million.[291]

Once again, the United Nations Development Programme (UNDP), the largest of the UN bureaucracies, is involved—this time as the sieve through which the UN money it administers lands in Iran with no strings attached. And Iran just happened to hold the presidency of the UNDP's Executive Board of the UNDP for 2009 and will be represented on the board at least through 2011.[292]

The UNDP Helps Iran to Evade Sanctions

The UNDP operates on a decentralized structure. Its local country offices define their priorities in concert with the host governments receiving the UNDP-administered funds. In aid recipient countries like Iran, the UNDP has a resident representative who also serves as the resident coordinator for all UN development-related projects in that country. In the case of Iran, the UNDP coordination responsibility covers seventeen UN agencies and programs.[293]

Who actually controls how the UNDP-administered money is being spent in Iran? The answer, according to an action plan agreement between the Government of the Islamic Republic of Iran and the UNDP, is *the Iranian government:* the "Ministry of Foreign Affairs of Iran coordinates all external aid and carries overall responsibility for the coordination of the UNDP Country Programme."[294]

While Iran flouts the current UN Security Council sanctions resolutions meant to deter its nuclear ambitions, the United Nations Development Programme is actively aiding Iran to obtain potential dual-use technology. It is doing so by enabling, in its own words, the "transfer of knowledge in science and technology through technology-based services," programs to "improve technological capacity in industries," and "joint international research projects."[295] The transfer will include "advance processing technologies and innovative system design."[296] There is no mention of any limitations on the types of technology eligible for transfer under the UNDP's auspices. Nor is there any mention of mechanisms to monitor whether the technology is being used to enhance Iran's military capacity, or whether Iran will share this technology with terrorist organizations it sponsors.

For example, the United Nations Development Programme, the World Health Organization and UNESCO have partnered with the Iranian Research Organization for Science and Technology (IROST), an innocent sounding scientific group. However, according to Iran Watch, the Japanese government has called IROST an "entity of concern" for biological, chemical and nuclear weapon proliferation.[297] The British government says IROST has procured goods and/or technology for weapons of mass destruction programs.[298] And it has reportedly acted as a front for the purchase of fungus from Canada and Netherlands, of the sort used for producing toxins.[299]

UN development bureaucrats prop up Iran's economy, observing that Iran's relative wealth due to its vast oil and gas reserves needs to be "translated into stronger economic performance in the long term."[300] UN bureaucrats hope that "the UN system will lend its support to the Iranian Government" by working to improve Iran's "economic performance and management."[301] The goal is to increase Iran's real economic growth by 8 percent per annum and to increase gross investment by 12.2 percent per annum.[302]

To achieve these objectives, the United Nations Development Programme is working with the Iranian terrorist sponsoring regime, to strengthen its export, import and production capacities and ultimately to help its accession to the World Trade Organization.[303] The UNDP's extensive activities on the Iranian regime's behalf, and the hard currency pumped into Iran's economy by the UNDP and its affiliated UN agencies, are operating at cross-purposes with the ongoing efforts by the UN Security Council and Western democracies to isolate Iran from the international financial community.

With all of its talk about tougher sanctions against Iran if it does not negotiate in good faith, the Obama administration is evidently doing nothing to stop continued UNDP assistance to the Islamic theocracy with nuclear ambitions.

The United Nations Development Programme has also partnered with Iran's biggest automobile manufacturer, Iran Khodro, which builds cars and commercial vehicles for domestic use and for export.[304]

Khodro is already the largest auto manufacturer in the Middle East, with lucrative partnerships with French, German and Chinese auto firms. Between 1996 and 2006, Khodro enjoyed an annual growth rate of 23 percent with a goal of manufacturing more than 650,000 cars.[305]

European firms doing business with Khodro should consider how their private self-interest conflicts with their own governments' stance against the Iranian regime. And Khodro's questionable dealings and associations should have given the UNDP pause—unless the goal all along was to undermine the economic sanctions imposed to date on Iran by the UN Security Council, the United States and the European Union.

For example, according to Iran Watch, the German government called Khodro "a risky end-user" in warnings to its exporters in 2004.[306] Also, it appears that one Manuchehr Manteqi, the name of the man who was chief executive and president of Iran Khodro until 2009, was also the name of a Brigadier General in the Islamic Revolutionary Guards Corps during the 1990s who served as a senior official of Iran's Defense Industries Organization.[307] Are they the same person? Apparently, the UNDP did not care.

What's more, a 2007 document issued by the United Nations Mission in Sudan referred without comment to an Iranian press report that Sudan and Iran—two regimes currently under UN Security Council sanctions—signed a memorandum of understanding to enhance defense cooperation, and that during his four day visit to Tehran, the Sudanese defense minister inspected Khodro's facilities![308]

And finally, Iran's Supreme National Security Council, which oversees the country's nuclear program, used Khodro to get around UN sanctions against purchasing massive amounts of carbon fiber.[309] Carbon fiber can be used in auto fuel tanks that run partly on compressed natural gas, but it also is a component of advanced centrifuges used to enrich uranium.[310]

Yet the United Nations Development Programme has declared that this Iranian front company is eligible for UNDP assistance!

The United Nations Development Programme also hypes its "good governance" agenda as its rationale for cooperating so extensively with the Iranian regime.[311] Improved economic conditions will help lessen corruption and increase openness, say UNDP propagandists. The precise opposite has occurred.

There is more political repression than ever in Iran, as evidenced by the brutal crackdown against Iranian citizens peacefully protesting the rigged June 2009 re-election of President Ahmadinejad. And when a member of the Iranian General Audit Office claimed that "a mafia-style group of mullahs" is "plundering the country and sending the proceeds to foreign banks," he was promptly arrested by the secret police, presumably on orders from "Supreme Guide" (or more accurately the "Cappo de Cappos") Ali Khamenei.[312]

Don't count on the UNDP's largesse to Iran reaching the needy anytime soon.

Islamists' Takeover of the UN's Largest Refugee Aid Program

The Islamists for all intents and purposes run the United Nations Relief and Work Agency for Palestinian Refugees (UNRWA), while we pay for it.

Based on 2006 figures, Western countries provided more than 95 percent of UNRWA's budget.[313] Arab donors, on the other hand, contributed less than 3 percent.[314] Since 1950, the United States has contributed more than $3.4 *billion* to UNRWA.[315] For fiscal year 2006, the US contributed more than $137 million of UNRWA's budgeted expenditures of $462 million. In fiscal year 2007, the US contributed $154 million, and in fiscal year 2008, $184 million.[316] By contrast oil-rich Saudi Arabia pledged a mere $1.2 million in 2007.[317]

And it only gets worse under the Obama administration. At an international donors' conference held in Egypt in 2009, to gather support for Palestinians after the Gaza conflict, Secretary of State Hillary Rodham Clinton pledged $900 million. Approximately $150 million of that will flow through UNRWA—on top of the $98.5 million the US already contributed to UNRWA in 2009.[318]

The United Nations Relief and Work Agency for Palestinian Refugees is about as old as the United Nations itself. The General Assembly created it in 1949 as a "temporary" relief agency providing humanitarian assistance to Palestinian Arabs, who had left their homes in Israel in 1948. [319] There were somewhere between 600,000 and 760,000 such refugees at the time.[320]

Sixty years later, UNRWA is a permanent UN fixture, far larger than any other United Nations sponsored humanitarian relief agency.[321] Palestinian refugees represent less than 18 percent of the world's refugees, yet UNRWA is the only UN agency devoted to just one refugee group, spending one third of all UN resources earmarked for refugees.[322]

Today, a fifth generation of Palestinian Arab refugees is served by UNRWA. Palestinian Arab refugees and their descendants registered with UNRWA now number around 4.6 million, and are scattered in throughout Gaza, Jordan, Lebanon, Syria, and the West Bank.[323] The refugees' neighboring Arab states have refused to provide permanent homes and citizenship to their fellow Arabs.

UNRWA gives these refugees false hope that they will all someday go back to Israel under some sort of "law of return." Said UNRWA Commissioner-General Karen Koning AbuZayd: "The refugees don't really want to be citizens of another country. Right now, they are waiting for a permanent, final status solution. Until a UN resolution says that they have the right of return or compensation, they and their descendants will continue in this state."[324]

As we saw in chapter five, the Israeli-Palestinian conflict is the Islamists' pet issue. UNRWA provides them the means to exploit the Palestinian refugees' suffering to fund their jihadist fighters, particularly Hamas.

Indeed, UNRWA and Hamas have become alter egos. The previous UNRWA Commissioner-General Peter Hansen admitted, without any show of concern, "Oh I am sure that there are Hamas members on the UNRWA payroll and I don't see that as a crime."[325]

Hansen's replacement as UNRWA Commissioner-General, Karen Koning AbuZayd, has picked up where Hansen left off. For example, at a 2006 Congressional briefing Commissioner-General

AbuZayd admitted to not checking the names of those who receive financial aid from UNRWA against any terrorist watch lists, noting that it would be too difficult because "Arab last names sound so familiar."[326]

She has taken Hamas' side, scolding the West for not dealing with the terrorist organization.[327] And she blamed Hamas' rocket attacks aimed at Israeli civilians on Israel's refusal to open all of the border crossings.[328]

Commissioner-General AbuZayd has also aligned herself with Syria—Iran's partner in helping the Hamas and Hezbollah terrorist organizations. According to a UN document summarizing Karen Koning AbuZayd's visit to Syria, she "expressed the UNRWA's appreciation over President al-Assad's continued support and over the Syrian people's solidarity, particularly during the Israeli aggression on Gaza."[329] And she presided over a UN agency that allows its schools to employ Islamic terrorists as teachers and administrators. A Palestine Press news agency report said parents contacted senior UNRWA official, John Ging, complaining that dozens of their children's teachers belonged to the Izz Al-Din Al-Qassam Brigades, Hamas's military-terrorist wing.[330] There is no report that the parents ever got any action on their complaint.

At a September 18, 2009 press conference, I asked Commissioner-General Zayad whether the UNRWA knew how many Hamas-affiliated teachers the agency employed. She replied that "we don't ask staff recruits about their affiliations"—a "don't ask, don't tell" policy, if you will. She also pleaded ignorance about those parent complaints sent to UNRWA officials.[331]

In fact, Hamas' grip on the UNRWA schools is tightening. A group affiliated with Hamas known as the Islamic Bloc controls the teachers' section of the UNRWA union in Gaza.[332] The Islamic Bloc runs its indoctrination programs in the UNRWA schools.[333] UNRWA schools use classroom materials that glorify terrorists, and which contain maps in which Israel has been erased.[334]

In the words of veteran UN reporter Claudia Rosett, UNRWA officials use "the UN stage as a megaphone to help elicit sympathy, drum up funds, denounce Israel and drape in UN baby blue the interests and demands of the Iranian-backed terrorists of Hamas."[335]

In short, American taxpayers have shelled out more than $3.4 billion dollars on a UN agency run by and for the Islamists, *and they are about to shell out hundreds of millions more under President Obama.*

CHAPTER SEVEN

The UN and the West Fall for the Fraud of Islamic Finance

A Strong Ethical Foundation?

"The major selling proposition of Islamic finance is its strong ethical foundation," claimed the president of the Islamic Development Bank, Ahmed Mohamed Ali.[336]

Nobel Prize winning economist Joseph Stiglitz, chairman of the *UN Commission of Experts on Reforms of the International Monetary and Financial System,* also praised the ethics of Islamic finance when I asked him about it at a United Nations press briefing.[337] Combine that sentiment with Stiglitz's promotion of the UN as the ideal overseer of world finances.[338] Stiglitz's article promoting the UN's leading governance role and his call for a new global reserve currency to replace the US dollar was singled out approvingly by the popular Muslim Web site Islamicity.[339]

Its defenders at the United Nations and elsewhere say Islamic finance is more ethical than Western capitalism, because it prohibits not just usury (*riba*), but forbids lending money at interest altogether.[340] In theory, Islamic finance prohibits banks from buying or trading debt itself. Instead, banks and their clients must invest in concrete assets and share the profits. Speculation is officially prohibited, too. These prohibitions derive from two religious sources regarding equitable distributive justice, permitted activities (*halal*), and public goods (*maslaha*).[341] This supposedly demonstrates the ethical and moral safeguards purportedly missing from the conventional capitalistic, free market system.[342]

Muslim Brotherhood spiritual leader Yusuf al-Qaradawi made this point when he claimed that the "collapse of the capitalist system, which is based on usury and securities rather than commodities in markets, shows us that it is undergoing a crisis and that our integrated Islamic philosophy—if properly understood and applied—can replace the Western capitalism."[343]

Western Leaders Buy into Islamic Finance

The Vatican Press

While its Eurocentric editorial slant doesn't necessarily reflect official Catholic Church teaching, even the venerable Vatican newspaper, *Osservatore Romano*, editorialized in March 2009: "The ethical principles on which Islamic finance is based may bring banks closer to their clients and to the true spirit which should mark every financial service."[344]

European Financial Leaders

As we have seen, European financial institutions have embraced Islamic finance. And consider that effusive praise from French Finance Minister Christine Lagarde, who extolled its "new principles for the international financial system based on transparency, responsibility and, I would like to add, moderation."[345] She added that "Islamic finance is calling out to us."[346]

Meanwhile, London is now an international center of Islamic finance.

"Islamic finance does demonstrate good banking behavior that has been perhaps lost over the last 10 years or so," said Neil Miller, head of Islamic finance at Norton Rose and an adviser to the British government. "Islamic banking is saying we are close to our clients and we're only going to do genuine transactions where we can see the asset, we understand the asset, we can make an assessment of that asset: whether it's financing a ship or an aircraft they will go and have a look at the business. It's giving guidance as to what banking should be."[347]

The US Treasury

Even more incredibly, the United States Treasury helped organize an Islamic finance forum in November 2008, in partnership with the Islamic Finance Project of Harvard University. The forum was "designed to help inform the policy community about Islamic financial services, which are an increasingly important part of the global financial industry."[348]

The target audience for this forum was staff from US banking regulatory agencies, Congress, Department of Treasury, and other parts of the Executive Branch.

Under President Obama, the Treasury is going one step further. It is defending its taxpayer-funded bail-out of insurance giant AIG (including its Bahrain-based sharia-compliant AIG subsidiary, AIG Takaful—Enaya) in a lawsuit filed by the Thomas More Law Center, on behalf of a former US marine who fought in Iraq and Afghanistan. The lawsuit alleges that AIG's sharia-compliant subsidiary "engages in Shariah-based Islamic religious activities that are anti-Christian, anti-Jewish, and anti-American."[349]

Treasury Department officials, who must have learned their lessons well at that Harvard seminar, have asked the federal district court to dismiss the lawsuit on the grounds that the Treasury Department doesn't control AIG. That's a curious argument, since the US government now enjoys a post-bailout 80 percent ownership interest in the company.

In other words, Obama's Treasury Department defends using American taxpayers' money to fund an operation that collects a religious tax, which in turn funds "charities" that funnel money to terrorists. This is not surprising considering that Obama's Treasury Secretary Timothy Geithner was very receptive to sharia-based finance when he was Federal Reserve Bank of New York president. Moreover, while representing the United States as Secretary of the Treasury on a visit to Saudi Arabia, Geithner praised Saudi Arabia's economy and told his royal hosts how much he wanted Saudi companies to increase their investments in the United States.[350] Apparently, like his boss, Geithner is not too worried about the religious taxing of profits for jihad that will almost certainly accompany those investments.

Islamic Finance Goes Global

Islamic finance is now a global phenomenon. Moody's Investor Service estimates that sharia-compliant finance accounts for around $700 billion of assets, and is growing at 10 percent to 30 percent a year. In a November 2009 note to its clients, Moody's said the purchase of sharia-compliant bonds and loans had grown 40 percent in the first ten months of 2009, year over year.[351]

Islamic Economic Injustice

Islamic finance promises to promote ethical business practices, and usher in a more equitable economic climate. However, in practice, there is no equitable system of wealth distribution in the Muslim world. Islamic finance is, in fact, a rigged system, benefiting a few wealthy rulers, petro-oligarchs and clerics while the poor in Muslim lands struggle just to survive.[352]

Despite the lofty rhetoric swirling around Islamic finance, a study by the Arab League Educational Cultural and Scientific

Organization found that 30 percent of the approximately 300 million people in the Arab World are illiterate.[353]

A World Bank report found that unemployment in the Arab world averaged 14 percent.[354] Despite having approximately 22 percent of the world population and 70 percent of its energy resources, the share of Organization of Islamic Conference (OIC) countries of the world's total outputs is only 5 percent. Nearly 40 percent of their population lives below the poverty level. Tellingly, twenty-two of the fifty least developed countries in the world are OIC member states.[355]

And women in sharia-compliant economies are often excluded from productive work and education outside of the home altogether.[356]

These are not the signs of a prosperous, just, and compassionate economic system.

Dr. Sami Alrabaa, a sociology professor and an Arab/Muslim culture specialist who has lived in Saudi Arabia, has observed:

> Saudi Arabia is the only country in the world that applies the Shari's (Allah's Law). And the Al Saud, the absolute rulers of the country, are proud of that. However, the banks in that country which call themselves "Islamic" are in reality banks like all the others across the globe. I lived in that country for six years and I know what I'm talking about.
>
> According to Human Rights Watch, Amnesty International, and all the human rights reports of the US State Department, Saudi Arabia has the highest rates of human trafficking in terms of domestic slaves and prostitutes... After all that Saudis go the mosque five times a day to pray in hopes that Allah would waive their atrocities. This is daily practice in all the oil-rich Arab countries. This is Islam in these countries on the ground.[357]

Clearly, western-style capitalist economies, with all of their faults, have nothing to learn from the way Islamic economies really operate "on the ground."

The Charade of Sharia-Compliant Finance

As for learning anything useful from sharia-compliant Islamic financial institutions, forget it. Under the Islamic system, unaccountable sharia boards consisting of one to three Islamic scholars (*ulama*) advise Islamic banks. These purported "experts" in economics or finance[358] are supposed to base their decisions upon their "human understanding" (*fiqh*) of the "divine law," but they answer to no one.[359]

Mufti Muhammad Taqi Usmani is one such Muslim scholar. A prolific writer on Islam and a former sharia judge in Pakistan's Supreme Court, Muhammad Taqi Usmani sits on sharia financial boards. He has served as an adviser to several global financial institutions, including Dow Jones (until he was terminated in 2008.)[360]

This "scholar" believes that "aggressive jihads were waged...because it was truly commendable for establishing the grandeur of the religion of Allah."[361] He also believes that Muslims should live peacefully in countries such as Britain only until they gain enough power to engage in battle.[362]

Along with twenty-nine other prominent Pakistani Islamic scholars, Muhammad Taqi Usmani signed a statement declaring that the "Taliban are not in fact terrorists."[363] The same statement criticized the Pakistani government for making progressive changes in education and women's rights. It even criticized the government for "promoting dancing, the Basant [kite festival], [and women's participation in] marathons..."[364]

Muhammad Taqi Usmani also signed a joint letter to the Organization of the Islamic Conference calling for the OIC to "take effective steps for bringing in an international law at the level of the United Nations, as per which blasphemy of the prophets and revealed books will be declared a criminal act."[365]

This is the kind of "scholar" serving on the Islamic banking boards.

Interpretations of what is prohibited under Islamic law vary according to these scholars' ideological bent.[366] Naturally, this leads to inconsistent decisions among sharia boards. There is no central regulator or court of last resort. And decisions are made behind closed doors with no oversight.

Here is an example of this ad hoc, unaccountable decision-making, taken from a Q&A exchange posted by Mufti Muhammad Taqi Usmani himself on the Islamic Web site, Albalagh:[367]

Q: "Seeing the name of Maulana Mufti Taqi Usmani in the Shariah Board and reading his fatwa on the permissibility of Meezan Bank products, I opened a saving account with Meezan Bank Limited. Now I have found out that there is a controversy on the subject and even Mufti Taqi does not recommend the bank now."

"Please guide me should I continue with the said bank or not? Where I should keep my money if even this bank is not Shariah compliant?"

A: "It is true that some ulama have issued a fatwa against the business of Meezan Bank, rather against Islamic banking in general, but after considering their arguments I could not change my view. *However, in case of disagreement between Muftis, one may act on the opinion of the Mufti that one believes to be more reliable.*" (emphasis added)

No doubt, Mufti Muhammad Taqi Usmani (the Taliban supporter, free speech basher and opponent of women's participation in sporting events) considers his own opinions the most "reliable." And, no doubt, he will keep issuing opinions on sharia compliance that reflect his retrograde Islamic ideology.

Zakat and Islamic Finance

Zakat (charity) is a central part of Islamic finance. According to the IslamBank Web site, a business is obliged to pay *zakat* in either of the following ways:

a) After covering his business expenses and taking care of his family needs, a trader should pay a minimum 2.5 per cent *zakat* on the net surplus, or,

b) "Evaluate the cost price of the inventory-in-trade…and pay a minimum 2.5 percent on this amount."[368]

As we have seen, Islamic charities collecting and dispensing *zakat* are often front groups that fund Islamic jihad, rather than legitimate humanitarian charities.

As one commentator put it,

> More often than not, it is people like [Muhammad Taqi] Usmani who are paid lucratively to sit on sharia-finance boards in order to determine what charities will receive the sharia-finance institutions' donations—and it's a fair bet that the March of Dimes is not among them.[369]

Nevertheless, President Obama wants to make it easier for these phony charities to collect tax-exempt donations within the United States!

The Shell Game

The financial instruments used by Islamic institutions for trading and extending credit are anything but ethical or moral. They are merely the components of a hypocritical shell game.

Chibli Mallat, a human rights lawyer and a former presidential candidate in Lebanon, explained the rank hypocrisy this way:

From a system which is informed by the moral unease in Islamic law toward speculative investment which is not underscored by labour, the current Islamic banks have engaged into a spate of dubious transactions with Arabic names that all but dupe the customer.[370]

Islamic financial institutions regularly find ways around the sharia prohibition against lending money at interest. They create equivalent instruments, which simply avoid the use of the words "interest" or "loan" to describe the underlying credit arrangements.

How Islamic Financing Really Works

One such instrument is called the Murabahah contract. As explained on the Web site of the Institute of Islamic Banking and Insurance, Murabahah is the single most popular form of Islamic financing.[371] It involves a "contract of sale between the bank and its client for the sale of goods at a price plus an agreed profit margin for the bank. The contract involves the purchase of goods by the bank which then sells them to the client at an agreed mark-up. Repayment is usually in instalments (sic)."[372]

The sequence of events in a Murabaha transaction is set out in a United Nations document entitled *Islamic Finance and Structured Commodity Finance Techniques: Where the Twain Can Meet.*[373] The authors of the document say that their purpose is "to inspire conventional bankers to incorporate Islamic financing structures into their credit packages, and Islamic bankers to adopt some of the innovations of structured finance to expand their lending and investment possibilities."[374]

Here are the steps:

(1)   After being approached by a buyer (who has already identified a supplier of the goods in which he is interested), the bank normally appoints the ultimate buyer as their agent for purchase of the required goods;

(2)   At the same time, the buyer executes an agreement with the bank binding himself to buy the requisite goods from the bank upon delivery, at a marked-up price on a deferred payment basis. The buyer may pay a non-refundable premium (called *urboun*) to secure his "promise to buy" (in most cases, this is the buyer's liability in case the deal is not finalized; other forms of guarantee payments also exist, however);

(3)–(4) The buyer, not the bank, enters into a sale contract with the supplier on behalf of the bank;

(5)–(9) The supplier arranges to transport the goods to the destination mentioned in the contract, along with documents including invoices, carrier's note and other papers, either to the buyer who is acting as agent of the bank or, more likely, through his (supplier's) bank for payment. In the latter case, prior to shipment, the supplier asks the buyer's bank to open a letter of credit, through which he will be paid after delivery;

(10)   The bank then offers the buyer the goods (of which it retains the documents, and thus, title) at the marked-up price. Its letter to the buyer clearly states the payment schedule. The mark-up rate is calculated from the date the bank paid for the goods to the dates the buyer pays. The bank also charges fees for its various services.

Note that there are technically two sale transactions—one through which the bank acquired the commodity, and the other through which it sold it to the client. They are supposed to be separate, even though in economic terms they constitute the same transaction.[375] In other words, the most popular form of Islamic finance is a shell game allowing the Islamic bank, which was never actually interested in purchasing the underlying commodity, to collect a set fee in return for making money available so the client who really wants that commodity can acquire it.

Still not convinced that Islamic financial instruments elevate form over substance? Here is how one Islamic bank describes the process of financing a house:[376]

- You identify the property you wish to buy and agree the purchase price with the seller of the property in the normal way.

- You approach us for assistance and complete an application form (*see section "do I qualify"*).

- If we are able to help, the bank will buy the property, after solicitors confirmed that everything is in order, and immediately sell it to you at a *higher price.*

- *The higher price* is calculated depending on the value of the property, the number of years you wish to pay us over and the amount of your first payment (*see "payment calculator" for an indication of the higher price*).

- When purchased, the property is registered in your name and the sale between yourself and the bank is recorded in the Murabaha Contract.

- Your first payment to the bank is made on the day of completion and is your initial contribution, normally a minimum of 17% of the purchase price.

- One month after completion your regular monthly payments will commence. These will be claimed by Direct Debit automatically from you (sic) normal bank account. (emphasis in the original)

This is simply a conventional mortgage in heavy Islamic garb. The only real difference may come down to how late payments are handled.

Instead of adding additional fees for late payments, an Islamic bank sometimes blackballs the customer by circulating his name to other Islamic banks.[377] This blackballing may continue even after the customer satisfies all of his payment obligations.[378]

A Rose by Any Other Name...

The Institute of Islamic Banking and Insurance tries to draw fine distinctions between interest-bearing loans and Murabahah contracts. For example, it says money exchanged for money plus interest is a usurious transaction involving the exchange of intangible commodities, while in "a Murabahah sale on credit the exchange is between unlike commodities, like goods and cash."[379] So what? It's still a credit transaction, with the bank receiving a fixed mark-up on the money it lays out on behalf of its client.

The Institute also argues that the Murabahah agreement, unlike a conventional Western-style loan agreement, "does not involve or imply a sale of something that one does not possess, because the agreement made with the buyer is concluded after actual possession."[380] Again, so what? With a security interest in the home or car being financed by a conventional interest-bearing loan, a bank shares the risk of a lower resale price should the client default and they are forced to repossess the collateral.

"Islam Is *Not* the Solution"

Obviously, United Nations experts, European financial leaders and the US Treasury have turned a blind eye to this hypocrisy in their eagerness to please the Muslim world. As we have seen, Nobel-prize winning economist Joseph Stiglitz's skepticism about Western-style capitalism has clouded his judgment regarding Islamic finance as an ethical alternative. Now, he is using his worldwide renown to promote a new global financial and economic architecture, to be overseen by the United Nations.

They all should pay heed to what Dr. Sami Alrabaa, the Arab/ Muslim culture expert whom I quoted earlier, has said about Islamic finance: "Islam is *not* the solution, it is rather a liability in both theory and practice. 'Islam is the solution' is hypocrisy and self-deception per excellence."[381]

The same goes for the United Nations. If we were to follow Dr. Stiglitz's suggestion to allow the UN to lead a new global financial and economic governance structure, the result will be economic self-destruction. And the Islamists will reap the spoils without having to fire a shot.

CHAPTER EIGHT

The UN and Obama Help Rebrand Organized Barbarism

To convince the world that sharia-based international norms don't present a threat to Western values, Islamists engage in the time-honored Muslim tradition of lying about their own faith to conceal its true nature. This form of deception is known as *taqiyya*.[382]

So we witness Islamists declaring with a straight face that Islam is a religion of peace, or that Islam is a tolerant religion.[383] And the Islamists regularly divert attention away from thoughtful questions about their religion, by attacking the questioner as an Islamophobe. Islamists insist that "inflammatory and misogynistic comments [in the Koran or in the oral traditions relating to the words and deeds of prophet Muhammad known as Hadiths] have been 'mistranslated,' misquoted or 'taken out of context.'"[384]

But Islamists get plenty of help with their *taqiyya* from the United Nations. Likewise, President Obama's Cairo speech on June 4, 2009, might as well have been an exercise in *taqiyya*.[385]

The Myths (i.e., the Taqiyya)

According to Barack Hussein Obama and the United Nations, the West harbors unfounded stereotypes of the Islam world that are preventing the development of harmonious relations between two great civilizations. Islam, they posit, is a tolerant, peaceful, and just religion that respects individual rights and the dignity of all human beings. President Obama and the United Nations have bought into an idealized conception of Islam that casts it as the precursor to the Enlightenment and modern day Western civilization.

What follows are a few examples from Obama's Cairo speech in June 2009, juxtaposed with excerpts from a report of a high level UN "Kumbaya" extravaganza known as the "Alliance of Civilizations."

The Alliance of Civilizations is a UN initiative intended to bridge the gap of understanding between the Western and Muslim worlds, through money-wasting forums and programs. Established in 2005 and cosponsored by Spain and Turkey, the Alliance focuses on four areas: youth, media, education, and migration.[386]

But, as veteran UN correspondent Claudia Rosett explains,

> the Alliance might more appropriately be called a U.N.-approved Slush Fund for Advancing Iranian and Other Islamic Interests. Both high profile and hard to pin down, it is first and foremost an Iranian brain child, which came to the U.N. by way of an earlier venture pitched in 1998 by Iran's then-president Mohammad Khatami for a "Dialogue of Civilizations."[387]

Recall that Khatami was that so-called "moderate" Iranian former president who called Israel a "terrorist, racist" regime.[388] Khatami also said that religion—specifically, Islam—should form "the foundations of a new civilization."[389] It sounds like he already knows how the "Dialogue of Civilizations" or the "Alliance of Civilizations"—or whatever you want to call such grand shows of faux moderation—must end.

In any case, President Obama was planning to attend this show of faux moderation during the Alliance of Civilizations' Istanbul conference in April 2009, but decided to pay a last-minute surprise trip to our troops in Iraq instead.[390] No matter. He was there in spirit, as evidenced by his Cairo address two months later containing myths about Islam which are uncannily similar to the Alliance's. The Obama administration has also since decided to formally join the UN's Alliance of Civilizations, with which Obama's views are so closely aligned:

Myth #1—
We have Islam to thank for Western civilization.

President Obama: "It was Islam at places like al-Azhar [University] that carried the light of learning through so many centuries, paving the way for Europe's Renaissance and Enlightenment."[391]

United Nations Alliance of Civilizations Report: "During medieval times, Islamic civilization was a major source of innovation, knowledge acquisition, and scientific advancement that contributed to the emergence of the Renaissance and the Enlightenment in Europe."[392]

Myth #2—
Islam is a tolerant religion.

President Obama: "And throughout history, Islam has demonstrated through words and deeds the possibilities of religious tolerance and racial equality."[393]

United Nations Alliance of Civilizations Report: "Historically, under Muslim rule, Jews and Christians were largely free to practice their faiths."[394]

Myth # 3—
Any tensions with the Muslim world stem from Western
colonialism and Israeli "occupation" of Palestine.

President Obama: "More recently, tension has been fed by colonialism that denied rights and opportunities to many Muslims and a Cold War in which Muslim majority countries were too often treated as proxies without regard to their own aspirations. Moreover, the sweeping change brought by modernity and globalization led many Muslims to view the West as hostile to the traditions of Islam."[395]

"...the Palestinian people, Muslims and Christians, have suffered in pursuit of a homeland. For *more than 60 years,* they've endured the pain of dislocation." (emphasis added)[396]

"Many wait in refugee camps in the West Bank and Gaza and neighboring lands for a life of peace and security that they have never been able to lead. They endure the daily humiliations, large and small, that come with *occupation*." (emphasis added)[397]

United Nations Alliance of Civilizations Report: "Selective accounts of ancient history are used by radical movements to paint an ominous portrait of historically distinct and mutually exclusive faith communities destined for confrontation. Such distorted historical narratives must be countered. More important for the purposes of this report is the fact that this history does not offer explanations for current conflicts or for the rise in hostility between Western and Muslim societies. On the contrary, the roots of these phenomena lie in developments that took place in the nineteenth and twentieth centuries, beginning with European imperialism, the resulting emergence of anti-colonial movements, and the legacy of the confrontations between them."[398]

"The partition of Palestine by the United Nations in 1947, envisaging the establishment of two states—Palestine and Israel—with a special status for Jerusalem, led to the establishment of the state of Israel in 1948, beginning a chain of events that continues to be one of the most tortuous in relations between Western and Muslim societies. Israel's continuing occupation of Palestinian and other Arab territories and the unresolved status of Jerusalem—a holy city for Muslims and Christians as well as Jews—have persisted with the perceived acquiescence of Western governments and thus are primary causes of resentment and anger in the Muslim world toward Western nations."[399]

Myth # 4— The West is to blame for negative stereotypes of Islam.

President Obama: "I have known Islam on three continents before coming to the region where it was first revealed. That experience guides my conviction that partnership between America and Islam must be based on what Islam is, not what it isn't. And I consider it part of my responsibility as president of the United States to fight against negative stereotypes of Islam wherever they appear."[400]

United Nations Alliance of Civilizations Report: "Assertions that Islam is inherently violent and related statements by some political and religious leaders in the West—including the use of terms such as "Islamic terrorism" and "Islamic fascism"—have contributed to an alarming increase in Islamophobia which further exacerbates Muslim fears of the West."[401]

President Obama and the United Nations both turn a blind eye to the organized barbarism that defines the Islamist worldview. They simply regurgitate and amplify the Islamists' phony messages of tolerance and victimhood. This lends credence to Islamist *taqiyya* or lies. If President Obama and the United Nations praise Islam and tout its supposed contributions to Western civilization, then why shouldn't Islamic legal precepts be incorporated into international law?

As the Egyptian-born British historian Bat Ye'or (the author of *Eurabia: The Euro-Arab Axis; Islam and Dhimmitude: Where Civilizations Collide*) put it, Obama and the United Nations are flattering "Muslim sensibilities" and expressing "the Muslim view of historical tolerance and cultural superiority over infidel civilizations."[402]

The Reality

We have seen the myths, repeated by President Obama and the United Nations. Then there is the very different, unsugarcoated view of how Islamic law destroys human lives from three Muslims who have actually lived for years under its yoke. They saw nothing to flatter, but plenty to condemn.

The Woman in the "Gender Cage"

The first is a Muslim woman who lived the first thirty years of her life in Egypt before she was able to emigrate to America. Her name is Nonie Darwish, whose father was regarded in the Muslim world as a *shahid* (martyr) for giving up his life more than fifty years ago in the jihad against Israel. [403]

"Growing up female in the Middle East," she said, "my life was impacted by the legacy of Sharia from the moment of birth."[404] And it was a stifling, degrading life to say the least. To escape the rigid sharia marriage laws, she emigrated to America in 1978 so that she could marry an Egyptian Coptic Christian. "Even so," Ms. Darwish explained, "it was necessary for him to convert to Islam in order to protect me from the long arm of Sharia law."[405]

After 9/11 brought the dangers of Islamist jihad to America's shores, Nonie Darwish decided to speak out publicly about her first-hand experiences living under "the most brutal, degrading, and humiliating laws in human history; laws that are obsessed with the sexuality of women, that subjugate and humiliate non-Muslims, and that ultimately produce a dysfunctional angry society."[406]

Ms. Darwish describes in painstaking detail the daily hardships imposed on Muslim women as a direct consequence of Islamic law and customs, patterned after Prophet Muhammad's own life. She did not rely on secondary sources or English translations of sharia and other Muslim texts. She went back to the Arabic language texts.[407] And she drew on her own personal experiences.

I will recount just a few of Ms. Darwish's examples:

- The sharia marriage contract is a document "granting sexual intercourse rights to the male and giving him total control over his wife or wives."[408] Or in the words of one of the most revered Muslim theologians of all time, Imam al-Ghazali, whom Ms. Darwish quotes: "Marriage is a form of slavery. The woman is man's slave, and her duty therefore is absolute obedience to the husband in all that he asks of her person."[409]

- A man is allowed up to four wives and can even enter into a temporary marriage contract to sanction a night of pleasure.[410]

- The husband is free to beat any of his wives if they are disobedient.[411]

- The husband can divorce his wives at will, but the wives are essentially stuck in loveless marriages at the pleasure of the husband they share.[412] The wives' shared husband is also favored in cases of custody of the children after the early years of childhood are over.[413]

- Men are granted the privilege to seek sexual gratification with children.[414] Muhammad placed his private parts between the thighs of six-year-old Aisha when she was six and consummated the marriage with her at age nine.[415] Iran's supreme leader, Ayotollah Khomeini, declared that it was perfectly okay under sharia for a man to sodomize a baby.[416]

Even disregarding female genital mutilation, sexual slavery, and honor killings, which still occur in parts of the Islam world, Islamic law stipulates a gender-segregated, patriarchal society in which women are treated as inferior beings. And that represents mainstream Islamic beliefs today, not a fringe extremist cult. No wonder the Organization of Islamic Conference is blocking the appointment of a new UN Human Rights Special Rapporteur to monitor laws that discriminate against women.[417]

Al-Azhar University, the Professor, and the Student

President Obama delivered his June 2009 speech to the Muslim world in Cairo, hosted by Al-Azhar University and the University of Cairo. During his "Cairo speech," proposing a new beginning in Islamic-US relations, Obama praised Al-Azhar University as a "beacon of Islamic learning," a place "that carried the light of learning through so many centuries, paving the way for Europe's Renaissance and Enlightenment."[418]

Alas, Obama left out the fact that the Grand Sheikh of Al-Azhar University, whom the BBC called "the highest spiritual authority for nearly a billion Sunni Muslims," approved suicide bombing based on Islamic law.[419]

Al-Azhar University was also the home of the Muslim Brotherhood's spiritual leader, Yusuf al-Qaradawi, whose incendiary writings I have quoted numerous times in this book. Despite his controversial *fatwas* (religious edicts), the Muslim scholars of the Al Azhar Islamic Research Council consider his membership an "enrichment to the Council's activities."[420]

Al-Qaradawi spared no time denouncing Obama's outreach speech to the Muslim world.

"The man [Obama] tried to quote from the Koran, as well as from the Torah and the New Testament," al-Qaradawi said. "He drew a parallel between the Koran and the Torah in their call for peace. He quoted the Talmud and the Torah as saying that the

Torah calls for peace. Never have I seen a single verse, paragraph, or sentence in the Torah which calls for peace. Everything in the Torah constitutes a call for war."[421]

That is how one of the world's major Muslim spiritual (and Muslim Brotherhood) leaders whom the Al Azhar Islamic Research Council considers an "enrichment to the Council's activities," responded to Obama's praise of Islam for its tolerance and respect of other religions. Has Obama noticed? I doubt it.

And Obama evidently did not speak with two Egyptian Muslims—a professor and student—who saw the dark side of Al-Azhar rather than the hype.

The Persecuted Professor

A professor of Islamic history at Al-Azhar University, Dr. Mustafa had started out teaching his students what he had learned himself, that "Islam is a religion of peace and only will fight against one who fights it."[422] But he could not square the idea of "an Islam of love, kindness and forgiveness" with the bombing of churches and killing of Christians that Muslim fundamentalists were committing all around him in the name of Islam.[423]

When the professor asked one of his friends, "Why are you killing our neighbors and countrymen whom we grew up with?" he received an answer that shocked him. "Out of all Muslims you should know," his friend replied. "The Christians did not accept the call of Islam, and they are not willing to pay us the *jizyah* (tax) to have the right to practice their beliefs. Therefore, the only option they have is the sword of Islamic law."[424]

The more Dr. Mustafa re-read the Koran and other texts of Islamic law, the more he saw what was "really causing a problem for my faith." He concluded that "Islam is full of discrimination—against women, against non-Muslims, against Christians and most especially against Jews. Hatred is built in to the religion. The history of Islam, which was my special area of study, could only be characterized as a river of blood."[425]

But that was only the beginning. When he raised questions about the Koran with his students, they reported him to university officials. What did Obama's beacon of Islamic learning and forerunner of the Enlightenment do next? It accused the professor of blasphemy, fired him, and turned him over to the Egyptian secret police, who imprisoned him.[426]

To force the professor to falsely confess to being an apostate for converting to Christianity—a crime punishable by death in Muslim lands—the secret police tortured him by pressing a red hot poker into the flesh of his left arm, beating him unconscious and immersing him in ice cold water, among other things.[427] Dr. Mustafa had not converted up to then, but that changed after he was finally released from prison. The secret police's false accusations became a self-fulfilling prophecy when the professor embraced Christianity.[428]

Assassins were sent to kill the professor, who was now a confirmed apostate under Islamic law. And when the professor's own father realized what his son had done, he became enraged, shouting to other members of the family that his son "has left the Islamic faith. I must kill him now!"[429]

The professor managed to escape the assassins and his own father. He ultimately came to the United States for religious asylum. But this Muslim scholar, who since his conversion to Christianity has gone by the name Mark Gabriel, does not want us to forget the central lesson of the personal pain he suffered under Islamic Law:

> I have never stopped crying for my Muslim people, whom I left behind, asking the Lord to deliver them from the darkness of Islam … It is the teachings of Islam that have produced terrorists who seem capable of any kind of evil in the name of Allah. Now the whole world wants to understand what Islam teaches. A great amount of misinformation has been shared in the media and on the Internet. My goal is to help you see plainly why these people do what they do.[430]

This is a far cry from the religious tolerance, education, and enlightenment that President Obama attributed to Islam generally and to Al-Azhar University specifically. Doesn't Obama realize his own embrace of Christianity despite his Islamic upbringing exposes him to charges of apostasy by that same university?

The Persecuted Student

A student at Al-Azhar University, Abdul Kareem Nabeel Suleiman (known as Kareem Amer), also found himself caught in the web of Islamic law.

Kareem grew up in a very religious family and attended the Al-Azhar religious school. As recounted on a Web site devoted to freeing Kareem from an Egyptian prison where he was detained for criticizing Islamic teachings and the religious extremism at his school, Al-Azhar's administration expelled Kareem and referred his case to state prosecutors. [431]

Kareem was arrested in November 2006 and subsequently sentenced to four years in jail for his Internet writings: three years for "contempt of religion" and one year for "defaming the President of Egypt." An appeal court upheld the four-year prison sentence, and the judge approved a civil claim filed by eleven lawyers who wanted to fine Kareem for "insulting Islam."[432]

Even one United Nations body, the UN Working Group on Arbitrary Detention, criticized his detention (although nothing of substance followed from this denunciation).[433]

What kinds of "insults" against Islam merited Kareem's expulsion from Al-Azhar University and subsequent detention in the eyes of his accusers and judges? For one thing, Kareem criticized the university's gender segregation policy.[434] He disagreed when Al-Azhar's Grand Sheikh pressured the Islamic Research Academy to pledge allegiance to Egyptian President Mubarak.[435] He criticized the teaching methods at his university, which he said was a school of "terrorism."[436] And he said that his conservative professors taught that freethinkers "end up in the dustbin of history."[437]

Kareem was charged by the university with contempt of religions in general, and specifically Islam; insulting the Grand Sheikh of Al-Azhar, as well as another professor; and atheism.[438]

The Egyptian government accused Kareem of the following crimes for which he was prosecuted and sentenced to the four-year prison term: (1) spreading data and malicious rumors that disrupt public security; (2) defaming the president of Egypt; (3) incitement to overthrow the regime upon hatred and contempt; (4) incitement to hate "Islam" and breach of the public peace standards; and (5) highlighting inappropriate aspects that harm the reputation of Egypt and spreading them to the public.[439]

During his detention, Kareem was "assaulted and then transferred to solitary confinement where he was placed in shackles and repeatedly beaten for two days."[440]

Just like the Al-Azhar professor I discussed earlier, Kareem was threatened with death by his own father. In this case, even though Kareem had not left Islam as the professor had done, just daring to criticize Islamic teaching was enough. His father "called for applying the Sharia on his son by giving three days to repent, followed by having him killed if he did not announce his repentance."[441]

All this Islamic student did was express his conscience. But *any* criticism of Islamic orthodoxy is considered blasphemy by Egyptian government officials, and by the Islamic university that Obama called the "beacon of learning."

The Islamists' Rebranding Campaign

The firsthand experiences of Nonie Darwish, Professor Mustafa (aka Mark Gabriel),and Abdul Kareem Nabeel Suleiman demonstrate that Islamic law is now a religious and ideological cover for organized barbarism. But the false Islamic narrative of misunderstood victimhood is winning out. Well-funded Islamists are rebranding their supremacist, misogynist Islamic ideology, rooted in sharia and in Muhammad's own life, into a nonthreatening pabulum more palatable to Western audiences.

The Islamists want to make sure that we are indoctrinated—or, as they would have it, "educated"—in their sanitized version of Islam. Only then will the West shed its oh-so-nasty racist Islamophobia.

We have a seen the role the United Nations plays in internationalizing the Muslim crime of defamation of religions. And the UN's Alliance of Civilizations, which the Obama administration has decided to join, is disseminating the Islamists' lies about their beliefs and intentions. But there is more to the UN's complicity in the Islamists' rebranding campaign, and sadly, it involves the education and welfare of children.

UNESCO Blames the West

The United Nations Educational, Scientific and Cultural Organization (UNESCO) is one of the UN's major outlets for the Islamists' "education" campaign.

UNESCO collaborates with the Organization of Islamic Conference mainly through the latter's specialized agencies such as the Islamic Educational, Scientific and Cultural Organization (ISESCO) and the Research Centre for Islamic History, Art and Culture (IRCICA).[442]

The trouble with UNESCO started during Amadou-Mahtar M'Bow's tenure as UNESCO's Director-General. M'Bow, an educator from the predominantly Muslim country of Senegal, was elected to the position in 1974 and re-elected in 1980.[443]

Two months after his re-election, M'Bow addressed an International Seminar on Islam. He praised Islam as a faith animated by such principles as "equality of all men before the Law" and "tolerance to others."[444] And then he repeated the Islamists' canard that "the image of Islam has been seriously distorted in the eyes of the people of non-Muslim countries."[445]

Under M'Bow's leadership, UNESCO adopted a resolution in 1982 calling for a "New World Information and Communications Order," or NWIOCO for short. The resolution was intended to redress what UNESCO considered distorted reporting and one-way flow of information from leading developed countries. In the usual UN double-speak, the resolution called for the "elimination of the imbalances and inequalities which characterize the present situation."[446] The resolution specifically sought to "reinforce co-operation in Unesco's (sic) fields of competence with the national liberation movements recognized by the Organization of African Unity and the Palestine Liberation Organization, recognized by the League of Arab States."[447]

The United States was troubled by the anti-Western direction UNESCO was taking under Amadou-Mahtar M'Bow, along with his mismanagement of the organization. When the Reagan administration's suggestions for reform were ignored, the US withdrew in December 1984.[448]

M'Bow's responded by denouncing "certain circles [which] wish to put into doubt the foundations of the international system."[449]

When the United States rejoined UNESCO nineteen years later during George W. Bush's first term, it was not welcomed with open arms. Eiji Hattori, Chargé de Mission to the Executive Office of the Director-General of UNESCO, declared that "UNESCO's stance and American globalism are incompatible."[450] He warned that for the US to play a constructive role in UNESCO, it "must discard isolationism and the American concept of justice as the universal justice … respect various cultures and traditions and modestly take the attitude to learn about them."[451]

Is this UNESCO ideologue basically saying that our system of constitutional liberties is no better than the Islamic system of law based on sharia? It certainly looks that way, given how UNESCO has sided with the Islamists in blaming the West for misrepresenting Islam.

And things almost got a whole lot worse, as hard as that may be to believe. Farouk Hosny, Egypt's "Culture" Minister, was a leading candidate to take over as Director-General of UNESCO in October 2009. Under the unwritten rule of regional rotation, it was the Arab region's "turn" to select a director-general.[452] And he had the backing of the Arab League, the African Union, and the Organization of the Islamic Conference.[453]

Mr. Hosny, among other things, told the Egyptian parliament in May 2008 what he wanted to do with any Israeli books found in the Alexandria library: "Let's burn these books; if there are any there, I will myself burn them in front of you."[454]

Anyone who wants to lead the world body dedicated to education should not even be thinking about burning books with which he disagrees, let alone advocating it openly in his country's parliament. But it took *five* rounds of voting before Hosny was finally defeated for the post by a former Communist, Irina Bokova of Bulgaria. Apparently, what finally did him in was the revelation that Hosny had boasted about helping the highjackers of the cruise ship, the Achille Lauro, escape from Italy in 1985—the same highjackers who had shot an elderly American Jewish tourist in a wheelchair and thrown him overboard.[455]

UNESCO's Collaboration with the Islamists' Image Makeover Campaign

UNESCO regularly excoriates the West for its allegedly one-sided, anti-Islam textbooks. For example, Eiji Hattori said the West was to blame for terrorism borne out of Muslim humiliation:

> The illusion that Western civilization is the one and only civilization has been shared not only by people of Europe and the United States, but also by non-Westerners until quite recently. Why? It is because textbooks written by colonial powers during the colonial period spread around the world. The singular view of "civilization" was fed to children through "education." This was the first globalization. The contribution of Muslims and Arabs to the human civilization ... was erased from textbooks.

People in the Arab world harbor deep "resentment" that their own culture, their human dignity, has thus been ignored. We should realize that this "resentment," or what Mahdi Elmandjra (of Morocco) calls "humiliation," is the very hotbed of terrorism. The cause of terrorism is not "poverty," though people often so simply define it as such. The root cause of terrorism is "unfairness," i.e. "injustice."[456]

And this was not just one UNESCO official's opinion. It was part of the organization's institutional DNA.

In December 2004, for example, UNESCO helped organize an international conference in Egypt entitled "The Image of Arab-Islamic Culture in European History Textbooks." It was a joint project with the Arab League, the European Program, and the Islamic Educational, Scientific and Cultural Organization.[457]

The central theme of this "image makeover" conference was the bad things Western textbooks say about Islam. The UNESCO co-sponsored international conference concluded, according to an Arabic publication's report of the proceedings, that European culture contained an "erroneous image, if not images" of Arabs, Muslims, Arab culture, Muslim civilization, and above all, of Islam.[458]

The report provided the gist of this UNESCO co-sponsored conference:

Many of the papers and documents presented to the conference, including a book entitled The Image of Arabs and Muslims in Textbooks Around the World, noted that Arabs are often portrayed as either filthy rich men who like to spend their petrodollars recklessly and fail to develop their countries adequately—especially in comparison to Israel—or as disturbingly poor, and often uncivilised individuals, who oppress women, indulge in polygamy and fail to address life in a realistic way, since they only believe in the heaven they are promised after death where they will have, as one European textbook notes, "much food, fun and sex."[459]

Sadly, as we have seen, this image is not the product of some made-up Western polemic against Islam. It comports with what Nonie Darwish experienced growing up in Egypt, and with sharia tenets she translated from her native Arabic.

Several conference participants were from Al-Azhar University—Obama's "beacon of learning" that punishes dissenting professors and students.

For example, Dr. Mustafa Al-Halwaji of Al-Azhar University explained to conference participants that misrepresenting Islam and Muslims in the European textbooks has negative effects on Muslim students:

> These students might be psychologically offended. They might even turn into fanatic defenders of their misrepresented religion in attempts to prove the validity of their religion.[460]

Dr. Al-Halwaji was so concerned about the alleged distortions of Islam in Western textbooks that he enlisted the help of UNESCO to correct them.[461] On his behalf, UNESCO contacted the ministries of higher education and of foreign affairs in countries around the world and asked them to provide their school history books for review by Al-Halwaji and other Muslim professors.[462]

Getting back to the Islamic "image makeover" conference in Egypt, Dr. Salah Ramadan El-Sayed of Al-Azhar University told the conference that Italian history schoolbooks handled the concept of jihad and the personality of Prophet Muhammad in a negative way.

Dr. Mohamed Mansour, also representing Al-Azhar University, declared that misunderstandings and misinterpretations of the Koran verses that address jihad, women, and other such issues occurred because "the verses were removed from their correct historical, geographical, social, cultural, military, and political context." He said, "A verse from the Qur'an should be read in the light of the Islamic principles and the rules of the Arabic language and rhetoric."

Yet that is precisely what professor Mustafa (aka Mark Gabriel) and student Abdul Kareem Nabeel Suleiman did. But when they spoke out about the real meaning of the Islamic principles—in context—they were expelled from the university and put in jail.

What's the point of having international conferences to foster better understandings of the Islamic world in the West when the world's leading Muslim university punishes its own professors and students for raising questions about their faith?

UNESCO does not bother to raise such questions at these conferences. It just cosponsors more of them, giving the Islamists platform after platform to whitewash their organized barbarism with loads of *taqiyya*.

In June 2005, for example, another conference was held in Rabat, Morocco—this time on "Fostering Dialogue among Cultures and Civilizations." The conference was jointly organized by UNESCO, the Islamic Educational, Scientific and Cultural Organization, the Organization of the Islamic Conference, the Arab League Educational, Cultural and Scientific Organization, the Danish Centre for Culture and Development, and the Anna Lindh Euro-Mediterranean Foundation for the Dialogue between Cultures.

The secretary-general of the OIC called for a review of textbooks and curricula in the West to counter an environment hostile to Islam. He got his way in the recommendations signed off by all of the participants, including UNESCO.[463]

UNESCO Ignores the Hate-Filled Muslim Textbooks

And what have leading Muslim countries such as Saudi Arabia done to remove hate-filled, supremist rhetoric from their own school textbooks? Nothing of significance. Do as we say, not as we do, is the Islamists' credo.

The "image makeover" conferences cosponsored by UNESCO run one way. They go after Western textbooks and downplay the far worse content in Muslim textbooks.

Consider the following examples of hateful teachings from Saudi textbooks used during the 2004–2005 academic year, as reported in the *Washington Post:*[464]

1. First Grade

   "Every religion other than Islam is false."

2. Fifth Grade

   "Whoever obeys the Prophet and accepts the oneness of God cannot maintain a loyal friendship with those who oppose God and His Prophet, even if they are his closest relatives."

3. Eighth Grade

   "As cited in Ibn Abbas: The apes are Jews, the people of the Sabbath; while the swine are the Christians, the infidels of the communion of Jesus."

4. Ninth Grade

   "The clash between this [Muslim] community (*umma*) and the Jews and Christians has endured, and it will continue as long as God wills."

5. Tenth Grade

   "Blood money [i.e., retribution paid to the victim or the victim's heirs for murder or injury] for a free infidel ... is half of the blood money for a male Muslim, whether or not he is 'of the book' or not 'of the book' (such as a pagan, Zoroastrian, etc.)."

   "Blood money for a woman: Half of the blood money for a man, in accordance with his religion."

Little has changed, according to a report of translated 2009 Saudi textbooks, documenting an ongoing pattern of hate, anti-Semitism, and violence taught in Saudi Arabian schools. The report was released by three congressional representatives:[465]

1   "The Prophet said, 'The hour [of judgment] will not come until the Muslims fight the Jews and kill them. [It will not come] until the Jew hides behind rocks and trees. [It will not come] until the rocks of the trees say ... O Muslim! O Servant of God! There is a Jew behind me. Come and kill him." [Source: Al Hadeeth wa Athaqafah (Sayings of the Prophet and Islamic culture.) Page 148, 2009. Taught in ninth grade, age fourteen.]

2. "The blood money for a Muslim woman is half of the blood money for a male Muslim, and the blood money for an infidel woman is half of the blood money for a male infidel." [Source: Fiqh (Jurisprudence.) Page 65, 2009. Taught in tenth grade, age fifteen.]

3. "The apostate (Muslims who convert, question or doubt Islam) is required to repent to the ruler. If he repents and returns to Islam, it is accepted and he is left alone. If he refuses it is mandatory that the ruler kill him." [Source: Towheed (Monotheism.) Page 33, 2009. Taught in twelfth grade, age seventeen.]

4. "The Goals of Zionist-Movement: Instill a fighting spirit among the Jews, as well as religious and nationalist fanaticism to challenge [other] religions, nations, and peoples; Establish Jewish control over the world; Incite rancor and rivalry among the great powers so that they fight one another, and kindle the fire of war among states so that all states are weakened and their state arises." [Source: Al Hadeeth wa Athaqafah (Sayings of the Prophet and Islamic culture.) Page 114, 2009. Taught in tenth grade, age fifteen.]

The American historian and author Dr. Richard Landes coined the term "demopaths" to describe those who display a radical imbalance between their insistence on asserting their own rights, and their lack of interest in defending the rights of others. These demopaths tell demonizing tales of those they brand the enemies of "human rights."[466]

Islamists fit this description to a tee. And UNESCO is their enabler busily focusing on Western textbooks that do not match the Islamists' rebranded self-image.

UNICEF Joins the Islamic Image Makeover Parade

UNICEF is the United Nations specialized agency devoted to the welfare of children. I remember, as a kid, collecting money on Halloween for UNICEF. In retrospect I should have taken the candy.

Shamefully, UNICEF co-authored a report with the International Islamic Center for Population Studies and Research of good old Al-Azhar University. The report made false claims about how well children were treated under sharia:

> Islam views childhood with hope and aspiration, seeing it as something to look forward to, seek and long for. When it is achieved, the fruit reaped is happiness of the soul, delight of the heart and elation of the chest...Hence, it is not surprising that Islamic Shariah (law) pays utmost attention to securing all that is needed to guarantee a wholesome psychological climate for the rearing of children, a climate wherein they learn about the world and formulate their customs and norms.[467]

The UNICEF- Al-Azhar report continues with more *taqiyya*, pointing out specific ways they claim Islamic law "protects" children:

Islam affirms:

- A child's right to health and life.

- A child's right to a family, kindred, name, property and inheritance.

- A child's right to healthcare and proper nutrition.

- A child's right to education and the acquisition of talents.

- A child's right to live in security and peace, and enjoy human dignity and protection under the responsibility of the parents.

- The caring role of society and the state to support all these rights and support families incapable of providing appropriate conditions for their children.

The Islamic Shariah states all of these rights, which are evident in the Quran and the sublime Sunnah of the Prophet Muhammad through his sayings and actions.[468]

Here is a more accurate statement of what Islamic law and custom "affirm" about children:

- Children are vessels to fill with hate of any enemy of Islam, particularly the Jews.[469]

- It's OK to sodomize small children and marry a child as young as 9 years old, just as Prophet Muhammad did.[470]

- Girls are taught that they don't deserve the same rights as boys because women are inferior to men.[471]

- In a divorce, the husband gets custody of the children automatically (for boys at age 7 and for girls from the start of menstruation), irrespective of the interests of the child.[472]

Challenge, Not Sugarcoat

President Obama and the United Nations are doing the Islamists' work for them, amplifying on a global stage their message that

Islamic law is compatible with the norms and values of democracy and universal human rights. They are complicit in the rebranding of a barbaric system that is the enemy of twenty-first century democratic civilized society.

Islamic law contradicts the notion that all human beings are entitled to be treated with equal dignity and have inalienable rights. Islamic law separates believers from nonbelievers, sanctioning inferior status, if not outright death, for the latter. In this worldview, religious tolerance is a one-way street. Women in Islam are degraded to submissiveness under misogynist laws. Children are taught to hate. Critical thought that questions official Islamic doctrines is regarded as the crime of defamation of Islam, punishable by death.

Apologists and the "makeover artists" insist that only extremist fundamentalists practice Islam this way, and that they are no different from extremist fundamentalists of every religion. Genuine Islam is gentle and peaceful, they say. But facts are stubborn things, especially when we learn them directly from Muslims who have personally suffered under Islamic law.

Obama and his friends at the United Nations are wasting time and resources pushing for more so-called dialogue to foster mutual understanding. There is really only one civilization that is represented at such discussions. The other side is simply making excuses for organized barbarism.

Before such a dialogue can accomplish anything, Muslims must first have a dialogue within their own faith. Muslims who truly believe their religion can embrace reason and modern-day humanistic values must openly challenge those retrograde ideologues whom they have permitted to define Islam today. I am not talking about just challenging the obvious nutcases such as Osama bin Laden, but about challenging the radical ideology of mainstream Muslim institutions such as Al-Azhar University, popular movements such as the Muslim Brotherhood and idolized spiritual leaders such as Yusuf al-Qaradawi.

Until Islam undergoes a reformation, Western democracies must challenge the ideas and methods of Islamists at every turn.

The White House and the United Nations are guilty of doing the opposite, by sugarcoating an evil ideology and amplifying the Islamists' *taqiyya*. They are betraying the brave Muslims like the three described earlier, who have endured personal suffering to tell the world the truth.

The result is to help the Islamists legitimize their legal norms based on sharia. With this wind at their backs, the Islamists can sail confidently toward global acceptance of sharia's incorporation into international law.

CHAPTER NINE

Flagellating the United States

Using the UN Whip

The Islamists are using the United Nations to tear down the moral standing of the United States. This complements their use of the UN to super-inflate their own image, as we have seen. Don't forget—this is the same United Nations with which President Obama wants to "re-engage."

For the task of trashing the United States, the Islamists turned to Dr. Doudou Diène from Senegal, a predominantly Muslim country and a member of the Organization of the Islamic Conference. As one of his final actions as the UN's Special Rapporteur on "contemporary forms of racism, racial discrimination, xenophobia and related intolerance," Diène conducted a three week "fact-finding" tour of the United States during the spring of 2008 to investigate racial conditions. Not surprisingly, he produced a highly critical report.

Diène's "investigation" followed accusations leveled against the United States by the UN Committee on the Elimination of Racial Discrimination (CERD). This committee oversees compliance with the UN Convention on the Elimination of All Forms of Racial Discrimination, to which the US is a signatory. CERD charged that the US was not meeting its treaty obligations, concluding that there were "stark racial disparities in US institutions, including its criminal justice system."[473]

In particular, the UN committee was

> deeply concerned about the increase in racial profiling against Arabs, Muslims and South Asians in the wake of the 9/11 attack, as well as about the development of the National Entry and Exit Registration System (NEERS) for nationals of 25 countries, all located in the Middle East, South Asia or North Africa... the Committee recommends that the State party [i.e., the United States] strengthen its efforts to combat racial profiling at the federal and state levels, inter alia by moving expeditiously toward the adoption of the End Racial Profiling Act, or similar federal legislation.[474]

But the report wasn't anti-American enough for the Islamists, so Dr. Doudou Diène came in to throw more UN-manufactured mud at the United States.

The UN's Special Rapporteur on Racism Fixates on Islamophobia

Diène was appointed Special Rapporteur in August 2002 by the Islamist-dominated UN Commission on Human Rights, the predecessor of the Human Rights Council, and served in that capacity through 2008. Before that, Diène worked in the UNESCO secretariat, where he held several positions including Director of the Division of Inter-cultural Projects.[475]

Diène's cultural and religious biases feed his obsession with Islamophobia and his animus against Western democracies. For example, in 2007 Diène told a UN committee on racism that "racial discrimination" was "now becoming a regular part of democratic systems, being blended in for example with the fight against terrorism."[476] Referring to the controversial depictions of the Prophet Muhammad in Danish newspaper cartoons and the violent reactions they inspired, he said "the cartoons illustrated the increasing emergence of the racist and xenophobic currents in everyday life."[477]

In other words, free speech equals racism if it is critical of Islam and its prophet. As Diène put it during a seminar organized by the United Nations in response to demands by the OIC, "[F]reedom of Expression is politically instrumantalised to propagate racist platforms."[478] Muslim violence and death threats intended to suppress free speech were of little concern to him.

For all of his work on Islamophobia and defamation of religions, Diène received the undying gratitude of the Organization of Islamic Conference:

> The OIC is particularly grateful to Mr. Doudou Diene, the Special Rapporteur on Contemporary Forms of Racism, Racial Discrimination, Xenophobia and related Intolerance, for his seminal work and his tireless commitment to addressing all issues relating to his mandate and in particular the question of the defamation of religions. His analysis and recommendations that have been somewhat recapitulated in the latest report reflect the extensive work that he has done on one of the most insidious forms of contemporary racism- Islamophobia. In the UN context, his work on the subject is truly of a path breaking nature ... Mr. Doudou Diene comprehensively defined Islamophobia as a term that refers to unfounded hostility and fear toward Islam and consequently fear and aversion toward all Muslims or the majority amongst them. It refers also to practical consequences of this hostility in terms of discrimination, prejudices and unequal treatment of which Muslims are the victims (whether individuals or communities) and their exclusions from important political and social spheres.[479]

And as his reward, Diène got another opportunity to beat up on the United States during his whirlwind, UN-paid junket across America in the spring of 2008. He visited government officials at the federal, state, and local levels during his "fact-finding" tour of the US. He even met Supreme Court Justice Stephen Breyer,[480] who advocates using international norms and foreign law to interpret the United States Constitution.[481]

But when he was not bending the ears of Justice Breyer and other government officials, Diène spent a considerable amount of his time visiting Muslim leaders in various cities, ostensibly to educate himself about racial conditions in the US.

For example, Diène attended a hearing held in Miami by Florida Muslim leaders to discuss Islamophobia and anti-Muslim discrimination.[482] At the end of the meeting, according to a report by participant and prominent Muslim civil rights advocate Ahmed Bedier, Diene called the rise of global Islamophobia alarming, and vowed that the issue would be included in the final report.[483]

> "We thank SR Diene for hearing our concerns about the rise in anti-Muslim bigotry in the United States, and we appreciate his concern about Islamophobia's growing threat to world peace," said Bedier. "Civilized nations must take concrete action to curb incitement of racial and religious hatred by supporting dialogue and education ..."[484]

Bedier is no stranger to the Islamists' cause. He was the founder and former executive director of the Tampa chapter of the Council on American-Islamic Relations (CAIR).[485] CAIR has a close relationship with the Muslim Brotherhood and financial ties to Saudi Arabia's supremist Islamic Wahhabi sect.[486]

Bedier condemns anyone in the United States who raises questions about Islamic law or Islamic organizations such as CAIR, branding these people "the lowest segment of our society."[487]

His "offense is the best defense" strategy is typical of Islamists, who use such epithets to attack those who dare criticize Islamic supremacism.[488]

Diène also attended a meeting in Anaheim, organized by the Islamic Shura Council of Southern California, to hear the Council's charges of Islamophobia, racism, and discrimination against Muslims. Shura Council chairman Muzammil Siddiqi, two representatives of CAIR, and Abdel Jabbar Hamdan—a former top fundraiser for the Texas-based Holy Land Foundation for Relief and Development—were part of this confab.[489] The Holy Land Foundation, by the way, was found guilty in 2008 of illegally funneling more than $12 million to Hamas.[490]

Diène's host Muzammil Siddiqi served as Department of Religious Affairs chairman at the Office to the United Nations of the al-Qaeda linked Muslim World League from 1976 to 1980. He warned Americans less than a year before 9/11: "If you continue doing injustice, and tolerating injustice, the wrath of God will come." [491]

Siddiqi has also suggested that the time will come when sharia will arrive in the United States. When Siddiqi was asked about implementing sharia in the US, he answered that "once more people accept Islam, insha'allah, this will lead to the implementation of Sharia in all areas."[492]

In Chicago (Obama's hometown), Diène presided over yet another hearing on alleged racial discrimination against Muslim Americans. CAIR-Chicago's Civil Rights director Christina Abraham presented cases of discrimination against Muslims in Chicago, as CAIR-Chicago reported on its Web site.[493] "This was an opportunity to address the issue of Islamophobia, how it is manifested, and to voice the concerns of Muslims in Chicago," said the CAIR director.[494]

Diène "balanced" his tour, so to speak, by meeting with far left human rights advocates in New York City, including the New York Civil Liberties Union and the Center for Constitutional Rights. The ACLU has its own brief against the United States, accusing this country of violating the UN Convention on the Elimination of All Forms of Racial Discrimination, to which it is a signatory.[495] Along with defending terrorist suspects, the ACLU is more than willing to help the Islamists make their case.

Surprise! Surprise! Diène Brands the US as a Deeply Racist Country

So what did Diène conclude after his "thorough" investigation? His report, presented to the UN Human Rights Council in June 2009 by the current Special Rapporteur Githu Muigai, concluded that "[R]acism and racial discrimination have profoundly and lastingly marked and structured American society."[496] While acknowledging that the United States has made progress in the battle against racism (as manifested by the election of President Obama), Diène found that the "historical, cultural and human depth of racism still permeates all dimensions of life of American society."[497]

Diène referenced a Gallup poll that had been quoted by CAIR in one of its reports on the status of Muslim civil rights in the United States to support the claims of Arab, Sikh, Middle Eastern, and South Asian leaders he met of the "overall negative perceptions of the American public toward Muslims."[498]

Diène objected to the special program requiring male noncitizens over the age of sixteen and from twenty-five countries to register with local immigration authorities because, he says, twenty-four of these countries have a majority Muslim population.[499] And he lashed out at "racial profiling" against "people of Arab, Muslim, South Asian or Middle-Eastern descent."[500] He recommended, among other things, that Congress adopt "the End Racial Profiling Act" and that "State Governments should also adopt comprehensive legislation prohibiting racial profiling."[501]

However, Diène did not criticize the Islamic terrorists who murdered nearly 3000 innocent people on 9/11, and he failed to acknowledge the legitimate fears of Americans that led to the very security measures he did criticize.

Diène Sees No Evil, Hears No Evil
Where Islamic Racism Is Concerned

Islamic racism has received scarce attention from the UN Rapporteur on racism. One limited exception was Mauritania, which Diène visited in January 2008. However, his criticisms of that Islamic country did not hold a candle to his indictment of US racism against Muslims.

In his report on Mauritania, Diène acknowledged that since achieving independence in 1960, "the Islamic Republic of Mauritania has been governed by authoritarian civilian or military regimes that created a political identity based on the Arabization of the country and Arab nationalism."[502] This manifested itself, he said, in "pervasive discrimination" against the black Moor and black African communities.[503] While officially outlawed, a legacy of slavery still persists in the form of "slavery-like practices," Diène wrote in his report.[504] Or as BBC put it more bluntly, "slavery remains Mauritania's best kept open secret."[505]

But Diène portrayed evidence of continued slavery in Mauritania as the exception rather than the rule. In fact, Diène's report said as many positive things about Mauritania as negative ones.[506]

Contrast Diène's superficial report on that country with the in-depth analysis of Mauritania conducted by a human rights consultant over thirteen years, in which he found not only that slavery was still practiced in Mauritania, but that the United Nations Development Programme and the World Bank had looked the other way while slaves were used in UN and World Bank sponsored projects![507]

"The World Bank and the UNDP could and should have taken the lead in doing something against Mauritanian slavery. But instead they supported the slave owners without asking any questions, they blinded their own research apparatus for slavery, they denied to the international community and their own bosses (sic) that slavery existed, and they advised the government of Mauritania to keep mute on the issue," concluded the human rights consultant.[508]

Why didn't Diène conduct his own in-depth investigation to check the veracity of these damning findings?

Most importantly, Diène's report makes it appear that the "slavery-like practices" in Mauritania, as he calls them, are a problem unique to that country. He fails to link Islam *as it is practiced today* with justifications for "slavery-like practices," not only in Mauritania, but in other countries where Islam is the official religion, such as Sudan, Libya, and on the Arabian peninsula. While governments in Muslim majority countries, including Mauritania, have technically outlawed slavery, the practice is too endemic in Islamic law to be abolished.

A leading Saudi government cleric and author of the country's religious curriculum, Sheik Saleh Al-Fawzan, stated bluntly several years ago that "[S]lavery is a part of Islam." [509] He went on to say that "[S]lavery is part of jihad, and jihad will remain as long there is Islam."[510] The sheik is a member of the Permanent Committee for Islamic Research and Fataawa, Saudi Arabia's highest religious body, a member of the Council of Religious Edicts and Research and a student of scholars from President Obama's favorite Islamic university, Al-Azhar University.[511]

In his book, *You Ask and Islam Answers,* Dr. Abdul-Latif Mushtahari, the general supervisor and director of homiletics and guidance at Al-Azhar University, says the following about Islam and slavery:

> Islam does not prohibit slavery but retains it for two reasons. The first reason is war (whether it is a civil war or a foreign war in which the captive is either killed or enslaved) provided that the war is not between Muslims against each other—it is not acceptable to enslave the violators, or the offenders, if they are Muslims. Only non-Muslim captives may be enslaved or killed. The

second reason is the sexual propagation of slaves which would generate more slaves for their owner.[512]

Islamist ideology, including the Arab supremacist culture within Islam, is inherently racist. To use Diène's phrase, "historical, cultural and human depth of racism still permeates all dimensions of life"[513]—not in the United States, as Diène alleges, but in the *Muslim* world.

But the truth would obviously interfere with the Islamists' dual propaganda strategies—to smooth over the hard realities of Islamic law while knocking down the moral standing of Western democracies on human rights. So the Islamists' handpicked UN Special Rapporteur on "contemporary forms of racism, racial discrimination, xenophobia and related intolerance" did the heavy lifting of deception for them.

Diène says Western-style racism against Muslims has caused the so-called clash of civilizations between the Judeo-Christian and the Islamic cultures.[514] But he never condemns Islamic fanatics whose faith demands the conquest and subjugation of Jews, Christians, Hindus, Buddhists, Bahá'ís, or atheists. Virtually all of the worst acts of terrorism in the world today are committed, financed, and led by radical Muslims who claim to act in the name of Allah.

And where is Diène's criticism of Saudi Arabia, the self-proclaimed guardian of the Islamic faith? Saudi Arabia is the fountainhead of religious intolerance, and demands the strict segregation of Muslims from non-Muslims, as well as men from women. Christians, Jews, and other non-Muslims are not permitted to worship in public. Non-Muslims are not even allowed into the cities of Mecca and Medina.[515] And if a hotel like the Makkah Hilton wants to stay in business, it has to remain "only accessible to visitors of the Muslim Religion."[516]

There is real human suffering caused by "racism, xenophobia, and intolerance," all of which are rampant in the Muslim world. But to speak the truth about Islamic law, rather than divert attention by focusing on the United States and other Western countries, would have been contrary to Diène's portfolio. He was obliged to use his position as the United Nations Special Rapporteur on racism to defend Islam and relentlessly attack the democratic West as the racist oppressor.

Western Transnationalists Buy into the Islamists' Narrative

All this matters because the Islamists are using the United Nations to infect our political and economic systems with sharia-based ideology. To do that, they have to foster a climate of receptivity amongst the Western elite to the idea that Western democratic values are not the appropriate governing standard for universal human rights. Their message to the elite is that the West is inherently racist, especially toward Muslims. Related to this message is the notion that a truly diverse, multicultural society must show its tolerant spirit of non-Western cultures by respecting the requirements of sharia.

The Islamists target their message to governmental leaders and influential opinion-makers. They need movers-and-shakers willing to embrace a global governance structure that treats Western democratic and capitalistic values as having less of a claim to serve as the basis for societal moral norms than Islamic values.

Samuel Huntington, the author of *Who Are We: Challenges to American National Identity* and of *The Clash of Civilizations and the Remaking of World Order,* called these leaders the "de-nationalized elites."[517] They think they are doing the world a favor by using transnationalism and multiculturism to "deconstruct" Western secular national identities and loyalties.[518]

As John Fonte (who coined the term "transnational progressives") explains, transnationalists divide the world into "oppressor vs. victim groups."[519] The values of our current democratic institutions must be "changed to reflect the perspectives of the victim groups," Fonte explained.[520] Indeed, Fonte says transnationalists have been "altering the definition of 'democracy,' from that of a system of majority rule among equal citizens to one of power sharing among ethnic groups composed of both citizens and non-citizens."[521]

Western transnationalists treat Muslims as part of the victim class, and insist it is wrong to link terrorism and Islam.[522]

And transnationalists are not just a European or far left problem. They occupy the highest government offices in the United States today.

When President Obama defensively apologizes to the Muslim world for America's supposed sins and then selects a transnationalist like Harold Koh as his top legal officer at the State Department, he is behaving like a member of the transnationalist, de-nationalized elite.

When Justice Stephen Breyer sits down with the UN spokesperson on racism, a man carrying out the Islamist agenda to attack the United States as a racist, Islamophobic country and then issues judicial opinions incorporating international norms into his constitutional interpretations, Breyer is also behaving like a member of the transnationalist, de-nationalized elite.

Indeed, the transnationalist, de-nationalized elite are ever ready to shill for the Islamists. It is not that Islamic ideology per se has any great attraction to non-Muslims in the West. It is all about righting all the terrible "wrongs" committed by Western society against the "oppressed victims" of the world, and not compounding those "wrongs" by stereotyping Islam as a violent, intolerant religion—which is precisely how it is being practiced by the Islamists today.

Here is how John Fonte illustrates the phenomenon:

> The transnational progressive response to radical Islam. This response has been twofold: Externally, it mostly takes the form of denial that terrorism is in any way connected to Islam. As Princeton University Dean Anne-Marie Slaughter put it: "Our enemy is not Islamic anything. The threat to our security comes from individual terrorists organized in global networks." At the same

time, internally within territorially based nations there is wide-spread accommodation to Islamist ideology, culture, and even, in some cases, sharia law across the West.

Thus, in March 2007 the *Daily Telegraph* reported that the European Union issued a classified handbook that banned the words "Islamic" and "jihad" in reference to terrorist attacks. Instead the EU directed public officials to replace concepts such as "Islamic terrorism" with words that are not "offensive" to Muslims.[523]

Obama's Flagellation

The Obama administration, as we have seen previously, is reluctant to use the phrase "war on terror."[524] When President Obama did make an exception and used a phrase like it during a television interview, he did so as part of his attempt to disassociate Islam from terrorism:

> Well, you know, I think it is very important for us to recognize that we have a battle or a war against some terrorist organizations. But that those organizations aren't representative of a broader Arab community, Muslim community.[525]

It is also now forbidden in Obama-land to use the term "jihad" to describe the ideological Islamic force we are fighting. President Obama's top homeland security and counterterrorism official, John Brennan, said it was inappropriate to use "jihad" in such a negative context because in the Islam religion, he claims, jihad means "to purify oneself or to wage a holy struggle for a moral goal." Brennan, certainly not a Muslim scholar himself, could have been reading right out of the UN's Alliance of Civilizations Report of the High-level Group praising the many positive connotations of jihad.[526] Don't forget—thanks to the Obama administration, the United States is now part of this United Nations-sponsored exercise in Islamic re-branding.

But when one considers the real meaning of jihad according to Islam's Prophet Muhammad from sources such as Bukhari (the Hadith, which are oral traditions relating to the words and deeds of Muhammad), Brennan's assertion is overwhelmingly disproved. The fact is that 97 percent of the jihad references are about war and 3 percent concern an inner struggle.[527] Also, the Koran itself is full of hate-filled violent passages. The Obama administration is helping the Islamists whitewash the words and deeds of the Islamists' own warrior prophet.

The following are just a sampling of Koran verses that sanction hatred and violence against non-Muslims:

- "Kill the disbelievers wherever we find them." (Koran 2:191)

- "O ye who believe! Take not the Jews and the Christians for your friends: They are but friends to each other." (Koran 5:51)

- "Shall I tell you who, in the sight of God, deserves a yet worse retribution than these? Those [the Jews] whom God has rejected and whom He has condemned, and whom He has turned into monkeys and pigs because they worshiped the powers of evil." (Koran 5:60)

- "I will inspire terror into the hearts of unbelievers: you smite them above their necks and smite all their fingertips off of them." (Koran 8:12)

- "When we decide to destroy a population, we send a definite order to them who have the good things in life and yet sin. So that Allah's word is proven true against them, then we destroy them utterly." (Koran 17:16–17)

Islamic scholars even teach that the Koran's more violent passages such as these supersede the peaceful passages written earlier in Muhammad's life. Of course, the Old Testament and other non-Muslim religious tracts contain their own share of inflammatory language. However, Islam has not undergone the internal re-examination and reformation that Western religions have. Today's Jewish and Christian leaders and thinkers do not interpret their religions' texts as literal justifications for violence against non-believers, as many Muslim immams and teachers still use the Koran and Hadith to do.

The common explanation of this difference is that Muslims are merely fighting back against their oppressors—the victims have simply turned into a freedom-fighting resistance movement, and who could possibly object to that?[528] Yet aside from the fact that Islam was a violent ideology from its inception under the warrior-prophet Muhammad, how does victimhood explain the violence Muslims unleash on other Muslims, including the killing of those who adopt another faith?

Sadly, President Obama's outreach to the Muslim world perfectly aligns with the Islamists' self-justifying victimhood narrative.[529] Veteran observer of Islamist hypocrisy, Anne Beyefsky, has called the president the "apologist-in-chief" for focusing on the United States' supposed failure to adequately protect Muslims' human rights instead of holding the Muslim world to account for its own problems.[530]

Bayefsky cited the examples Obama used: "the 'prison at Guantánamo Bay,' 'rules on charitable giving [that] have made it harder for Muslims to fulfill their religious obligation,' and impediments to the 'choice' of Muslim women to shroud their bodies."[531]

As we have seen, the truth is at odds with Obama's tales of poor, put-upon Muslim victims. Women in Muslim lands often have no choice in any sphere of their lives because of the commands of Islamic law.[532] Islamic charity is often diverted to funding terrorism—hence the need for tightened security regulations.[533] And nothing that goes on at Guantánamo compares to the torture and wanton killings the Koran commands devout Muslims to perform as part of jihad.[534]

Yet President Obama used his Cairo speech to the Muslim world to engage in a verbal flagellation of his own country!

Weaving the Fabric of International Norms

Let's connect some dots here. The Islamists play the race card. They win over gullible transnationalist, multiculturalist governmental leaders and opinion-makers in Western democracies, including, most importantly, the president of the United States. And they do all this with the help of the UN, which Obama has made a critical part of his policy to "re-engage" with the world.

As we have seen, UN agencies such as UNESCO and UNICEF are used to burnish a falsely benign image of Islam. Meanwhile, the UN Human Rights Council and General Assembly shield Islam from criticism. And at the same time, UN-appointed investigators of racism attack the West, particularly the United States, to undermine its moral standing. This helps the Islamists project an apocryphal narrative that aligns Muslims with the oppressed victims of alleged Western institutional racism. The Islamists deftly use the UN to exploit Western guilt about its racist past, to immunize Islam itself from critical scrutiny.

Islamists also take advantage of Western elites who romanticize the United Nations as the only international institution that can help make amends to the alleged victims of Western racism. Senator John Kerry (who chairs the Senate Foreign Relations Committee) exemplified this effusive embrace of the UN during the Senate hearing to confirm Susan Rice as the United States' UN ambassador. He exclaimed that the "United Nations ... advances important international norms that will benefit all nations."[535]

Susan Rice, whom President Obama elevated to cabinet status to demonstrate his reverence for the United Nations, has said that, "our security and well-being can best be advanced in cooperation and in partnership with other nations. *And there is no more important forum for that effective cooperation than the United Nations*" (emphasis added).[536]

But UN lovers refuse to acknowledge or simply fail to understand that with their control of the UN General Assembly and its human rights apparatus, the Islamists can now dictate the outcomes they wish. They are not interested in "effective cooperation" to solve multinational issues, only in advancing their own agenda. And they are succeeding.

So when a US Supreme Court Justice like Stephen Breyer—Obama's model Supreme Court justice—says that the laws of the United States and other nations are merely pieces of a "larger fabric,"[537] watch out. The Islamists are interweaving sharia-friendly international norms into the UN fabric, which the transnationalist elites in the White House and our courts are busy stitching into the law of our land.

CHAPTER TEN

Moral Equivalency, Multiculturalism, and the Radical Muslim Agenda

We have seen how President Obama's Cairo speech to the Muslim world set the stage for more accommodation of Muslim demands. And, of course, the United Nations' leadership liked what it heard. Secretary General Ban Ki-moon said, "President Obama's message will herald the opening of a new chapter in relations between the United States and the Islamic world" and that the Cairo speech is "a crucial step in bridging divides and promoting intercultural understanding, which is a major objective of the United Nations."[538]

Obama and the UN leadership are speaking the same language. That is, the West must accommodate Muslim sensibilities in every respect. Little is asked from the Muslim world in return, except unheeded pleas to curb the terrorists who act in the name of Islam.

The "new chapter in relations between the United States and the Islamic world" being written by Obama with the enthusiastic backing of UN leadership, is "bridging divides" by capitulation. This strategy reflects three dangerous trends that have been developing for decades.

Moral equivalency and *multiculturalism* now profoundly affect how both the United Nations and the United States interact with the Muslim world.

And, as we shall see in the next chapter, these two trends have paved the way for the third trend: what I call *manic multilateralism* and the transnationalists' legal mumbo jumbo that goes with it.

By giving in to these trends and neutering our own democratic values and institutions to accommodate Islamic demands, we are becoming patsies for the Islamists' cause. And the United Nations—one of Obama's favorite institutions—is also one of the Islamists' principal tools for manipulation.

Moral Equivalency

The Saul Alinsky Model

Saul Alinsky, President Obama's idol and an inspiration for 1960s student radicals and for self-styled iconoclasts ever since, was the notorious radical rabble-rouser who developed and popularized the political tactics of confrontation and infiltration for "community organizers." His two best-known works were *Reveille for Radicals* and *Rules for Radicals*.[539]

Alinsky was an apostle of moral equivalence. He taught that the "judgment of the ethics of means is dependent upon the political position of those sitting in judgment."[540] He also said that "[Y]ou do what you can with what you have and clothe it with moral garments" and that "[G]oals must be phrased in general terms like 'Liberty, Equality, Fraternity,' 'Of the Common Welfare,' 'Pursuit of Happiness,' or 'Bread and Peace.'"[541]

Alinsky's most famous tactic involved portraying one's political opponent as the essence of evil. "A war is not an intellectual debate, and in the war against social evils there are no rules of fair play," said Alinsky. "In our war against the social menaces of mankind there can be no compromise. It is life or death."[542]

Alinsky believed in infiltrating and co-opting established institutions, as part of his community "organizing" campaigns. Religious institutions—including mosques—were no exception. The Council of Islamic Organizations of Greater Chicago is a founding member of United Power for Action & Justice, which is an affiliate of Industrial Areas Foundation—Alinsky's own organization.[543] The black nationalist Muslim leader Malcolm X praised Alinsky as "the most effective organizer in the country."[544] Alinsky was also commended for his work in the Nation of Islam newspaper *Muhammed Speaks*. And Alinsky was told that "if the Muslims think you're o.k. you must be o.k."[545]

Obama, Alinsky, and the Islamists

Barack Obama was heavily influenced by the teachings of Saul Alinsky, in his own early career as a community organizer on the south side of Chicago. Obama went on to teach these organizing tactics to other organizers. These tactics were often referred to as Alinsky's "rules for radicals" after the title of his 1971 book.[546]

Years after Alinsky's death, we see his fingerprints all over Obama's presidential rhetoric and policies. And the Islamists are reaping the benefits. They rely on moral equivalence to undermine any objective or empirical discussion of good and evil, and reject the moral superiority of Western civilization to their own oppressive, misogynist, racist and life-negating ways based on sharia law. The Islamists will not compromise or coexist with Western values, any more than Alinsky would compromise with capitalism. Their war, like Alinsky's, is one of life and death.

Alinsky was clear about why he wrote *Rules for Radicals:* "What follows is for those who want to change the world from what it is to what they believe it should be. 'The Prince' was written by Machiavelli for the Haves on how to hold power. 'Rules for Radicals' is written for the Have-Nots on how *to take it away*" (emphasis added).[547]

President Obama, who received between 67 percent and 90 percent of the Muslim vote—probably nearer the higher end—is letting Islamists *"take away"* America's moral standing and leadership position, by repeatedly apologizing for America's alleged wrong-doings.[548]

Alinsky cynically manipulated the rhetoric of moral values. He taught that in order to most effectively cast themselves as defenders of moral principles and human decency, organizers must react with "shock, horror, and moral outrage" at their opponents' proposals.[549] This sets up the paradigm of victim versus oppressor. By adopting the Islamic victimhood narrative as his way to reach out to the Muslim world, Obama helps Islamists play the race card and demand more special accommodations. For example, Obama said in a speech to the NAACP that "the pain of discrimination is still felt in America" among African-Americans and *Muslim-Americans.*[550]

> "Make the enemy live up to their own book of rules," said Alinsky. "You can kill them with this, for they can no more live up to their own rules than the Christian Church can live up to Christianity. No organization, including organized religion, can live up to the letter of its own book. You can club them to death with their 'book' of rules and regulations."

This strategy defines the core of the UN-istan Intifada that I described at the outset of this book. The Islamists know how to push all the right buttons to exploit our system of laws and rules to their advantage. They use all the means discussed in this book to infect international law with sharia-friendly ideology, which they then leverage to manipulate our own political and judicial institutions. This strategy has been called "lawfare," or the use of Western legal institutions to achieve the Islamists' radical agenda.[551]

Obama plays right into this strategy with his obsessive regard for world opinion and international law, as we shall see in more detail in the next chapter.

America's Moral Force for Good Is Reviled

The United States is the most powerful nation in the history of the world. We may ultimately take second place economically to China, but that will take decades, if it happens at all.

Yet, in spite of its mistakes, this country uses its immense power for good and has liberated millions from the twin totalitarian evils of fascism and communism.

As the commentator Charles Krauthammer observed,

> the "use of the word 'empire' in the American context is ridiculous. It is absurd to apply the word to a people whose first instinct upon arriving on anyone's soil is to demand an exit strategy…That's because we are not an imperial power. We are a commercial republic. We don't take food; we trade for it. Which makes us something unique in history—an anomaly, a hybrid—a commercial republic with overwhelming global power. A commercial republic that by pure accident of history has been designated custodian of the international system."[552]

No Difference between the United States and the Worst Dictatorship

Nevertheless, starting in earnest during the 1960s with the protests against the Vietnam War and continuing to this day, the United States is accused of having imperialist ambitions. Using force to protect our national interests, whatever the reasons or results, is portrayed as proof of such ambitions and, portrayed, according to Charles Krauthammer, as a "form of grand national selfishness."[553] Capitalism has become a dirty word because it does not guarantee economic and social equality. Our failures at all times to live up to our own ideals and rules, be it the infamous My Lai Massacre in Vietnam,[554] the abuses of detainees by some US soldiers at the Abu Ghraib prison in Iraq,[555] or the recent upheavals on Wall Street, are raised again and again as proof of America's intrinsic evil.

This notion of moral equivalency is taken right out of Saul Alinsky's playbook. Context matters not. Values matter not. Results matter not. America is as bad as the worst dictatorial regimes, as lawless as the most lawless societies.

Former US ambassador to the United Nations, the late Jeane Kirkpatrick, wrote that those who "criticize liberal democratic societies measure our practices by our standards and deny the relevance of their practices to judgments concerning the moral worth of our own society."[556]

Kirkpatrick recalled how the Soviet Union used the rhetoric of Western democratic values to attack Western democracies:

> First, it involves a demonstration of the failure of Western democracies to meet their own standards which are regarded as utopian measuring rods. Second, it proceeds by continuous falsification of Soviet practices and assertions of Soviet loyalty to basic Western values. At the same time that it is suggested that we do not respect our own values, it is claimed by the Soviets that they do. Our flaws are exaggerated, theirs are simply denied. Third, the conclusion is, of course, inexorably arrived at, that there is, at best, not a dime's worth of difference between these two regimes.[557]

The Useful Idiots in Our College Campuses

But this strategy could never succeed without the help of our own intellectual elite. As Soviet dictator Joseph Stalin once declared, "Clearly, simpletons cannot help the proletariat to fight for socialism, to build a new society. I do not underestimate the role of the intelligentsia; on the contrary, emphasize it."[558]

The 1960s cultural and political tumult in the United States, with its anti-authority bent, turned academia into a viral carrier of the far left's moral equivalency message.[559]

Fast forward more than two decades since Kirkpatrick wrote her incisive analysis of Soviet strategy. The Islamists are now using that same strategy. The difference is that they have been even more successful at turning the liberal Western vocabulary of racism, oppression, genocide, and tolerance against critics of reactionary Islam.

We have seen how the Islamists use the United Nations as the stage where they act out their fictions of Zionist and Western crimes against them. Zionist Israel and its "Big Satan" protector, the United States, are cast as arch villains conspiring to control the world. Defenders of the Islamic faith are cast as champions of human rights in this twisted morality play. Naturally, any human rights violations alleged to exist in the Muslim world are either denied altogether or shrugged off in comparison to the supposed inhumanity of Israel and Western democratic societies. Suicide bombers "do not suffer from mental health problems," a UN spokesman told the press on World Suicide Prevention Day 2009.[560] Then exactly who are they? In the United Nations, which doesn't dare define the word "terrorism" accurately, the Islamic suicide bombers are morphed into heroic resistance fighters. And, as we have seen, they will not be subject to prosecution in the International Criminal Court for the international crime of "aggression."

But remember the endgame of the UN-istan Intifada: to use the United Nations to penetrate and transform the secular norms of international law, then infect our political and economic systems with sharia-friendly ideology. While transnationalist judges and politicians are increasingly receptive to moral equivalency and victimhood messages, the broader society must be receptive as well. Only then can the Islamists achieve a lasting socio-political consensus around fundamental changes in societal norms. To disseminate their message to the broader population and influence our culture, the Islamists need credible allies among the so-called thought leaders and opinion-makers on our campuses and in the media.

Fortunately for the Islamists, the campuses and mainstream media are in the hands of leftists who dismiss Western values as hypocritical covers for racist, neo-colonialism. These leftists are the perfect carriers of the Islamists' moral equivalency message. It doesn't bother them that they are privileging suicide bombings, the killing of apostates, the suppression of free speech, and the subordination of women over a philosophy that values innocent life and the equal right of all individuals to live in freedom. They are the Islamists' "useful idiots."

Islamic Indoctrination on Campus

Leftist campuses today are playgrounds of Islamists propaganda, not just Marxist-inspired ideology.

> "Anti-Western professors," Islamic expert Robert Spencer noted, "often backed up by Saudi money, have turned Middle Eastern Studies departments into propaganda mills for the view that Westerners themselves, and Americans in particular, are ultimately to blame for the actions of Islamic terrorists. Meanwhile, extremist Islamic student groups are not only tolerated on campuses, but are financially supported by guilt-ridden university officials."[561]

Professor Said's Pseudo-Intellectual Critique

University professors and administrators legitimize Islamic ideology by elevating its moral standing and denigrating Western civilization. The late professor Edward Said of Columbia University helped lay the groundwork for this brand of Islamic supremist, anti-American pseudo-intellectualism with his 1978 book *Orientalism*.[562] He taught that academic scholarship in the West concerning Islam was characterized by negative racial stereotypes and anti-Arab and anti-Islamic prejudice. Said's book had the desired effect of chilling research and writing that questioned the premises of Islamic ideology. Self-criticism by Islamic scholars was heresy; blaming all of the ills of society on the evil West was now de rigeur.

There is now an Edward Said Chair in Arab Studies at Columbia University, which is endowed, not surprisingly, by the United Arab Emirates.[563]

Said's Lemmings

Just as predictably, one of those who've held the chair, Professor Rashid Khalidi, justified jihad terror attacks against Israeli civilians as "resistance to occupation" which is "legitimate in international law."[564]

Khalidi, by the way, is an old pal of Barack Obama, going back to the days when they taught together at the University of Chicago. At a farewell dinner for Khalidi attended by the Obamas, held before Khalidi departed Chicago for Columbia University, Barack Obama praised Khalidi for broadening his perspective. "It's for that reason," said a grateful Obama, "that I'm hoping that, for many years to come, we continue that conversation—a conversation that is necessary not just around Mona [Khalidi's wife] and Rashid's dinner table," but around "this entire world."[565]

Khalidi is right at home at Columbia. Hamid Dabashi, chair of the University's Department of Middle East and Asian Languages and Cultures, has called Zionism a "ghastly racist ideology" and contended that "the so-called pro-Israeli lobby is an integral component of the imperial designs of the Bush administration for savage and predatory globalization."[566]

Columbia Professor Joseph Massad's class on Palestinian and Israeli politics and society is described this way in the university catalogue: "The purpose of the course is not to provide a 'balanced' coverage of the views of both sides." Massad's writings have dismissed Arab anti-Semitism as "a Zionist-inspired propagandistic claim."[567]

When Massad taught at Harvard, he penned this masterpiece of moral equivalency:

> The word "torture" seems to be a difficult word for Americans to utter when they are caught in the act of committing it. But political language has always been a malleable thing in America just as

it was in Orwell's 1984 ... for the rest of the world, the horrifying torture to which Iraqis have been subject will remain pure torture. The only "abuse" being committed here is the abuse of language by the American government and its subservient media.[568]

The real "abuse" of truth is Massad's denial of the barbarity of Islamic law which justifies torture, killing of apostates and infidels, and debasement of women. Yet, in June 2009 this "scholar" was granted tenure by Columbia University.

The moral equivalency virus is not confined to Columbia University. For example, Professor Omid Safi of Colgate University offered a class entitled "Islam and modernity," which consisted of a diatribe against so-called "islamophobes, Neo-Cons, Western triumphalists, etc."[569]

Bruce D. Larkin, Professor Emeritus of Politics at the University of California, Santa Cruz, offered a course entitled "The Politics of the War on Terrorism" that asks the loaded question: "How did Bush and Cheney build the fiction that al-Qaeda was a participant in the 9/11 attacks?"[570]

The University of Arizona freshman composition English 101 class has required readings from the blame-America-first crowd, who believe the US-led war on terrorism is a war on innocent people in other countries, not to mention an imperial project. The *Communist Manifesto* is thrown in for good measure.[571]

On campuses across the country, Israelis are compared to Nazis as part of a hate campaign being orchestrated by Islamic groups against Israel in particular and Jews in general.[572] There is growing anti-Semitism even at that pinnacle of higher education, Harvard University, where, as on other campuses, students and professors have demanded that the university remove all Israeli investments from its endowment.[573]

And speaking of Harvard, its Muslim chaplain advised students asking about the punishment for apostasy in Islam that the "preponderant position in all of the 4 sunni madhahib (and apparently others of the remaining eight according to one contemporary `alim) is that the verdict is capital punishment."[574] He also told them that "[D]ebating about religious matter is impermissible, in general."[575]

> "I would finally note that there is great wisdom (hikma) associated with the established and preserved position (capital punishment)," said the Muslim chaplain Taha Abdul-Basser, "and so, even if it makes some uncomfortable in the face of the hegemonic modern human rights discourse, one should not dismiss it out of hand."[576]

And finally, to shut off any consideration of "hegemonic modern human rights discourse," the Harvard chaplain closes with "And Allah knows best."[577]

College students across the country are being indoctrinated in the moral equivalency—if not superiority—of Islamic ideology vis a vis "hegemonic" Western values. And this thinking is reverberating in our broader culture through the mainstream media and the Internet.

The New York Times Downplays Islamic Links to Terrorism

The New York Times is a case in point. The newspaper, whose slogan is "All the News That's Fit to Print," ran thirty-two front-page articles on the Abu Ghraib in Iraq.[578] The measures taken by the Bush administration to combat terrorism were regularly excoriated as flagrant violations of international law, but the *Times* has less to say about the barbarian Islamic terrorists whose actions precipitated these measures in the first place.

The New York Times' lead stories in the immediate aftermath of the Mumbai, India massacres that occurred in November 2008 omitted the central fact that the terrorists who murdered more than 170 innocent people were fanatical Islamists. The *Times* referred to them simply in generic terms as "gunmen," "attackers," and "militants."[579]

The only hint of any Muslim connection to Mumbai was reported in *The New York Times* on November 27, 2008, and that was a complaint from two of the attackers about the treatment of Muslims in India and about hostilities in the disputed territory of Kashmir. The *Times* actually gave one of these cold-hearted terrorists a platform for his pose as the real victim in question.

The truth makes no difference to the politically correct crowd at *The New York Times* and other left-wing media in the West. They refuse to acknowledge the centrality of Islamic religious dogma to the scourge of international terrorism.

Shortly after the 9/11 al Qaeda attack on our homeland, a regular columnist for *The New York Times,* Nicholas D. Kristof, wrote a piece entitled "Terrorism beyond Islam."[580] He opined that the "defiant and violent antagonism to the West that we now associate with Islamists was for centuries linked instead to places like Japan, Korea and China." Such violence, he said, was not inherent to Islam as a religion but rather was caused by "frustration at the humiliating choice faced by once-great civilizations heartsick at the pressure to discard bits of their own cultures to catch up with the nouveaux riches in the West."[581]

Claptrap like this, coming not only from our colleges but also from the West's most prestigious newspaper, creates a homegrown base of opinion that the Islamists are happy to build upon.

Multiculturalism

Multiculturalism is a close cousin of moral equivalency.

Multiculturalism exalts the diversity of cultural values as an end in itself. It emphasizes the equal collective rights of different groups, rather than the rights of each individual. It demands deference by the authorities to the differentiated needs of each culture, even if doing so tramples on the rights of other individuals. The idea of America as the great "melting pot" of different cultures, races, and religions is anathema to the die-hard multiculturalist.

A Twisted Definition of Discrimination

In a multicultural society, immigrants do not have to adapt to the ethos of their host country; rather, the host country must adapt to each immigrant group's differences and demands. Thus, it becomes discriminatory to deny requests for special accommodations for Muslims. It makes no difference if the request violates a core defining principle or norm of the host country's political and social system, norms that have kept it cohesive and stable thus far.

Without a shared set of moral and social values, a country will disintegrate. Freedom of speech, freedom of religion, and respect for the individual—the hallmarks of Western democratic societies—are life-affirming values that are far superior to Islamic law and ideology. Allowing Islamists to impose their atavistic practices on our institutions is tantamount to surrendering our core values in the service of a warped notion of "tolerance."

As Bruce Bawer, the author of *While Europe Slept: How Radical Islam Is Destroying the West from Within,* observed:

> Multiculturalism has become official dogma in much of Western Europe, and the word is routinely used as if it were a synonym for equal rights or ethnic pluralism or colorblind democracy. Of course, it isn't. It's a grotesque expression of cultural self-contempt and self-destructiveness. Multiculturalism compels self-declared anti-fascists to blind themselves to the most chillingly fascist phenomena of our time. It compels feminists to accept the subjugation and abuse of women by men who believe they have the right to rape, beat, and murder them. It compels gay activists to embrace as allies people who, given the chance, would drop a wall on them.[582]

Bawer explains that if

> you're a multiculturalist, it's verboten even to notice, acknowledge, and express concern about murderous hatred directed against you and yours by the officially oppressed. For a multiculturalist, any act or statement by a member of an officially oppressed group,

however morally reprehensible, is to be understood either as a legitimate reaction against "our" prejudice (or our forebears' colonialism) or as a legitimate aspect of an alien culture that we, in our pitiful narrowness, have failed to understand and respect—which is, of course, our obligation.[583]

Multiculturalist Accommodation of Islam in the United States

The United States is going down the same multiculturalism road as Bawer has traced for Europe. We see it in the public funding of school programs extolling Islam, for example, which would be clearly prohibited if the programs taught Judeo-Christian beliefs.[584]

Special Accommodations to Muslims in American Schools

In Minnesota, for instance, a charter school receiving public money called Tarek ibn Ziyad Academy has close ties with the Muslim American Society which, in turn, is the US alter ego of the Muslim Brotherhood.[585]

Seventh-graders at a San Francisco-area school were required to "become Muslims" for two full weeks as part of California's world history curriculum. This included professing as "true" the Muslim belief that "the Holy Quran is God's word," reciting the Muslim profession of faith—"Allah is the only true God and Muhammad is his messenger"—and chanting "Praise be to Allah."[586] Just imagine what would happen if a public school told Muslim students to become Jews for two weeks and recite the traditional Jewish prayer: "Hear, O Israel: the Lord our God, the Lord is one." That school would not be standing after the first day.

Yet the Ninth US Circuit Court of Appeals in California dismissed a case brought by outraged parents even though Supreme Court decisions have kept religion out of public schools for decades.[587] In a brief memorandum opinion, the appeals court concluded that the activities did not constitute "overt religious activities that raise Establishment Clause concerns." The Supreme Court apparently forgot its own precedents when it refused to take an appeal from the Ninth Circuit decision.[588]

A San Diego public school set aside fifteen minutes of classroom instruction time for Muslim students to pray, and the school cafeteria banned pork and other foods Islam considers unclean.[589] The San Diego chapter of the Council on American-Islamic Relations explains that America "is transforming demographically, religiously" and must "now accommodate things that are not traditionally accounted for before."[590]

The Ninth Circuit apparently agrees. The same court that allowed Islamic indoctrination in public schools upheld another public school's ban on a student performance of an *instrumental* version of "Ave Maria" at their high school's graduation, because the performance could be seen as endorsing religion.[591] These judges—in an effort "to accommodate things that are not traditionally accounted for before" as CAIR put it—saw no inconsistency in allowing Islam prayers in the classroom, while upholding the banning of a one-time performance of a Christian-themed instrumental classic. What's next on the banned list? "The Battle Hymn of the Republic"?

The palpable discrimination in favor of Islam displayed by one of our country's most influential courts—and the Supreme Court's failure so far to redress it—should shock every American concerned with preserving what is left of our distinct national and cultural identity.

Special Accommodations to Muslims in the American Workplace

Special accommodations are also granted to Muslims in the American workplace. A Muslim chief executive of a Floridian telecommunications company, for example, fired a Catholic employee for violating a rule against eating pork on company premises. Since pork is considered "unclean" in the Islam religion, religious accommodation in this case meant enforcing a religious rule *against* a non-Islamic employee.[592]

And now the federal government is enforcing special accommodations for Muslims employed by non-Muslim owned companies. In response to complaints filed by Somali Muslim employees with the help of Chicago-based Council on American-Islamic Relations (Barack Obama's hometown), the Equal Employment Opportunity Commission (EEOC) decided that JBS Swift violated their civil rights by dismissing those who refused to work during Ramadan because they were not permitted to take special time off during work hours for prayer. The demand would have disrupted work schedules, leaving their fellow non-Muslim workers to pick up the slack. The EEOC chose to send its decision by letter directly to the Islamist CAIR organization, showing their close relationship in the Obama era.[593]

There are many more examples of special accommodations to Islamists' demands, but the most interesting concerned two top universities, who chose to sacrifice core Western values rather than "offend" Muslim sensibilities.

Harvard Segregates the Sexes and Yale Censors Free Speech

Harvard University administrators have set aside six women-only hours at the university gym so Muslim women can swim without the presence of men. Segregation by gender is suddenly considered acceptable by one of America's most prestigious universities, in the name of multiculturalism.[594]

Yale University Press removed reproductions of the twelve infamous Danish cartoons parodying Muhammad *in a book about the controversy*, entitled *The Cartoons That Shook the World*.[595] In addition, Yale University Press didn't include any other illustrations of the prophet, including an ancient Ottoman print, in deference to Muslim sensitivities.[596]

Yale University and Yale University Press reached this decision after consulting with a number of authorities on how the Muslim world would react to the publication of the cartoons in particular. They all advised against publication. One of these authorities was Ibrahim Gambari, special adviser to the United Nations Secretary General and former minister of Nigeria. "You can count on violence if any illustration of the prophet is published," Gambari warned. "It will cause riots, I predict, from Indonesia to Nigeria."[597]

Gambari knows all about Islamic violence. His home country of Nigeria is constantly riven by attacks against Christians by radical Islamists, including a group called "Boko Haram," which translates to "western education is sin."[598]

The director of Yale University Press, John Donatich, took the UN official's advice to heart in deciding to omit all images of Muhammad from the book. He explained his decision to accommodate Muslim sensitivities by saying that "when it came between [freedom of the press] and blood on my hands, there was no question."[599]

And so one of America's most prestigious liberal arts institutions decided not to risk hurting the Islamists' feelings—or, for that matter, putting Yale property and students in jeopardy from the violence that could erupt as a result of those hurt feelings. Yale cowered after taking the advice of an Islamic United Nations official.

Eating Away at Our Moral Pillars

Jeane Kirkpatrick astutely observed that in order to "destroy a society it is first necessary to delegitimize its basic institutions so as to detach the identifications and affections of its citizens from the institutions and authorities of the society marked for destruction."[600]

Multiculturalism and moral equivalence are the termites within our societal structure that are eating away at its pillars, one by one.

Semantic Tricks

The Islamists manipulate the terms we use to describe our values, then turn this language against us. We begin to doubt the worth of our own institutions and our inherent rights as self-governing people operating under our own set of laws. The semantics of universal human rights are turned against the most faithful practitioners of human rights by the most flagrant *violators* of human rights. Words become weapons to deconstruct liberal democratic norms and to call for an alternative global order based on perverted, archaic values.

As Jeane Kirkpatrick explained,

the "theft of words like genocide and the language which appears in documents like the United Nations Charter and the Geneva Convention are ... examples of systematic comprehensive effort at semantic rectification ... What further complicates this is the effort not only to redefine values but to eliminate any epistemological standard—any standard of proof—by which events might be objectively observed and through which we might have appeal to the double bind in which the semantic falsification puts us."[601]

Obama's Shameful Bow

President Obama not only literally bowed in deference to Saudi King Abdullah as he greeted him at the opening of the G20 meeting in London in April, 2009.[602] He metaphorically bowed to the Islamists in his Cairo speech when he apologized for the United States' efforts to defend freedom. And he rewrote history by asserting that "Islam has demonstrated through words and deeds the possibilities of religious tolerance and racial equality."[603]

As we have seen, Islam as practiced in Muslim lands demonstrates precisely the opposite of "religious tolerance and racial equality." Islamic ideology and theocracy are at odds with the exercise of human reason and self-government.

Yet Obama wants to remake the United States into a multicultural society where an oppressive burden placed on women in Muslim society—the wearing of the burqua—becomes a virtue to be encouraged. He is willing to subordinate American values of individual liberty, freedom of expression, and equal treatment under the law to a system that accommodates Muslims' special demands in "practicing religion *as they see fit.*" [604]

"Islam in America Brand"— Courtesy of Obama's State Department

Want more evidence of the lengths to which the Obama administration will go in order to engage with the Islamists? Incredibly, Obama's State Department has announced that the "Bureau of International Information Programs (IIP) has assembled a range of innovative and traditional tools to support Posts' outreach activities during the Islamic holy month of Ramadan... America.gov will publish a 'Multicultural Ramadan' feature."[605]

The Bureau was tasked with publishing:

> three articles for Ramadan 2009 addressing the concept of *an Islam in America 'brand';* advocacy (civic and political) of the Muslim American community; and community innovation/ community building. The writer will contact Muslim American experts in each of these fields. These articles will be available on America.gov in English, Arabic, and Persian. (emphasis added)[606]

The Obama State Department's campaign to help Islamists rebrand their ideology in America parallels the UN's rebranding of Islam discussed in chapter eight.

While promoting the Islamic "brand" and a multicultural celebration of Ramadan, the Obama administration asked Georgetown University, a Catholic institution, to cover over the name of Jesus inscribed on a pediment on the stage when President Obama spoke there in April 2009.[607] Apparently, *covering up Christian sym-*

bols when Obama speaks is part of his definition of multiculturalism as well.

It is time to stop obscuring the Judeo-Christian and Enlightenment roots that have allowed us to advance far beyond the fundamentalist-dominated Muslim world, simply to comply with the dubious and ever-changing demands of multiculturalism.

Obama's special guests at the White House Ramadan Banquet

You can learn a lot about someone by the company he keeps—or, in President Obama's case, the people he invites to dinner at the White House. Consider, for example, Obama's White House Ramadan banquet, held in September 2009, attended by such senior administration officials as Defense Secretary Robert M. Gates and Attorney General Eric Holder.[608]

One nongovernmental guest at Obama's banquet was Dr. Ingrid Mattson, president of the Islamic Society of North America (ISNA).[609] ISNA, like CAIR, was named as an unindicted co-conspirator of the Holy Land Foundation for Relief and Development, an Islamic "charity" which was convicted in 2008 by a federal jury for giving more than $12 million to the Palestinian terrorist organization Hamas.

Another of President Obama's dinner guests at the White House Ramadan banquet was Jameel Jaffer, a litigator for the American Civil Liberties Union and Director of the ACLU's National Security Project.

Jaffer is a darling of the far left who has litigated cases against the United States in support of terrorists' rights. He has also fought to allow radical Islamists such as Tariq Ramadan entry into the US. Tariq Ramadan, the grandson of Hasan Al-Banna who founded the fundamentalist Muslim Brotherhood in Egypt, had been barred from entering the US since 2004 because of his alleged financial contributions to Palestinian groups designated as fundraising agencies for Hamas by the US Treasury Department—that is, until the Obama administration decided to let him into the country as mentioned further below.[610]

Jaffer led the ACLU's battle seeking public disclosure of highly sensitive documents regarding America's interrogation of suspected terrorists. He won a major victory on April 16, 2009, when the Obama Justice Department released four key memos produced by the Office of Legal Counsel in 2002 and 2005, against the advice of the president's national security team.[611] Now this radical ACLU litigator wants more:

> We will argue that, yes, to the extent that the government has disclosed and acknowledged facts about the CIA's interrogation program, at the very least documents that relate to those facts can't be properly withheld. I don't think the government is going to dispute that proposition…we're still hopeful that the new administration has made a decision not just that these memos can be released, but that certain information about the CIA's program that, until now, has been withheld, not just can be released, but should be released to the public.[612]

Jaffer also won a victory for Tariq Ramadan, when the Second Circuit Court of Appeals overturned his visa denial and remanded the case to the lower court for further evidentiary proceedings. The ACLU expressed hope that the Obama administration would end Ramadan's exclusion without further litigation.[613] Its wish was granted by Secretary of State Hillary Clinton, who signed an order lifting the Bush-era ban for Ramadan to enter the United States. Jaffer praised the decision: "We see [S]ecretary Clinton's decision as a recognition that the (exclusion was) illegitimate to begin with." Jaffer, by the way, had the honor of introducing Tariq Ramadan at his first public appearance in the United States after the lifting of the ban–a panel discussion held at New York's Cooper Union in April 2010. Joining Jaffer and Ramadan for this celebration of the ACLU's victory and the Obama administration's cave-in was none other than the Obama White House's very own Muslim advisor, Dalia Mogahed! [614]

It does not stop there. One of Jaffer's National Security Project staff attorneys, Denny LeBoeuf, is in turn the director of the ACLU's notorious John Adams Project.[615] This project has endangered the lives of covert CIA agents, whose photos have been shared with the attorneys for detained terrorist suspects, as well as with the suspects themselves. Even the Obama Justice Department is currently "investigating" whether the John Adams Project has broken any laws.[616] President John Adams must be rolling in his grave.

The ACLU has also filed a petition in Dallas federal court to have the Islamic Society of North America removed from the list of unindicted co-conspirator s in the Homeland Foundation charity case.[617]

So it seems highly irregular, to say the least, for an attorney currently engaged in sensitive litigation against the US government, along with one of his Islamic clients, to be feasting with the president of the United States and high-level administration officials, including the Attorney General, without any record of what they may have talked about.

Did Jaffer, for example, lobby President Obama or other government officials attending the Ramadan banquet to release more of the CIA documents?

Did he argue on behalf of Tariq Ramadan and try to persuade President Obama to let him into the country, leading eventually to Hillary Clinton's decision to reverse the ban on his entry?

Did Jaffer try to persuade President Obama or Attorney General Holder to drop the Justice Department's investigation of the John Adams Project?

Did Jaffer and ISNA's president Dr. Mattson discuss the naming of ISNA as an unindicted co-conspirator with President Obama at the White House banquet?

And did they urge the President and Attorney General to read the ACLU report published a couple of months prior to the dinner, carrying a title sure to grab Obama's attention—*Blocking Faith,*

Freezing Charity: Chilling Muslim Charitable Giving in the "War on Terrorism Financing?"[618]

The ACLU, citing several *United Nations treaties,* argued in its report that the United States was in violation of international law because its terrorism financing policies and enforcement actions "have a discriminatory effect on Muslims"—any national security concerns notwithstanding.[619]

Perhaps Obama has already read the ACLU report. It reinforces his own inclination to ease up on measures cracking down on Islamic charities that channel donations to terrorists, as he promised the Muslim world he would do in his Cairo speech. And it plays right into his concerns about not violating the UN's notion of international law.

Debasing the Medal of Freedom

Once again bowing at the altar of multiculturalism and moral equivalence, in 2009 Obama awarded the nation's highest civilian award, the Medal of Freedom, to a shining example of both trends, and a long-time Israeli basher: Mary Robinson.

Mary Robinson is a former UN Commissioner for human rights and former president of Ireland. She presided over the UN's anti-Semitic, pro-Palestinian romp known as Durban I. In early 2002, she said that "What emerged from the World Conference was an historic document of enormous importance." She praised "the victim-oriented approach in addressing the problems of racism and racial discrimination." Of course, the "victims" singled out for special recognition were the Palestinians.[620]

Later that year, she praised Durban I's outcome as "remarkably good, including on the issues of the Middle East."[621]

At an international diversity conference cosponsored by the UN in 2005, Ms. Robinson said that acknowledging what another UN official called the "multicultural base of democracy" should start in primary school.[622] By the way, that other UN official who coined the phrase "multicultural base of democracy" was Jomo Kwame Sundaram, from the UN's Department of Economic and Social Affairs. Recall that this is the same Malaysian economist discussed in chapter two, leading the UN's drive to build a radically different global economic and financial architecture.

Robinson is now the president of the International Commission of Jurists, and presided over an ICJ panel which—in a fit of moral equivalence—concluded that counterterrorism measures adopted after 9/11 "threaten[s] the very core of the international human rights framework."[623]

Robinson's panel also concluded that "the conflation of acts of terrorism with acts of war was legally and conceptually flawed."[624] Accordingly, it asked President Obama to "immediately and publicly renounce" the characterization of counterterrorism as a "war against terror," and to investigate human rights abuses against terrorism suspects.[625]

The panel wants the military detention center at Guantánamo Bay closed in "a human rights compliant manner" and says that "persons held there should be released or charged and tried in accordance with applicable international law standards."[626] The panel urged President Obama to "fully uphold and faithfully apply *international humanitarian law* (the laws of war)" and to "repudiate any policies or practices associated with the 'war on terror' paradigm which are inconsistent with *international humanitarian and human rights law*" (emphasis added).[627]

"Seven years after 9/11, it is time to take stock and to repeal abusive laws and policies enacted in recent years. Human rights and international humanitarian law provide a strong and flexible framework to address terrorist threats," said Mary Robinson when her International Commission of Jurists panel report was released in February 2009. "It is now absolutely essential that all states restore their commitment to human rights and that *the United Nations takes on a leadership role in this process*. If we fail to act now, the damage to international law risks becoming permanent," she added (emphasis added).[628]

Obama is not only following the Mary Robinson panel's recommendations. In awarding her the Medal of Freedom, he has blessed her panel's blurring of fundamental moral distinctions between those fighting for freedom and those who are the enemies of freedom. Robinson's handiwork reflects the transnationalist, multilateralist mania, which awaits us as President Obama's foreign policy takes hold.

CHAPTER ELEVEN

The UN and Obama in Pursuit of Manic Multilateralism

President Obama has embraced the United Nations, the epicenter of the kind of manic multilateralism that strives for the least common denominator by global consensus.[629] His UN ambassador, Susan Rice, said in her first address to the Security Council that "the United Nations is at the center of our collective efforts to promote respect for international humanitarian law"—whatever that is.[630] With the Islamists now shaping UN-created international norms, particularly regarding "human rights," relying on the United Nations for leadership is like relying on an arsonist to put out his own fire.

Manic Multilateralism versus Rational Multilateralism

Manic multilateralism is an uncritical deference to global norms and consensus, irrespective of the consequences. Charles Krauthammer described its ultimate purpose: to "reduce American freedom of action by making it subservient to, dependent on, constricted by the will—and interests—of other nations. To tie down Gulliver with a thousand strings."[631] This mindset includes a "mania for treaties," and "the slavish pursuit of 'international legitimacy'—and opposition to any American action undertaken without universal foreign blessing."[632]

This is not to say that we must always choose between the unilateral pursuit of America's national interest on the one hand, versus multilateralism on the other. Rather, the choice is often between rational multilateralism and *manic* multilateralism. Striving for lowest common denominator consensus often keeps us from reaching practical solutions to manageable problems. Intelligent cooperation does not mean acquiescence to whatever other countries think, no matter the cost.

It's time to retire the romantic fictions that the UN is the only claimant to multilateral "legitimacy," or that Islamists will ever adhere to the rules-based, verifiable reciprocity necessary to form a durable multilateral arrangement. Their real objective at every turn is to game the system.

Islamists Do Not Regard Treaties with Unbelievers to Be Binding

Islamists do not consider treaties entered into with *kaffars* (unbelievers) to be durable binding commitments. Recall that they are masters of deception, or *taqiyya*. The most one can realistically expect from Islamists are temporary truces known as *hudna*, which they enter into for tactical reasons to gain advantage over their enemies.[633]

Our Founding Fathers learned that lesson the hard way. They tried the treaty route to get American ships back from the Muslim pirates. After a Treaty of Peace, Friendship, and Ship-Signals was signed with one Muslim nation in 1786, and an American ship was released, another Muslim nation (part of the same loose confederation) promptly seized the same ship for ransom.

I have already quoted the Muslim leader with whom Thomas Jefferson and John Adams had met in London to seek a peaceful solution, but his words bear repeating because nothing has changed in over two hundred years.[634] He explained candidly that it was the Muslims' "right and duty to make war upon whoever (sic) they could find and to make Slaves of all they could take as prisoners, and that every Mussulman [Muslim] who should be slain in battle was sure to go to Paradise."

The problem ended when Thomas Jefferson became president and decided to use military force—unilaterally.

Islamists who prefer death over life, who have turned lying into an art form, who believe their way is the only way and that *kaffars* do not deserve freedom or life are not prime candidates for rational multilateralism.

Only a manic multilateralist who believes in multilateralism for its own sake would risk innocent peoples' lives by letting Islamists tie our hands while they operate as they please. But that is precisely what President Obama is doing, whether he is fully conscious of it or not.

Obama Puts American Lives at Risk to Please Global Opinion

Let's take a look at an example of manic multilateralism in action. It involves the detention of alien enemy combatants, an area where President Obama is seeking the stamp of "international legitimacy."

Closing Guantánamo

As he promised during the campaign, President Obama signed an executive order directing the closure of the detention facilities at Guantánamo Bay by early 2010—a deadline that has proven elusive, by the way. White House officials said the move is part of an effort to repair America's image abroad.[635]

It was a move that has been well received at the United Nations, where UN High Commissioner for Human Rights Navi Pillay described Obama's action as representing a good day for the rule of law.[636]

As it happens, Obama signed the order on the same day that a Saudi-born former Guantánamo terror detainee named Said Ali al-Shihri, who had been sent to enroll in a Saudi "rehabilitation program" for former *jihadists,* was reported to have returned to his old terrorist ways instead. That should be no surprise, since Saudi Arabia is an incubator of terrorism.[637]

Al-Shihri left Saudi Arabia and quickly became an al Qaeda commander in Yemen, which is re-emerging as another terrorist safe-haven.

Al-Shihri is not the only Guantánamo alumnus who has resumed terrorist activities. The Pentagon believes dozens of former Guantánamo detainees have "returned to the fight" against America, although the precise number is disputed.[638]

Obama will either release most of the remaining detainees or try them under the full constitutional protections afforded criminal defendants in American courts. What about dangerous captives who cannot be tried for risk of revealing intelligence secrets in open court, or because evidence against them was elicited under coercive interrogation techniques? Some of them may be released on legal technicalities. If no other country agrees to take them, they may actually be permitted to remain in the United States, where they will be able to set up sleeper al Qaeda cells.

And if the United Nations has its way, former captives may be awarded damages for their pain and suffering during detention. The UN Special Rapporteur on Torture, Manfred Nowak, has claimed, for example, that inmates freed from Guantánamo should sue the United States if they have been "mistreated."[639]

Giving the 9/11 Mastermind His Day in Civil Court with Full Constitutional Protections

The most dramatic example of this dangerous lunacy of treating alien terrorist suspects like ordinary criminals is the Obama administration's plan, as of the writing of this book, to try Khaled Sheikh Mohammed and his al Qaeda cohorts in civil federal court. Military commissions, operating under procedures approved by Congress and subject to review by the federal courts, already provide alien enemy detainees with sufficient due process protection, without creating a propaganda circus for al Qaeda to exploit.

We are at war with a ruthless enemy that wants to destroy the very Constitution the Obama administration is now misusing in the name of "full legal protections." Any blood that spills directly or indirectly as a result of this circus will be on the hands of President Obama and Attorney General Eric Holder.

Obama's High-Stakes Gamble: End Tough Interrogation That Could Prevent Another 9/11

President Obama has kept another of his campaign promises by making the *Army Field Manual* the rulebook governing interrogation techniques for all United States Government personnel including the CIA.[640] With very limited undefined exceptions, the enhanced interrogation techniques that have helped keep us safe since 9/11 are a thing of the past.

The *Army Field Manual for Human Intelligence Collector Operations* is a publicly available document.[641] Therefore, it actually tells terrorists how they are likely to be interrogated and the expected psychological outcomes. Hardened terrorists will have little problem in learning to manipulate their interrogators.

In other words, Obama has removed the element of surprise from future interrogations. Keeping the enemy guessing about what we do and how we do it is essential in an asymmetric war with an enemy that relies upon the element of surprise. Publicly available rules that spell out what terrorist suspects can expect while in detention remove their incentive to cooperate.

The toughest sanction in the *Army Field Manual* is the limited separation of an unlawful enemy combatant from his fellow detainees, which requires higher levels of approval before it can be imposed.[642] Again, this will have little effect on terrorists trained to handle such conditions.

Separation of enemy combatants can mean solitary confinement. It may also include feelings of isolation and loss of a sense of control brought on by perceptual or sensory deprivation, sleep deprivation, the induction of fear and hopelessness, and the use of sensory overload, temperature, or environmental manipulation.[643]

However, the *Army Field Manual* prohibits the use of "excessive noise," "excessive dampness," or "excessive or inadequate heat, light or ventilation."[644] And the manual bans sleep deprivation—unless it provides a detainee at least four hours of sleep a night.[645] (Before you shout "torture," consider how many American college students survive on less than four hours a night of sleep.)

The *Army Field Manual* states:

All prisoners and detainees, regardless of status, will be treated humanely. Cruel, inhuman and degrading treatment is prohibited. The Detainee Treatment Act of 2005 defines "cruel, inhuman or degrading treatment" as the cruel unusual, and inhumane treatment or punishment prohibited by the Fifth, Eighth, and Fourteenth Amendments to the US Constitution. This definition refers to an extensive body of law developed by the courts of the United States to determine when, under various circumstances, treatment of individuals would be inconsistent with American constitutional standards related to concepts of dignity, civilization, humanity, decency and fundamental fairness.[646]

Under Army interrogation rules, interrogators cannot even mock those passages in the Koran that serve as the basis for the most dangerous *jihadists*' fanatical beliefs, much less deprive them of these incendiary religious tracts altogether.[647]

The UN's "Torture" Expert Wants to Double-Down on Obama's Gamble

Yet UN officials such as its torture "expert" Manfred Nowak are not satisfied. They want to increase the risks to American lives even further.

Nowak believes, for example, "[W]hen isolation regimes are intentionally used to apply psychological pressure on detainees, such practices become coercive and should be absolutely prohibited."[648] He also warned the American Psychological Association that psychologists' continued presence at Guantánamo Bay and similar detention settings violates international law. He threatened to revoke the association's UN accreditation as a Non Governmental Organization if it did not order its members to discontinue their presence at Guantánamo Bay.[649]

In the world of manic multilateralism represented by the United Nations, an unaccountable self-described torture "expert" can make up international law as he goes along and declare that using even conventional psychological methods to elicit information from detainees is forbidden.

Will Obama give in to international opinion and let UN charlatans like Manfred Nowak have their way? Probably. We know, for example, that Nowak had several meetings with Obama State Department officials within a month of Obama's inauguration, and that Nowak came away very pleased with the outcome.[650]

And take the Obama's Justice Department appointment of a special prosecutor to re-open cases of alleged abuses by CIA interrogators, whom had already been investigated with a determination not to prosecute.[651] Even Obama's national security team opposed this decision. And seven former CIA directors who served both Republican and Democratic presidents have asked President

Obama to end the Justice Department's criminal probe.[652] But Obama has ignored them.

Evidently, it was more important that the Obama Justice Department's decision had earned instant praise from the United Nations.

> "I warmly welcome this responsible decision by the US Government to open a preliminary investigation," said the United Nations High Commissioner for Human Rights, Navi Pillay. "I hope there is a swift examination of the various allegations of abuse made by former and current detainees in Guantánamo and other US-run prisons, and if they are verified, that the next steps will involve accountability for anyone who has violated the law."[653]

In the Alice-in-Wonderland world of the UN, which the Obama administration wants so badly to engage at full throttle, the word of likely terrorists is given equal or greater credence than the word of CIA agents trying to prevent another 9/11.

Separating Manic Multilateralism from Reality

The 1949 Geneva Conventions are the core of international humanitarian law, the body of multilateral treaties regulating the conduct of armed conflict.[654] The United States is a party to the Geneva Conventions and honors them—when they apply.

The Geneva Conventions consist of four primary parts, along with a "Common Convention" that cuts across the entire treaty, which the International Red Cross summarizes as follows:[655]

1. The first Geneva Convention protects wounded and sick soldiers on land during war.

2. The second Geneva Convention protects wounded, sick and shipwrecked military personnel at sea during war.

3. The third Geneva Convention applies to prisoners of war.

4. The fourth Geneva Convention affords protection to civilians, including in occupied territory.

The Geneva Conventions require that "*[P]risoners of war* who refuse to answer may not be threatened, insulted, or *exposed to unpleasant or disadvantageous treatment of any kind*" (emphasis added).[656] A prisoner of war must be treated like a member of the US armed forces and granted the same living conditions.

The *Army Field Manual* follows this protocol only for detainees who actually qualify as prisoners of war. Detainees eligible for POW status are provided with privileges and procedural protections that go beyond the baseline prohibition of cruel, inhuman, and degrading treatment that extends to all detainees, including unlawful enemy combatants.[657]

However, not all detainees are eligible for POW status. Under the Geneva Convention on Prisoners of War, combatants are entitled to the additional protections of POW status only if they meet certain conditions, namely that they are:

- members of the armed forces or

- a militia belonging to a party to the conflict.

They must be organized under a command structure, wear a fixed distinctive sign or emblem recognizable at a distance, carry their arms openly and conduct their operations in accordance with the laws and customs of war.

Al Qaeda and other terrorist detainees do not even begin to meet these minimum qualifications. They deliberately target innocent civilians, in violation of the most elementary laws of war. They set off bombs, impersonate civilians or police, hide among civilians, and use mosques as terrorist sanctuaries. It is simply laughable to think that denial of POW status equates to torture, or any other form of truly inhumane treatment. On the contrary, it means denying special privileges and procedural protections to individuals who refuse to abide by even the most minimal civilized norms and laws of war, not to mention the Geneva Conventions themselves.

The Global War Against Armed Global Terrorist Networks Is Not an International Armed Conflict According to the UN—and the US Supreme Court

In the alternative reality occupied by the United Nations, its torture "expert" Manfred Nowak pointedly avoids the entire POW eligibility issue for another reason entirely. The Geneva Convention on Prisoners of War only applies to international armed conflicts. Nowak thinks the issue is irrelevant because "I do not consider this so-called 'war on terror' as an international armed conflict."[658]

Also, he thinks terrorists deserve some understanding. He blames Islamic jihadist suicide bombings on poverty, the conflict in the Middle East and "the arrogance of the north in this kind of 'clash of civilisation' (which is a bit of a self-fulfilling prophecy)."[659] Islamic supremacist ideology has nothing to do with it, according to Nowak.

Under Nowak's logic, it makes no difference that the POW provisions of the Geneva Conventions are inapplicable to the suspected terrorists in Gitmo. These detainees are protected anyway under Common Article 3, since it covers situations of *non-international armed conflicts*. This part of the Geneva Conventions requires humane treatment for all persons in enemy hands. It prohibits, among other things, murder, mutilation, torture, cruel, humiliating and degrading treatment, the taking of hostages, and "the passing of sentences and the carrying out of executions without previous judgment pronounced by a regularly constituted court, affording all the judicial guarantees which are recognized as indispensable by civilized peoples."[660]

Nowak glides over the fact that all of these horrible acts are regularly committed by the terrorists themselves.

The Supreme Court Endorses Nowak's Wacky Views

Nothing compels us to take Nowak's opinions seriously. But the United States Supreme Court has used the same logic as this UN torture guru when it invalidated the special military tribunals set up by the Bush administration to try enemy combatants held at Guantánamo Bay. Accepting without analysis the proposition that the global war on terror was not part of an international armed conflict, the Court applied the benefits of civilian protection under Common Article 3 to suspected terrorists, including al Qaeda.[661] It concluded that the detainees were entitled to "protections recognized by customary international law," which included at minimum that "an accused must, absent disruptive conduct or consent, be present for his trial and must be privy to the evidence against him."[662]

The Supreme Court reached this decision after consulting a Friend-of-Court brief filed by 271 United Kingdom and European parliamentarians. Their brief referred to the Geneva Conventions five times.[663]

> "Even assuming that Hamden [the detainee] is a dangerous individual who would cause great harm or death to innocent civilians given the opportunity," the Supreme Court said, "the Executive nevertheless must comply with the prevailing rule of law in undertaking to try him and subject him to criminal punishment."[664]

The Supreme Court admitted that the phrase *"all the guarantees... recognized as indispensable by civilized peoples"* in Common Article 3 is not defined. And it could not explain how fighting the global Islamic terrorist network that trained and funded the 9/11 attackers from bases in Afghanistan and from cells in the Middle East and Europe is a "local" conflict. Nevertheless, it applied the

UN paradigm of criminal law protections for suspected alien terrorist detainees, and listened to European parliamentarians, rather than defer to the elected US Congress and the commander-in-chief on how best to prosecute the war

More Legal Mumbo Jumbo from the World of Manic Multilateralism

The United Nations Convention Against Torture and Other Cruel, Inhuman or Degrading Treatment or Punishment of 1984, to which the United States is a party, establishes a regime for international cooperation in the criminal prosecution of torturers.[665] Each member state is required either to prosecute torturers found in its territory or to extradite them to other countries for prosecution.

When the US Senate ratified the treaty in 1994, it stated its understanding of torture as an act "specifically intended to inflict severe physical or mental pain or suffering," which is the definition of torture in the UN Convention itself. The Senate went on to define mental pain and suffering as "prolonged mental harm" resulting from such causes as "the intentional infliction or threatened infliction of severe physical pain or suffering or the threat of imminent death."[666]

The Senate also included the reservation that the US would understand "cruel, inhuman, or degrading treatment or punishment" to mean "the cruel, unusual and inhumane treatment or punishment prohibited by the Fifth, Eighth, and/or Fourteenth Amendments to the Constitution of the United States."[667]

But the United Nations does not defer to the lawfully constituted processes of each sovereign member state. It has its own definitions of torture or degrading treatment. Torture guru Manfred Nowak insists that the United Nations Convention Against Torture severely limits "how the fight against terrorism, even global terrorism of the type of al-Qaeda, has to be fought, in a democracy in particular."[668]

Wacky Nowak Makes Up International Law as He Goes Along

Nowak maintains, without any established legal precedent to support his position, that the UN Convention Against Torture requires the US to prosecute Bush administration lawyers who drafted legal opinions justifying the use of enhanced interrogation tactics on terrorist suspects.[669] These memos authorized such techniques as sleep deprivation; keeping detainees naked, in standing positions, in cold cells or in a cramped box filled with harmless insects; prolonged shackling; open-hand slapping; and, its best-known method, waterboarding.

According to the circular reasoning of the UN's "expert" on torture, these techniques clearly constituted torture; therefore, the lawyers' legal justifications made them participants in torture. "[O]n the basis of these memoranda, then orders would be given, and persons would be subjected to these kind of interrogation techniques," Nowak said, which "one should know actually can easily amount to torture."[670]

Yet Nowak has yet to present a legally binding definition of torture which excludes any of these enhanced interrogation techniques. These techniques, remember, were used in very limited circumstances, and in a carefully controlled environment, to elicit information that could save thousands of lives, after less harsh alternatives were tried and failed. There is no definition barring their use in such circumstances in the UN Convention itself or in US law.

None of the enhanced interrogation methods used by the Bush administration were techniques that "one should know actually can easily amount to torture" under the US Senate's definition when it ratified the treaty.[671] And that's what counts.

The Bush-era legal memos placed strict limits on when and how to apply the techniques to avoid any severe long-term physical or psychological harm. They also provided for monitoring of the interrogations and high-level signoffs in writing on a case-by-case basis. Moreover, these techniques were reserved only for detainees whom we suspected possessed valuable, time-sensitive intelligence.[672]

The harsh interrogation methods condemned by Nowak provided the CIA interrogators with enough actionable intelligence that the government was able to thwart an imminent terrorist attack on Los Angeles. Khalid Shaikh Mohammed, the 9/11 mastermind, gave up vital information that led to the capture of the leader of a plot to hijack passenger planes and fly them into the tallest building on the West Coast, the Library Tower in Los Angeles. Khalid Shaikh Mohammed also provided information that led to the disruption of an al Qaeda cell planning anthrax attacks inside the United States.[673]

Such information did not freely flow from Khalid's lips during a friendly interrogation session. In his initial interrogation by CIA officers, according to former CIA Director George Tenet, Khalid Shaikh Mohammed had defiantly told them, "I'll talk to you guys after I get to New York and see my lawyer."[674] Waterboarding changed his mind, and the information he subsequently supplied saved thousands of lives. Now Obama is seriously considering giving this 9/11 ring leader the opportunity to go to New York, or wherever his trial ends up taking place, and meet with his legal team, who will no doubt exploit poor Khalid's suffering during the subsequent propaganda circus.

As for Nowak, he rejects the "ticking bomb" scenario as justification for harsh interrogation techniques.[675] And the current UN High Commissioner for Human Rights, Navi Pillay, believes, like Nowak, that detainees "are entitled to an expeditious and fair trial before the regular courts."[676]

International Law Has "Absolute Priority"

I took the liberty of confronting Nowak, the UN's Special Rapporteur on torture, at a press conference at UN headquarters on October 20, 2009.

When I asked whether the United Nations' view of international law would trump a contrary decision by the highest court of a functioning democracy such as the United States, Nowak said international law has "absolute priority." His rationale was that a UN member state that voluntarily signs and ratifies a treaty is bound by the obligations of that treaty. Any reservations or carve-outs from a member state's treaty obligations as conditions to its ratification, such as the US Senate included in its ratification of the UN Convention Against Torture, were illegal, according to Nowak, if the UN human rights committee in charge of monitoring compliance decided they were illegal. In other words, he believes, along with much of the UN establishment, that neither the US Senate nor our judiciary has the final say as to how the United States' treaty obligations should be interpreted and administered. That privilege belongs to the UN itself.

Then I asked Nowak how he would react if the US Supreme Court decided that a coerced confession from a high-level al Qaeda suspect was admissible at trial because the coercion, while psychologically intense, did not amount to torture and the suspect was not entitled to all of the constitutional protections afforded in ordinary criminal trials. Would Nowak assert the primacy of the UN's unaccountable international law apparatus over the Supreme Court?

At first, Nowak bobbed and weaved, but in the end, he simply couldn't resist picking a fight with the highest court in the US. He replied that the UN's "monitoring bodies have the power to decide whether a member state is in compliance." In his view, the Constitution as interpreted by the Supreme Court cannot be used to justify an action at variance with international law as interpreted by the relevant UN bodies.

The Supreme Court Again Goes Along
with the UN's Wackiness

As shocking as such a bold assertion of power by a UN functionary is to Americans who believe in self-government and national sovereignty, Nowak and his UN colleagues may win by default. UN officials are filing so-called Friend-of-Court briefs with the Supreme Court on human rights issues and the Court increasingly defers to their views.

We have already seen how the Supreme Court used the same logic as the UN torture guru Nowak when it decided to invalidate the special military tribunals set up by the Bush Administration to try enemy combatants held at Guantánamo Bay. Let's also consider the Supreme Court's evident acceptance of the UN's criminal law paradigm when dealing with detained Islamic terrorist suspects. When the Court decided that such alien detainees must be granted full habeas corpus rights and declared that the procedures for military trials which Congress passed and President Bush signed were insufficient, it made this decision on the advice of the Canadian jurist Louise Arbour. At the time, Arbour was the United Nations' High Commissioner for Human Rights. Her Friend-of-Court brief mentioned habeas corpus five times.[677]

Arbour advised the Supreme Court that the UN International Covenant on Civil and Political Rights required them to reverse the Court of Appeals decision denying the detainees' petition for habeas corpus:

> In exercise of the mandate entrusted to her by the international community, the High Commissioner calls on this Court to give full effect to the United States's international obligations in adjudicating the questions presented ... the obligation of the United States arising from Article 9(4) [of the UN Covenant] is neither fully defined by nor dependent on constitutional provisions or federal statutes affording access to habeas relief per se. Hence, in order to ensure compliance by the United States with its obli-

gations under the Covenant, the judicial access afforded by the United States to persons it has detained must be assessed for compliance with each of the requirements set forth in Article 9(4)...If United States law were as construed by the Court of Appeals to preclude habeas corpus, however, the United States would be in breach of its obligations under the Covenant.[678]

Sure enough, the Supreme Court listened to the UN High Commissioner for Human Rights and incorporated her notion of international law into its decision interpreting what was required under the United States Constitution.

Obama Also Goes Along with the UN's Wackiness

And Obama has also been listening to the UN. In fact, his administration is making it very difficult to gain timely intelligence from high-value Islamic jihadist detainees. *Terrorists detained in Afghanistan have even reportedly been read Miranda warnings.*[679] Yes, you read that right. These are the same Miranda warnings which require American law enforcement officers to inform criminal defendants in the US of their right to remain silent, and their right to an attorney! Recall that after only a brief interrogation, the Obama administration also "Mirandized" the al Qaeda-affiliated Christmas Day bomber who almost blew up an airplane on the way to Detroit with explosives hidden in his underwear. Not surprisingly, Umar Farouk Abdulmutallab then clammed up.

It has taken a series of potential catastrophes on our home soil, including the attempted car-bombing in Times Square, to finally convince even the Obama administration to *consider* modifying Miranda protections to deal with the global terrorist threat. That's one small step in the direction of common sense if it should actually come to pass. Meanwhile, the administration is making terrorist suspects' lives easier in other ways.

For example, Obama and his Attorney General Eric Holder have been planning to put terrorist in chief Khaled Sheikh Mohammed on trial as a criminal defendant in a federal civil court rather than in military court where he belongs. If Obama goes through with this plan, it would be perhaps his most atrocious decision to date. As president and commander in chief, Obama's first and foremost duty is to protect the security of all Americans. Yet he is considering risking the security of American citizens to extend the full protections of the Constitution to one of its most dangerous sworn foreign enemies. And wherever Khaled Sheikh Mohammed is ultimately tried, other alien terrorist suspects such as the Christmas Day bomber are being accorded the full array of constitutional rights by the Obama administration in our federal civil court system, despite the viable alternative of a military tribunal.

The Constitution applies, as its preamble states, to "*We the People of the United States.*" Not to the *foreign enemies* of the United States. The preamble says that "*We the People of the United States*" have established the Constitution to "provide for the common defence" (sic) and to "secure the Blessings of Liberty to ourselves and our Posterity." There is nothing in the preamble, or anywhere else in the Constitution, that guarantees these blessings of liberty to foreign terrorists who have declared war on the United States. Yet that is precisely what Obama is doing.

Under Obama's administration, the war against Islamic terrorists has been turned into a criminal law proceeding, with full constitutional rights extended to the enemy. This legal mumbo jumbo is the fruit of the manic multilateralism embraced by Obama, the Supreme Court, and the UN.

Listen to Winston Churchill
Instead of the United Nations

President Obama has praised Winston Churchill for upholding democratic values and the rule of law even when London was being "bombed to smithereens."[680]

But if the president wants to use Winston Churchill as a reference point for his own policies, he ought to pay heed to what Churchill had to say both about Islam and the United Nations.

Churchill's Warnings on Islam

Winston Churchill did not buy the myth that Islam was either a truly tolerant or a peaceful religion. He saw through the façade that Obama is either unwilling or unable to pierce:

> ...the Mahommedan religion increases, instead of lessening, the fury of intolerance. It was originally propagated by the sword, and ever since, its votaries have been subject, above the people of all other creeds, to this form of madness... Individual Moslems may show splendid qualities, but the influence of the religion paralyzes the social development of those who follow it. No stronger retrograde force exists in the world. Far from being moribund, Mohammedanism is a militant and proselytizing faith.[681]
>
> How dreadful are the curses which Mohammedanism lays on its votaries! Besides the fanatical frenzy, which is as dangerous in a man as hydrophobia in a dog, there is this fearful fatalistic apathy. Improvident habits, slovenly systems of agriculture, sluggish methods of commerce, and insecurity of property exist wherever the followers of the Prophet rule or live. A degraded sensualism deprives this life of its grace and refinement; the next of its dignity and sanctity. The fact that in Mohammedan law every woman must belong to some man as his absolute property—either as a child, a wife, or a concubine—must delay the final extinction of slavery *until the faith of Islam has ceased to be a great power among men.* (emphasis added)[682]

Churchill added that "civilisation (sic) is confronted with militant Mahommedanism. The forces of progress clash with those of reaction. The religion of blood and war is face to face with that of peace. *Luckily the religion of peace is usually the better armed*" (emphasis added).[683]

Churchill's Warnings on the United Nations

Churchill helped to create the UN, along with President Franklin Delano Roosevelt, but he was under no illusions. He warned about the danger of a false peace built on sand:

> We must make sure that its work is fruitful, that it is a reality and not a sham, that it is a force for action, and *not merely a frothing of words,* that it is a true temple of peace in which the shields of many nations can some day be hung up, and *not merely a cockpit in a Tower of Babel.* Before we cast away the solid assurances of national armaments for self-preservation we must be certain that our temple is built, not upon shifting sands or quagmires, but upon the rock. (emphasis added)[684]

Unfortunately, President Obama is doing the precise opposite. He told the UN General Assembly during his September 2009 address that the United States under his administration has "re-engaged the United Nations" and has broken with the Bush Administration's "unilateral" approach. He promised to address America's "priorities" in the UN and warned that not following "the United Nation's demands" (sic) would make "all people less safe."[685]

He would rather join the United Nations' Tower of Babel styled "Alliance of Civilizations" with Islamists, instead of ensuring that we do not get entrapped by the Islamists' agenda at the UN.

As EYEontheUN.com editor Anne Bayesfsky put it, "[T]he Obama administration has made repeated efforts to curry favor with rogue regimes, and in particular, the Arab and Muslim states that control the balance of power in many UN bodies."[686]

Forsaking Our Allies and Coddling Our Enemies

The UN and the Obama administration apply different standards when judging Islamic countries as opposed to our democratic allies. Israel is the most obvious case. We have already discussed the UN's double standard when dealing with the Palestinian issue. The Obama administration compounded the problem when it pressured Israel to freeze settlement construction.[687]

Then consider the accusations leveled against Israel by a UN Human Rights Council "fact-finding" mission in Gaza headed by Judge Richard Goldstone of South Africa. This UN mission looked into the alleged human rights violations committed during Israel's Operation Cast Lead launched to end the terrorist rocket attacks fired from Gaza against Israeli civilians.

The Goldstone report declared that "Israel committed actions amounting to war crimes, possibly crimes against humanity." The report recommended that the UN Security Council require Israel to launch its own investigation, which the Security Council would monitor. If Israel did not investigate and take action to the Security Council's satisfaction, the Security Council should refer the matter to the International Criminal Court prosecutor.[688]

Although the Goldstone report did criticize Hamas and other terrorist groups for their rocket attacks, most of the report focused on strident accusations against Israel.

As Harvard law professor Alan Dershowitz wrote on the *Jerusalem Post*'s Double-Standard Watch, the Goldstone report was "so filled with lies, distortions and blood libels that it could have been drafted by Hamas extremists." Then he added, "Wait—in effect, it was!"[689]

Dershowitz explained that one member of the group is a

"Hamas lackey who before being appointed as an 'objective' judge had already reached the conclusion—without conducting any investigation or hearing any evidence—that Israel's military actions 'amount to aggression, not self defense' and that 'the manner and scale of its operations in Gaza amount to an act of aggression and is contrary to international law.'"

"Other members," Dershowitz continued, "were accompanied on their investigations in Gaza by actual Hamas activists who showed them only what Hamas wanted them to see. The group was eager to find or manufacture 'evidence' to support what the Human Rights Council itself had directed them to find."[690]

The investigation was so bad that even Mary Robinson had refused to participate.[691]

What was the Obama administration's reaction to the Goldstone report? I asked Ambassador Susan Rice after she emerged from a closed Security Council session on the Middle East. "We have very serious concerns about many recommendations in the report," she said in the first official American response to the Goldstone report.[692] That was encouraging. But then in the next breath, she punted the whole matter back to the Human Rights Council, which was responsible for the travesty to begin with: "We will expect and believe that the appropriate venue for this report to be considered is the Human Rights Council."[693]

The United States, let's remember, is now a member of the UN Human Rights Council, where double standards are standard operating procedure. Predictably, the Human Rights Council ignored our representative's objections and endorsed the Goldstone report. It then was taken up by the General Assembly, where it was also endorsed and then referred back to the Security Council. So much for trying to exert a rational influence on the Human Rights Council from within. Thanks to Obama, the United States is now a full-fledged member of this notorious club.

A Tale of Two Countries: Honduras and Iran

Another example of the double-standard is the zero tolerance displayed by both the UN and the Obama administration toward

Honduras' interim change in government, while at the same time Obama and the UN effectively ratified the "legitimacy" of Iran's fraudulent election.

It seems the only regimes Obama and the UN are willing to play real hardball with are the likes of a democratic nation like Honduras—and, of course, Israel.

On September 15, 2009, the United Nations Human Rights Council heard an update from the UN High Commissioner for Human Rights, Navi Pillay, on what she regarded as the salient human rights issues of the day. Pillay mentioned the "marred" election in Afghanistan, along with her claim—shared by the United Nations General Assembly, Secretary General Ban Ki-moon and the Obama administration—that "constitutional order had been subverted and democratic space undermined" in Honduras. But somehow, the fraudulent presidential election in Iran did not rise to this same level of concern in Pillay's mind.

In fact, Pillay turned the fraudulent election and the protests that followed into a positive demonstration of "the vitality of Iran's civil society and political life." To her credit, Pillay at least acknowledged "the towering constraints that peaceful activism faces" in Iran.[694] But that is too little too late for the dissidents being murdered and imprisoned there. Honduras was much higher up on her list of priorities.

Shortly before Pillay addressed the Human Rights Council, the Council's president barred the Permanent Representative of Honduras in Geneva from participating, which is the right of every UN member state, because he was not the "accredited representative of President Zelaya's Government."[695] The fact that Manuel Zelaya had been replaced by the current interim president pursuant to Honduras' constitutional processes, and with the full support of its elected legislative body and its civilian high court, was overlooked.

The United States sided with the opponents of Honduras' constitutional processes in support of Zelaya, who had pulled a trick out of Venezuelan strongman Hugo Chavez's playbook by trying to give himself another term in office through a referendum. The US even revoked the Honduras' interim president's visa, along with the diplomatic and tourist visas for fourteen Honduran Supreme Court judges.[696]

Meanwhile, Iran's illegitimate government's right to participate at the UN was never challenged. Ahmadinejad was not denied a visa to the United States, but treated as a duly authorized world leader entitled to speak at the fall 2009 United Nations General Assembly.[697] As usual, his speech attacked Israel, prompting a few countries, including the United States, to walk out. He also played down the violence on the streets of Iran, declaring that "[O]ur nation has gone through a glorious and fully democratic election, opening a new chapter for our country in the march toward national progress and enhanced international interactions." Congratulating himself on his "glorious" victory, he added that Iranian voters had "entrusted me once more with a large majority."[698]

When Ahmadinejad finished, he was loudly applauded by those who had remained in the General Assembly Hall.[699]

UN Secretary General Ban Ki-moon had already legitimized Ahmadinejad's disputed electoral victory by congratulating him on his re-election, and sending him a diplomatic letter on the occasion of his inauguration.[700]

Although B. Lynn Pascoe, Under Secretary General for Political Affairs, told me that Ban's letter to Ahmadinejad had not congratulated him on his re-election, the Mehr News Agency Persian service had reported to the contrary that the "UN Secretary General congratulated the re-election of Dr. Ahmadinejad." It also reported that Ban Ki-moon said he wanted to strengthen the UN's interaction with Ahamdinejad, and that he praised Iran's role in the promotion of social and economical development in the world, and confronting terrorism.[701] I asked the Secretary General Spokesperson's office to provide me with a copy of the secretary general's letter to Ahmadinejad but they refused.

It should also be noted that the secretary general subsequently met privately with Ahamdinejad during the Iranian presidential pretender's 2009 UN visit.[702]

I asked Ban Ki-moon at his monthly press conference on September 17, 2009, whether he saw any double standard between the UN's denial of credentials to representatives of the interim government in Honduras, and welcoming Ahmadinejad. He replied that he deferred in such matters to the General Assembly credentials committee. But a few minutes later, he launched into a full-throated defense of Zelaya.[703]

Ban Ki-moon declared that

> when a leader [is] elected constitutionally, through a transparent election process, then his authority and office should be protected and guaranteed. This is the principle of the international community and the United Nations. For that, all the Member States of the United Nations have supported President Zelaya. I would like to reaffirm that again.[704]

However, Zelaya was removed legitimately through Honduras' constitutional process, which should be respected just as much as the constitutional process under which he was elected initially. And Ban Ki-moon ducked my question as to why Ahmadinijad—who certainly was not elected "through a transparent election process"—should be recognized by the UN as Iran's legitimate leader.

While taking a hard line against little Honduras' interim government, the Obama administration rewarded Mahmoud Ahmadinejad by agreeing to sit down with Iran as part of the so-called "5+1" talks (the 5 permanent members of the Security Council plus Germany).[705] This is part of Obama's engagement-without-conditions policy, which has disappointed Iranian dissidents looking for support from the United States.[706]

And Iran—like Obama—wants to discuss complete worldwide disarmament but has declared that suspension of its own nuclear program is off the table.[707]

Driving Toward Total Nuclear Disarmament

President Obama has called for "a world without nuclear weapons" and says the United States has a "moral responsibility" to lead the way, as the only nation ever to use them.[708]

The US has nothing to apologize for

Obama should read the diary of President Harry Truman, the last Democratic president who understood the world for what it truly was, not what he fantasized it to be. Truman considered the atomic bombings of Japan an absolute last resort, used only after it was clear that Japan had no intention of surrendering:

> We were approaching an experiment with the atom explosion. I was informed that event would take place within a possible thirty days. I then suggested that after that experimental test of the fission of the atom, that we give Japan a chance to stop the war by a surrender. That plan was followed. Japan refused to surrender and the bomb was dropped on two targets after which event the surrender took place.[709]

Truman believed Japan's refusal to surrender would cost 250,000 more American lives if we had to invade Japan.[710] He used the bomb to end a war that Japan had initiated against the United States when it attacked Pearl Harbor, and that it would not end on its own. We have nothing to apologize for.

How can Obama think that the United States should lead the way to complete nuclear disarmament while North Korea is testing its nuclear bombs, and Iran is trying to attain them?

Obama Comes to the UN to Push for Disarmament

Once again, Obama is looking to the United Nations to play a central role in his manic multilateralism exercise. He is leading efforts to create a potential new international organization overseeing nuclear weapons reductions.[711] And he personally presided over a heads-of-state discussion of a nuclear-free world at a special session of the UN Security Council.[712]

When I asked UN Ambassador Susan Rice whether the US would be contributing a concrete proposal to guide the special session's outcome, since it was being led by President Obama, she had no substantive response. Here is her non-answer:

> We're obviously chairing the Council and chairing that summit. We proposed this initiative. We have an interest in the quality of its outcome. And obviously, what we are suggesting and consulting with our colleagues on reflects the thinking and the aims of the US government. But obviously, any product of the Council is a product of 15, and I'm simply reflecting that reality in saying that this will be a process of consultation and discussion; and what, if anything, emerges will be a consequence not only of what the United States might propose but what others embrace.[713]

Ambassador Rice then said that "the session will be focused on nuclear nonproliferation and nuclear disarmament broadly, and not on any specific countries."[714]

Obama's Virtual World

The Security Council disarmament session ran along the lines that Rice laid out—a lot of sound and bombast but few specifics. President Obama mentioned the two rogue countries with dangerous nuclear ambitions, Iran and North Korea, only once during his speech, but immediately added that "[T]his is not about singling out individual nations."[715]

Kudos to French president Nicolas Sarkozy for trying to ground the session in some foundation of reality. After Obama outlined his vision of a nuclear-free world, Sarkozy replied:[716]

"We live in the real world, not the virtual world. And the real world expects us to take decisions.

President Obama dreams of a world without weapons ... but right in front of us two countries are doing the exact opposite.

Iran since 2005 has flouted five security council resolutions. North Korea has been defying council resolutions since 1993.

I support the extended hand of the Americans, but what good has proposals for dialogue brought the international community? More uranium enrichment and declarations by the leaders of Iran to wipe a UN member state off the map."

The Toothless Disarmament Resolution

Before that special Security Council disarmament session, the United States circulated a draft UN Security Council resolution calling on *all* countries with atomic weapons to get rid of them.[717] To achieve the desired outcome of a unanimously passed resolution, the draft resolution did not name the two key players involved—Iran and North Korea—or mention sanctions.

The final version of the resolution that passed followed this approach.[718] It called for a treaty "on general and complete disarmament under strict and effective international control" without specifying what that meant or providing any real teeth to the resolution. It mentioned in passing the Security Council's "particular concern at the current major challenges to the non-proliferation regime"—presumably an oblique, indirect reference to Iran and North Korea without naming them—but contained not a word about sanctions.[719]

"For international rules and laws to be effective," George Bush said back in 2004 when dealing with the same issue in a much more realistic fashion, "they must be enforced."[720]

So why is Obama now wasting time, and our country's prestige, with meaningless discussions and toothless resolutions? The answer is Obama's naïve reliance on the authority of the United Nations and his own powers of persuasion. We will take the UN treaties seriously. The Irans of the world will not. This is an example of lethal engagement at its worst.

As EYEontheUN editor Anne Bayefsky concluded, Obama's conflation of total disarmament and non-proliferation

> shamelessly panders to Arab and Muslim states. It is a familiar recipe for stonewalling efforts to prevent Iran or other Muslim and Arab states from acquiring nuclear weapons until Israel is disarmed or Israel's (unofficial) nuclear capacity is exposed and neutralized. It is also a frequent tool of those whose real goal is to stymie America's defenses.[721]

A Nuclear-Free World—Except for the Rogue States

And what exactly is the UN's role on nuclear disarmament? UN Secretary General Ban Ki-moon is promoting his own plan to achieve a nuclear-weapon-free world, which calls for all parties to the Nuclear Non-Proliferation Treaty to pursue negotiations "in good faith," either through a new convention or through mutually reinforcing instruments backed by credible verification.[722]

As the old proverb goes, the road to hell is paved with good intentions. When it comes to the UN, even the good intentions part is usually missing.

For example, a representative from Iran, which flouts UN Security Council resolutions regarding its nuclear program, was elected as a vice chair of the UN Disarmament Commission in 2007. A Syrian representative was chosen to serve as the Rapporteur.[723] Allowing Iran—one of only eleven nations subject to Security Council enforcement sanctions—to serve as vice chair of a body charged with making recommendations on nuclear proliferation and disarmament made a mockery of both the UN Disarmament Commission and of the Security Council resolutions aimed at Iran.[724]

How can anyone take the United Nations seriously when governments that break its rules are entrusted with enforcing them?

Apparently, Obama does. He told the UN General Assembly that "a world in which IAEA [UN International Atomic Energy Agency] inspections are avoided and the *United Nation's (sic) demands* are ignored will leave all people less safe, and all nations less secure" (emphasis added).[725] And he assured his motley global audience, which included dictators like Mahmoud Ahmadinejad, Moammar Qadaffi, and Hugo Chavez, that the United States would "address our priorities" at the UN.[726]

Meanwhile, in the real world (rather than the virtual world that Obama inhabits), the UN International Atomic Energy Agency, led by Egyptian diplomat Mohamed ElBaradei, has censored published reports to exclude evidence of Iran's military nuclear program.[727] This follows a report in March 2009 by the Government Accountability Office which found that "[N]either [the Department of] State nor IAEA seeks to systematically limit TC [technical cooperation] assistance to countries the United States has designated as state sponsors of terrorism," including Iran, Sudan, and Syria.[728]

Mohamed ElBaradei has headed the UN's chief nuclear watchdog agency for twelve long years, a term that has finally come to a close. Explaining why forceful action against the Islamic theocracy would be a mistake, ElBaradei told a French magazine that the

> Muslim world is angry, feels humiliated ... The Iranian nuclear problem is only part of a complex situation involving the Middle East and Muslim world security. To establish confidence between parts, you have to talk about Iraq, Afghanistan, Palestine, Lebanon, you have to talk about extremism, human rights, poverty ... This people' 11(sic) become extremists. Because they have nothing to loose (sic), because they feel humiliated.[729]

Mohamed ElBaradei then suggested that "uranium enrichment should be submitted to *multilateral control, even for Western countries.* Western super powers have to understand that if they want a long-term system, it must be fair" (emphasis added).[730]

President Obama is hopping aboard this manic multilateralist disarmament train. When talking about Iran during his Cairo speech to the Muslim world, Obama said:

> I understand those who protest that some countries have weapons that others do not. No single nation should pick and choose which nations hold nuclear weapons. That is why I strongly reaffirmed America's commitment to seek a world in which no nations hold nuclear weapons. And any nation—including Iran—should have the right to access peaceful nuclear power if it complies with its responsibilities under the nuclear Non-Proliferation Treaty. [731]

President Obama made this statement and then decided to negotiate with Iran on Iran's terms, despite full knowledge of Iranian lies and deception. For months, before finally disclosing Iran's deception to the public on September 25, 2009, Obama had been aware of a secret Iranian nuclear enrichment plant deep inside a mountain base of the Iranian Revolutionary Guards, near the religious center of Qum.[732] Yet valuable time was lost as he continued his quixotic quest for unconditional talks with Iranian officials. Even if tougher sanctions were effectively imposed with the full cooperation of Russia and China, it would be too little too late at this point.

Global nuclear disarmament treaties do not work when rogue regimes like Iran and North Korea flout the obligations imposed by the treaties they sign. Iran may claim it is complying with its responsibilities under the nuclear Non-Proliferation Treaty. However, outside of the Iranian regime itself and its most ardent supporters, only the most naïve would give the Islamic Republic of Iran the benefit of the doubt in this regard.

And it is equally naïve to rely on the United Nations to serve as the principal forum for negotiating and enforcing nuclear non-proliferation, test ban, or disarmament treaties, as Obama does, when the UN selects Iran to serve as a vice chairman of its Disarmament Commission!

As Anne Bayefsky put it, President Obama's "group-hug theory of diplomacy deserves the disdain of anyone who can separate rhetoric from reality."[733]

Sadly, there are too few people in positions of political influence today at the United Nations or in the United States government with enough common sense to tell the difference. Certainly, Obama cannot separate his rhetoric and fantasies of a nuclear-free world from reality—and his pursuit of lethal engagements is putting all of us at risk.

CHAPTER TWELVE

Where Are We Now and Where Do We Go from Here?

Ironically, as I was preparing to write this book, President Obama was awarded the 2009 Nobel Peace Prize. The Nobel Prize Committee said of their newest laureate, who'd been in office at that point a mere nine months: "Obama has as president created a new climate in international politics. Multilateral diplomacy has regained a central position, with emphasis on the role that the United Nations and other international institutions can play."[734] Committee chairman Thorbjoern Jagland also singled out Obama's efforts to heal the divide between the West and the Muslim world.[735]

Not surprisingly, Obama received this once most prestigious of international awards for his embrace of manic multilateralism, and his appeasement of Islamists. In his UN General Assembly speech on September 23, 2009, for example, President Obama said the United Nations can either be "a place where we indulge tyranny, or a source of moral authority."[736] Clearly, he has already decided— the UN will be the source of "moral authority" the United States will now follow.

However, as presently structured, the United Nations can *only* be a place that indulges tyranny. And that is what it does day after day. Fewer than half the member states in the General Assembly are bona fide democracies.[737] Meanwhile, the Human Rights Council is dominated by the radical, belligerent Islamic bloc. Despite blatantly flouting a series of Security Council resolutions, Iran is protected by its trading partners, China and Russia, from any meaningful punishment. Adding insult to injury, Iran is even awarded leadership positions in UN agencies and forums dealing with disarmament, development, and human rights!

As a consequence, the United Nations has completely squandered its moral authority. Obama is nevertheless putting his faith in the United Nations as "an indispensable factor in advancing the interests of the people we serve."[738] It should be clear based upon such declarations, and everything we have revealed in this book, that because of Obama's policy of lethal engagements America is now in grave danger of losing its national sovereignty and moral identity.

The United States was founded upon a set of "self-evident truths" set forth in the Declaration of Independence, that "*all men are created equal, that they are endowed by their Creator with certain unalienable Rights, that among these are Life, Liberty and the pursuit of Happiness.*"[739]

Government, our Founding Fathers believed, is set up "to secure these rights" and derives its "just powers from the consent of the governed." We have fought tyrants abroad and a bloody civil war at home to ensure that "Life, Liberty and the pursuit of Happiness" remain our "unalienable rights."

However, the best military in the world will not help us hold on to our freedoms if we let alien values infect our system from within. As we have seen time and again, radical Islamic ideology is the polar opposite of the "self-evident" truths upon which this country was founded. Islamism is a supremist, racist, misogynist ideology that denigrates human reason, individual freedom, and self-government.

The father of our country, George Washington, warned in his farewell address against allowing "foreign influence and corruption" to subject "the policy and the will" of our country "to the policy and will of another."[740] In the twenty-first century, we are now allowing ourselves to be subjected to the policy and will of the Islamists.

The United Nations is the Trojan horse the Islamists are using to transform international law into a more sharia-friendly version, particularly on human rights and freedom of expression. The Islamists are coming after us, using the United Nations—and relying heavily upon Obama's obsession with that global body and our transnationalist judges' willingness to turn the US Constitution into a reflection of international law.

As mentioned before, Obama is dedicated to addressing America's "priorities" at the United Nations. He has promised to "re-engage" the UN and submit the United States to its whimsical dictates regarding international law. He is enabling a global institutional framework influenced by Islamists' ideology to undermine our "unalienable rights," which is accelerating with every transnational judge he sends to the federal courts to transform the US Constitution into a reflection of international law.

Instead of trumpeting this country's exceptional generosity of spirit and its commitment to human freedom, President Obama is constantly apologizing for our real or imaginary mistakes. Instead of declaring that religious freedom in America neither negates our Judeo-Christian roots nor justifies special accommodations for Islam, Obama boasts that the United States is "one of the largest Muslim countries in the world."[741]

Some will accuse me of concocting an alarmist "blue helmet" conspiracy theory linking President Obama, the Islamists, and the UN in a nefarious scheme to impose one-world government under sharia. Those critics have missed the entire point of this book. What I have described, with plenty of documentation, is the undeniably shared worldview at the United Nations and within the Obama administration. Whether they consciously intend to help the Islamists carry out their plans is beside the point. The United Nations/Obama administration approach to major conflicts—demonstrated by word and deed—is the lethal kind of engagement more properly described as appeasement. By indulging the Islamists, they are letting them win the UN-istan intifada at the United Nations and here at home.

We simply need to compare the Islamists' intentions expressed in their own words with the actions and rhetoric of the UN and the Obama administration.

	Islamists' World-View	United Nations and Obama Administration Words and Actions	
Free Expression	OIC Plank: "Endeavor to have the United Nations adopt an international resolution to counter Islamophobia."	UN Human Rights Council and General Assembly pass UN Resolutions defining "defamation of religions" as a violation of international law.	U.S. joins UN Human Rights Council and co-sponsors Egyptian resolution to combat media "religious stereotypes."
	Muslim Brotherhood website: "intellectual freedom can't be cited in matters related to beliefs."		
	OIC Secretary-General: "confronting the Danish cartoons...we sent a clear message to the West regarding the red lines that should not be crossed."[i]		President Obama: "I consider it part of my responsibility as president of the United States to fight against negative stereotypes of Islam wherever they appear."[ii]

Islamic Terrorism	Hamas-Hezbollah are freedom fighters, not terrorists.	No agreement on definition of terrorism.	Refuses to link "War on Terror" with fight against Islamic terrorists.
	Muslim Brotherhood Movement Home Page: "Jilhad is our way. To die in the way of Allah is our highest hope."	Terrorists exempt from new international crime of "Aggression."	Refuses to use the term "jihad" in the context of Islam-inspired violence.
Islamic Tolerance	Koran 9:29: "[F]ight those who believe not in Allah... now acknowledge the Religion of Truth until they pay the Jizya with willing submission, and feel themselves subdued."	UN Alliance of Civilization: "Historically, under Muslim rule, Jews and Christians were largely free to practice their faiths." [iii]	President Obama: "And throughout history, Islam has demonstrated through words and deeds the possibilities of religious tolerance..." [iv]
The West Must Adapt To Islam And Apologize For The Past	Muslim Brotherhood Project: "...channel thought, education and action in order to establish an Islamic power [government] on the Earth."	UN Alliance of Civilization: "Assertions that Islam is inherently violent and related statements by some political and religious leaders in the West...have contributed to an alarming increase in Islamophobia which further exacerbates Muslim fears of the West." [vi]	President Obama: "...tension has been fed by colonialism that denied rights and opportunities to many Muslims." [v] "...in the United States rules on charitable giving have made it harder for Muslims to fulfill their religious obligation." [vii]

	"...collect sufficient funds for the perpetuation of *jihad*."[viii]	UN issues reports calling U.S. a racist society.[ix]	Obama apologizes for racial and religious stereotypes in the U.S.[x]
New Global Financial Order	Sheikh al-Qaradawi, spiritual leader of the Muslim Brotherhood: "[T]he collapse of the capitalist system...shows us that it is undergoing a crisis and that our integrated Islamic philosophy - if properly understood and applied - can replace the Western capitalism."[xi]	UN Commission of Experts endorses global economic governance and replacing the dollar with new international reserve currency.	Obama agrees to IMF surveillance of the U.S. economy and expanded use of IMF-created international reserve asset. Obama lets the dollar slide in value, leading to calls for a new global reserve currency.

i George Orwell meets the OIC By Robert Spencer, Jihad Watch (June 25, 2008).

ii Text of Obama's speech in Cairo, op.cit.

iii United Nations Alliance of Civilizations, Report of the High-level Group, op. cit., p. 11.

iv Text of Obama's speech in Cairo, op.cit.

v Ibid.

vi United Nations Alliance of Civilizations Report of the High-level Group, op. cit., p.13.

vii Text of Obama's speech in Cairo, op.cit.

viii The Muslim Brotherhood "Project" By Patrick Poole FrontPageMagazine. com (May 11, 2006) (quoting an English translation of S/5/100 report 1/12/1982)

ix Concluding observations of the Committee on the Elimination of Racial Discrimination: UNITED STATES OF AMERICA, op. cit.; Report of the Special Rapporteur on contemporary forms of racism, racial discrimi-

222 — Joseph A. Klein

nation, xenophobia and related intolerance, Addendum: Mission to the United States Of America By Doudou Diene, op. cit.

x   Text of Obama's speech in Cairo, op.cit.; Obama to NAACP: Progress made but much still to accomplish, CNN, op. cit.

xi   Islamic Finance System 'Can Replace Capitalism' By Patrick Good-enough, CNSNews.com, op. cit.

We Must Reverse Course Before It Is Too Late

We are stuck with the Obama administration until at least January 20, 2013. And unless the American electorate elects a strong alternative candidate in 2012—one who believes in American exceptionalism and muscular diplomacy rather than apologies and manic multilateralism—we will continue to spiral toward UN-istan for four more years.

A Platform to Recapture Our Independence

The tea parties and town hall protests have begun mobilizing Americans to stop this madness. We now need a mass movement, whose platform is based on the enduring principles laid down by our Founding Fathers in the Declaration of Independence and the Constitution.

1.   End dependency on foreign borrowing and strengthen the dollar by drastically reducing the federal deficit: The deficit for fiscal year ending on September 30, 2009, reached an obscene all-time high of $1.42 trillion. As a portion of our nation's total economy as measured by the gross domestic product (GDP), the budget deficit stood at 10 percent, which is the highest since World War II![742] As a result, we are borrowing and printing money at record rates, driving the value of the dollar down to ridiculous lows. The world is reacting by considering replacing the dollar as the global reserve currency. We cannot let that happen. We must call for a constitutional amendment allowing a line item veto, and prohibiting a budget deficit that is in excess of 3 percent of our country's GDP, except in a time of an emergency as declared by at least two-thirds of both houses of Congress.

2. *End reliance on foreign and international law as the basis for interpreting our Constitution:* Our Founding Fathers declared independence so Americans would no longer be subjected "to a jurisdiction foreign to our constitution." Neither the United Nations nor the International Criminal Court must ever be allowed to subject this country's laws to their jurisdictions, which are "foreign to our constitution."

Transnationalist judges should not be in any position to interpret the United States Constitution through the lens of foreign and international law. And we must reverse the damage already done by transnationalist Supreme Court decisions. Use the constitutional amendment process if necessary; for example, we must call for a national defense amendment that overturns the Supreme Court's disastrous Geneva Convention and habeas corpus decisions and prohibits the trial of alien enemy combatants in civil court.[743]

3. *End accommodation to alien values that threaten our inalienable rights:* We must stop kow-towing to Islamic demands where they conflict with core American values. We need to ensure, through statute or, if necessary, by adding clarifying language to the First Amendment, that the United States does not recognize "defamation of religions" or its equivalent as either a criminal or civil offense. Our inalienable right of free expression is not negotiable.

4. *End dependency on foreign oil:* If the West had never helped Muslim countries develop their vast oil reserves, they would have remained primitive tribal-based, pre-industrial economies. And that's where we want them to return. In the short run, we must tap our own vast oil and natural gas resources by more aggressive drilling right at home. Ultimately we should replace oil and

other fossil fuels with alternative sources of energy on a significant scale. If we do so, the Islamic economies will shrivel. And without oil money to burn, the Islamists will be unable to fund their terrorist and stealth jihads.

5. *Last but not least, end the manic multilateralism that looks to the United Nations for validation of American foreign policy:* We are wasting many billions of dollars on this dysfunctional organization. The non-political agencies that truly help people in need should be spun off from UN control. The rest of the UN is too far gone to save. It should be thrown on to the scrap heap of history like the failed League of Nations or moved to Dubai which said that it is prepared to host the UN headquarters on its soil. Let the Islamists and their friends have fun in Dubai. We should start over with an organization consisting only of true democracies.

Protest, Sue and Elect to Protect Common Sense American Values

We need to expand the tea party protests to protest such lunacies as the trial of Khalid Shaikh Mohammed and his co-terrorists in federal civil court.

We need to start using the courts as aggressively as the ACLU and its co-Islamic advocates. This includes bringing lawsuits to challenge their tax-exempt status, because their political propagandizing makes them ineligible for such status under the Internal Revenue Code.[744] We should stop waiting until after they sue school districts and employers for discriminating against Muslims on specious grounds. Instead, we need to be proactive, and bring lawsuits on behalf of plaintiffs whose rights are violated through pro-Muslim discrimination.

For example, the next time a public school forces its students to participate in Islamic rituals, it should be sued by non-Muslims, and not only on "establishment clause" grounds but also for violating the rights of students being pressured into uttering words that contradict their beliefs. If a student cannot be forced to say the pledge of allegiance (as the Supreme Court has ruled), a student should not be intimidated into reciting Islamic prayers or participating in other rituals. Moreover, unless the school conducts similar programs in Jewish, Christian, and other faiths' rituals, the non-Muslim students can then claim that their equal protection rights under the Fourteenth Amendment are being violated.

Meanwhile, segregating men and women in gyms to accommodate Muslim sensibilities—whether in a publicly owned or privately owned facility—should be challenged under federal law prohibiting gender-based discrimination.

Finally, we need to remove loony leftists from all levels of elected government, including boards of education, city councils, state legislatures, and of course, Congress. The 2009 governors' races in New Jersey and Virginia, and the election of Republican Scott Brown in Massachusetts to take the "Kennedy" seat in the US Senate, demonstrated that a backlash is building against the left-leaning members of the Democratic Party.

As Newt Gingrich told Newsmax.TV, "[W]hether it's Speaker [Nancy] Pelosi or Majority Leader [Harry] Reid or President Obama, all of them are arousing the American people to defend America against very left-wing, radical ideas."[745]

If Obama himself isn't turned into a one-term president, then at least he should have as few friends in Congress as possible. And by reversing, or at least reducing, the left's control of the Senate, it will be easier to thwart Obama's opportunity to pack the federal courts with transnational judges.

A New Peoples' Constitutional Convention

All of these steps will help restore our country to its moral foundation. But I am afraid they may not be enough.

Americans who care about what is happening to this country need to mobilize support for a new *Peoples' Constitutional Convention to Save America*. This constitutional convention will reaffirm America's foundational governing principles by using the constitutional amendment process to ensure that they are unequivocally stated.

For example, the first three planks in the platform outlined above would require or benefit from constitutional amendments. In addition, Georgetown constitutional law professor Randy E. Barnett recommends a new "Federalism Amendment," which would "provide tea-party enthusiasts and other concerned Americans with a concrete and practical proposal by which we can restore our lost Constitution."[746] This amendment would include a provision requiring that the Constitution be interpreted according to its original meaning.[747]

Under Article V of the Constitution, Congress is required to call a Constitutional Convention whenever two-thirds (currently thirty-four) of the states apply. If three-fourths of the states approve an amendment, it is added to the Constitution. Neither Barack Obama nor the Democratic-controlled Congress can stop the convening of a Constitutional Convention or interfere in its decision-making process.

Some of the most intense *opposition to the Constitutional Convention idea* comes from fringe groups on the right and the left such as the John Birch Society and the American Civil Liberties Union who oppose the very idea of a Constitutional Convention.[748] They all fear that such a convention will be high jacked by their respective ideological enemies.

Fortunately, the vast majority of Americans do not belong to either extreme. We just want what Abraham Lincoln promised in his Gettysburg Address—"that this nation, under God, shall have a new birth of freedom—and that government of the people, by the people, for the people, shall not perish from the earth."[749]

Islamists fervently believe that freedom and self-government are false idols that must be destroyed and replaced with unquestioned obedience to Allah. There is no middle ground with what we fervently believe and with what generations before us have pledged to protect with their "lives," their "fortunes" and their "sacred honor."

Our freedom will perish if we continue on President Barack Hussein Obama's present course of lethal engagement with radical Islam and its carrier—the United Nations. If it takes a constitutional convention to right our ship of state, so be it. The American people must be heard now, loud and clear to save our nation from morphing into an alien state of UN-istan.

Endnotes

Chapter One

1 Stealth Jihad: How Radical Islam is Subverting America Without Guns or Bombs By Robert Spencer, Regnery Publishing, Inc. (2008).

2 Merriam-Webster Online Dictionary (2009).

3 "Barack Obama's speech in Cairo," New York Times (June 4, 2009). http:// www.nytimes.com/2009/06/04/us/politics/040bama.text.html?_r=1 See also Guest list for Obama's White House Ramadan dinner, Los Angeles Times (September 1, 2009). http://latimesblogs.latimes.com/washington/2009/09/ obama-ramadan-dinner-white-house.html

4 "Federal Jury in Dallas Convicts Holy Land Foundation and Its Leaders for Providing Material Support to Hamas Terrorist Organization," US Department of Justice Press Release (November 24, 2008). http://justice.gov/opa/ pr/2008/November/08-nsd-1046.html

5 "Obama's Top Legal Pick Supports Sharia" By Meghan Clyne, Islam in Action Web site (March 31, 2009). http://islaminaction08.blogspot.com/2009/03/ obama-top-legal-pick-supports-sharia.html

6 "Global Trends 2025: A Transformed World," National Intelligence Council (November 2008).

7 Organization of Islamic Conference Web site.

8 "Ten-Year Programme of Action to Meet The Challenges Facing the Muslim Ummah in the 21st Century," Third Extraordinary Session of the Islamic Summit Conference, Section 1(II, 3) (December 7–8, 2005).

9 "Who Leads the United Nations?" By Brett D. Schaefer (Heritage Lecture #1054), Heritage Foundation (December 4, 2007).

10 Federation of American Scientists Intelligence Resource Program Web site (January 2002), http://www.fas.org/irp/world/para/mb.htm.

11 "The Principles of The Muslim Brotherhood," The Muslim Brotherhood (Ikhwan) Official English Web site, http://www.ikhwanweb.com/Article.asp ?ID=813&LevelID=2&SectionID=116.

12   Stealth Jihad: How Radical Islam is Subverting America Without Guns or Bombs, op. cit. at p. 15.

13   "The Muslim Brotherhood 'Project'" By Patrick Poole FrontPageMagazine.com (May 11, 2006) (quoting an English translation of S/5/100 report 1/12/1982 [December 1, 1982] entitled "Toward a worldwide strategy for Islamic policy." Translation prepared by Scott Burgess and was first published in serial form by The Daily Ablution in December 2005). http://www.frontpagemag.com/readArticle.aspx?ARTID=4476

14   Ibid.

15   "Obama's Muslim Brotherhood Links Deserve Second Look," International Analyst Network (June 11, 2009). http://www.analyst-network.com/article.php?art_id=2972

16   Ibid.

17   Ibid.

18   "President's Envoy to Islamic Conference Admits Having Made Controversial '04 Remarks," ABC News (February 19, 2010) http://blogs.abcnews.com/politicalpunch/2010/02/presidents-envoy-to-islamic-conference-admits-having-made-controversial-04-remarks.html

     "Obama's Islamic Envoy Admits Prior Support For Convicted Terrorism Supporter 'Ill-Conceived' or 'Not Well-Formulated,'" Centrist.net (February 20, 2010). http://centristnetblog.com/daily-news/obamas-islamic-envoy-admits-prior-support-for-convicted-terrorism-supporter-ill-conceived-or-not-well-formulated-2004-transcript-confirms-hussain-as-close-friend-of-al-arain-family/

     "Muslims Welcome Removal of LAPD's Mapping Program," Muslim Public Affairs Council (November 16, 2007). http://www.mpac.org/article.php?id=563

     See also http://www.discoverthenetworks.org/individualProfile.asp?indid=2401

19   http://atlasshrugs2000.typepad.com/atlas_shrugs/2009/06/obama-appointment-arif-ali-khan-asst-secretary-dhs.html

20 "Islamism Grows Stronger at the United Nations" By David Littman, Middle East Quarterly (September 1999). http://www.meforum.org/477/islamism-grows-stronger-at-the-united-nations

21 "Discussion of religious questions now banned at UN Human Rights Council," International Humanist and Ethical Web site, http://www.iheu.org/node/3193 (June 23, 2008).

22 "Reading into The Muslim Brotherhood's Documents," The Muslim Brotherhood (Ikhwan) Official English Web site, http://www.ikhwanweb.org/Article.asp?ID=818&LevelID=2&SectionID=116.

23 "The Organization of the Islamic Conference and Eurabia" By Fjordman, FaithFreedom.org (September 19, 2008).

24 "Ten-Year Programme of Action to Meet The Challenges Facing the Muslim Ummah in the 21st Century" Third Extraordinary Session of the Islamic Summit Conference, Section 1 (VII, 3) (December 7–8, 2005).

25 http://www.un.org/News/Press/docs/2008/ga10801.doc.htm
Also see "U.N. assembly again votes against defaming religion" By Patrick Worsnip, Reuters (December 19, 2008). Such resolutions have been passed by the Human Rights Council or its predecessor, the Commission on Human Rights since 1999 (including in 2009), and by the General Assembly itself since 2005.

26 "George Orwell meets the OIC" By Robert Spencer, Jihad Watch (June 25, 2008).

27 "Does Turkey Still Belong in NATO?" By Daniel Pipes, Philadelphia Bulletin (April 6, 2009).

28 For the text of the resolution see: http://www.eyeontheun.com/assets/attachments/documents/FOEsep307936.pdf
See also "You Can't Say That At the UN, the Obama administration backs limits on free speech" By Anne Bayefsky, The Weekly Standard (October 5, 2009). http://weeklystandard.com/Content/Public/Articles/000/000/017/043ytrhc.asp

29 "Gag The Internet!An Obama Official's Frightening Book About Curbing Free Speech Online" By Kyle Smith, New York Post (July 11, 2009).

30 "Bill would give president emergency control of Internet" By Declan McCullagh, CNET News (August 28, 2009). http://news.cnet.com/8301–13578_3–10320096–38.html

H. R. 1966: To amend title 18, United States Code, with respect to cyberbullying
http://thomas.loc.gov/cgi-bin/query/z?c111:H.R.1966:

31 "FCC's New Hire Targeted Conservative Radio Stations in Writings," Foxnews. com (August 10, 2009). http://www.foxnews.com/politics/2009/08/10/pub-fccs-new-hire-previously-targeted-gop-radio-stations/

32 Prologue to a farce: Communication and democracy in America By Mark Lloyd, University of Illinois Press (2006) at p. 20. See also "The Structural Imbalance of Political Talk Radio" By John Halpin, James Heidbreder, Mark Lloyd, Paul Woodhull, Ben Scott, Josh Silver, S. Derek Turner, Center for American Progress (June 20, 2007). http://www.americanprogress.org/issues/2007/06/talk_radio.html

33 "Father Zakaria Botros on CAIR's radar," Jihad Watch (January 30, 2009). http://www.jihadwatch.org/archives/024645.php

"FOX TV coerced into providing stations with 'nice Muslim' spots made by group linked to terrorism,"
Militant Islam Monitor (January 15, 2005). http://www.militantislam-monitor.org/article/id/376

34 "CAIR Tenth Anniversary Report - 1994–2004," op. cit., p. 75.
"US Muslims Guide Ill-informed Media," Islamonline (November 15, 2007). http://www.islamonline.net/servlet/Satellite?c=Article_C&cid=11950 32319619&pagename=Zone-English-News/NWELayout

35 "CAIR Tenth Anniversary Report - 1994–2004,," op. cit. p. 43.
http://www.cair.com/Portals/0/pdf/10th_anniversary_report.pdf

36 EyeontheUN Web site, http://www.eyeontheun.org/facts.asp?1=1&p=61

37 United Nations General Assembly Resolution 3314, adopted during the twenty-ninth session on December 14, 1974. "Aggression" is defined as "the use of armed force by a State against the sovereignty, territorial integrity or political independence of another State." This resolution's definition of "aggression" is being used by the Special Working Group on the Crime of Aggression as the basis for the defining the international crime of aggression by individual leaders of a "State" within the jurisdiction of the International Criminal Court. Non-state members of terrorist organizations will not be covered.

38 Press Conference by Christian Wenaweser, Chairman of the Special Working Group On Crime Of Aggression (United Nations New York Headquarters, February 12, 2009). Mr. Wenaweser is Permanent Representative of Liechtenstein and President of the Assembly of States Parties to the Rome Statute of the International Criminal Court. As of the writing of this book, Prince Zeid Raad Zeid Al-Hussein, Ambassador of Jordan to the US, is serving as the Chairman of the Inter-Sessional Meeting on the Crime of Aggression.

39 Remarks At "Townterview" Hosted by CNN and KTN, Hillary Rodham Clinton Secretary of State, Conducted by Fareed Zakaria of CNN and Beatrice Marshall of KTN, University of Nairobi, Kenya (August 6, 20( ). http://www.state.gov/secretary/rm/2009a/08/126954.htm

40 "The Global Impact of the Gold Dinar," By Philip J dge, Anglo Far st Bullion Company (Research Department) www.anglofareast.com (September 2003).

41 "Islamic Banks Surge, Thanks to Financial Crisis" By James Joyner, *Atlantic Council* (December 24, 2008). http://www.acus.org/new_atlanticist/islamic-banks-surge-thanks-financial-crisis

42 International Centre for Education in Islamic Finance Web site, http://www.inceif.org/discover/faqs/faqs.php?intPrefLangID=1&

43 Opening speech by Dr Zeti Akhtar Aziz, Governor of the Central Bank of Malaysia, at the 5th Annual Islamic Finance Summit, London (January 24, 2006).

44 Governor's Speech at the Seminar on Islamic Finance - "Toward Gaining Global Growth Potential of Islamic Finance" by Dr Zeti Akhtar Aziz (January 15, 2008).

45 "Asia split over China's 'war of nerves' with U.S." By Tetsushi Kajimoto and Yoo Choonsik, The US Daily (March 30, 2009).

46 "Malaysia, Iran bank on dollar alternative" By Kalinga Seneviratne, Asia Times (July 4, 2003).

47 See http://www.un.org/ga/president/63/commission/members.shtml

48 See http://www.un.org/ga/econcrisissummit/background.shtml

49 "Facts on new UN assembly head D'Escoto," Reuters (June 4, 2008).

50 "Latin radicals take centre stage at UN summit snubbed by the West" By James Bone, Timesonline (June 22, 2009). http://www.timesonline.co.uk/tol/news/world/us_and_americas/article6550305.ece

51 "US 'demonizes' Iranian leader," Kuwait Times (March 19, 2009). See also http://www.alarabiya.net/articles/2009/03/18/68676.html

52 An example of Jomo Kwame Sundaram's writings on Islamic finance is "Islamic economic alternatives: critical perspectives and new directions" By Jomo K. S. (Jomo Kwame Sundaram), Macmillan Academic and Professional (1992).

53 "Jomo urges overhaul of financial system," The Star Online (February 18, 2009).

54 "The EU's Global Mission" By Joseph E. Stiglitz, Project Syndicate (March 2007). http://www.project-syndicate.org/commentary/stiglitz85

55 "The Malaysian Miracle" By Joseph E. Stiglitz, Project Syndicate (September 2007). http://www.project-syndicate.org/commentary/stiglitz91

56 Press conference by Chairman of Commission of Experts on International Monetary, Financial Reform Recommendations to General Assembly (March 26, 2009).

57 "Recommendations by the Commission of Experts of the President of the General Assembly on reforms of the international monetary and financial system" (draft report for the UN Conference on the World Financial and Economic Crisis and its Impact on Development, June 2009), pp. 18–20, 38, and chapters 4 and 5.

58 Ibid., pp. 93–97.

59 "World Economic Situation and Prospects 2009—Global Outlook 2009," Chapter 1. http://www.un.org/esa/policy/wess/wesp2009files/wesp2009pr.pdf

60 Ibid.

61 UNiFEED (December 1, 2008). http://www.unmultimedia.org/tv/unifeed/detail/10541.html

62 MEMRI Iranian Media Blog (June 24, 2009). http://www.thememriblog.org/iran/blog_personal/en/17642.htm

63 "Outcome of the Conference on the World Financial and Economic Crisis and Its Impact on Development" (A/RES/63/303). http://www.un.org/ga/search/view_doc.asp?symbol=A/RES/63/303&Lang=E

   "Report of the Commission of Experts of the President of the United Nations General Assembly on Reforms of the International Monetary and Financial System."

64 See Statement by John F. Sammis, Alternate Head of Delegation, on the adoption of the outcome at the United Nations Conference on the World Financial and Economic Crisis and Its Impact on Development (June 26, 2009). See also Remarks by Ambassador Susan E. Rice, US Permanent Representative to the United Nations, at the Conference on the World Financial and Economic Crisis and Its Impact on Development, in the General Assembly Hall (June 24, 2009).

65 "UN Climate Change Report On Global Warming" By Elaine McKewon, Center for Research on Globalization (January 31, 2007). http://www.globalresearch.ca/index.php?context=va&aid=4655

Chapter Three

66 Text of Obama's speech in Cairo, New York Times (June 4, 2009). http://www.nytimes.com/2009/06/04/us/politics/040bama.text.html?_r=1

67 "Obama tells Turks that US is not at war with Islam" by Tom Rau, Associated Press (April 6, 2009).

68 "Obama Bombs American History 101 Sorry, Barack, But There Were No Muslims On The Mayflower" By Paul L. Williams, Ph.D. (June 6, 2009). http://community.comcast.net/comcastportal/board/print?board.id=news&message.id=768714&format=one

69 Ibid.

70 "'Global War On Terror' Is Given New Name" By Scott Wilson and Al Kamen, Washington Post (March 25, 2009).

71 "The Dysfunctional Human Rights Council," New York Times editorial (April 11, 2009).

72 "Why the US decision to rejoin the U.N. Human Rights Council is self-defeating" By Anne Bayefsky, Foreign Policy (April 3, 2009).

73 For example, see Roper v. Simmons, 543 US 551 (2005) (citing several human rights treaties in determining that laws permitting the execution of juvenile offenders are unconstitutional irrespective of whether the treaties were ratified by the United States Senate).

74 Transnational progressivism is a term coined by Hudson Institute Fellow John Fonte in 2001 to describe the world view that endorses the ideas of postnational global citizenship and the authority of international institutions

over the sovereignty of individual nation-states. See "Global Governance vs. the Liberal Democratic Nation-State: What Is the Best Regime?" By John Fonte, Encounter at 10: The Power of Ideas, 2008 Bradley Symposim (June 4, 2008). http://pcr.hudson.org/files/publications/2008_Bradley_Symposium_Fonte_Essay.pdf

75 Roper v. Simmons, supra. At least four Supreme Court justices have written or concurred in opinions that make significant use of foreign and international laws in the interpretation of constitutional provisions—Justices Breyer, Ginsberg, Kennedy, and Stevens. The fifth justice who has expressed support for using foreign and international law in US judicial decisions is Justice Sonia Sottomayor. The justice who is most opposed to this trend is Justice Scalia.

76 Hamdan v. Rumsfeld, 548 US 557 (2006). This case, together with the Geneva Conventions Common Article 3 on which it relied, will be discussed more extensively in Chapter Eleven.

77 Boumediene v. Bush, 553 US ___ (2008). See also Brief Of Amicus Curiae United Nations High Commissioner For Human Rights In Support Of Petitioners (August 24, 2007). http://ccrjustice.org/files/Brief%200f%20 Amicus%20Curiae%20United%20Nations%20High%20Commissioner%20 for%20Human%20Rights%20In%20Support%200f%20Petitioners.pdf?php MyAdmin=563c49a5adf3t4ddbf89b

78 Stephen Breyer, Keynote Address at Proceedings of the Ninety-Seventh Meeting of the American Society of International Law, 97 Am. Soc'y Int'l L. Proc. 265, 267 (2003).
      "Breyer, Souter are Obama's Models for Supreme Court Choices, Advisor Says" By Pete Winn, CNSNews.Com (October 31, 2008). http://www.cnsnews.com/news/article/38533. The Muslim Public Affairs Council Press Release "MPAC Rep. Attends Obama's Announcement of Supreme Court Nominee" (May 10, 2010). http://www.mpac.org/article.php?id=1116. "Kagan: Shill for Shariah?" By Frank Gaffney, Big Government (May 19, 2010) http://biggovernment.com/fgaffney/2010/05/19/kagan-shill-for-shariah/. Confirmation Hearings On The Nominations Of Thomas Perrelli Nominee To Be Associate Attorney General Of The United States And Elena Kagan Nominee To Be Solicitor General Of The United States Before The Committee On The Judiciary United States Senate One Hundred Eleventh Congress First Session (February 10, 2009), p. 167. "Obama Nominates Elena Kagan to the U.S. Supreme Court" By Tyler Lewis, Leadership Conference on Civil and Human Rights web site (May 10, 2010) http://www.civilrights.org/archives/2010/05/971-kagan-nomination.html. For a description of the Muslim Public Affairs Council's radical ideology see "Muslim

Public Affairs Council: Behind the Façade" By The Investigative Project on Terrorism (2005).

79 "Indonesia Hosts World Islamic Forum As Momentum Builds Up," The Jakarta Post (March 2, 2009).

80 "Islamic Finance and Global Security," Al Bawaba (March 10, 2009).

81 "Islamic Finance System 'Can Replace Capitalism'" By Patrick Goodenough, CNSNews.com (October 13, 2008).

82 "New reserve currency idea needs work-German minister" By Louis Charbonneau, Reuters (March 27, 2009).

83 "Replace capitalism with Islamic financial system: cleric," Breitbart.com (October 12, 2008).

84 "Is the Dollar's Value the Most Important Contributor to the Price of Oil?" By Dr. James Hamilton, Seeking Alpha (August 11, 2008).

85 "Is the Falling Dollar behind Oil Price Rises?" By Jeff Vail (June 2, 2008). http://www.jeffvail.net/2008/06/is-falling-dollar-behind-oil-price.html

86 "Replace capitalism with Islamic financial system: cleric," op. cit.

87 "Crisis towers over the dollar" By W Joseph Stroupe, Asia Times (November 25, 2004).

88 "World Islamic Trade Organization: briefing, Parliamentary Monitoring Group, South Africa" (April 16, 2003).

89 "London Summit—Global plan for recovery and reform," Official Communique (April 2, 2009). http://www.londonsummit.gov.uk/resources/en/news/15766232/communique-020409

90 "The demise of the dollar - In a graphic illustration of the new world order, Arab states have launched secret moves with China, Russia and France to stop using the US currency for oil trading" By Robert Fisk, The Independent (October 6, 2009). http://www.independent.co.uk/news/business/news/the-demise-of-the-dollar-1798175.html

91 Press briefing By Chairman of the UN Commission of Experts, supra (UN headquarters, March 26, 2009).

92 "The Almighty Renminbi?" By Nouriel Roubini, New York Times (May 14, 2009).

Chapter Four

93 Text of Obama's speech in Cairo, New York Times (June 4, 2009). http://www.nytimes.com/2009/06/04/us/politics/04obama.text.html?_r=1

94 Stealth Jihad, op. cit. at 42.

95 Islam Online Web site. http://www.readingislam.com/servlet/Satellite?cid=1123996016410&pagename=IslamOnline-English-AAbout_Islam/AskAboutIslamE/AskAboutIslamE

96 Koran, 9:29

97 Ibid.

98 "There Is No Such Thing as 'Moderate' Islam.' Continued Conversations with Nonie Darwish," Chesler Chronicles (January 19, 2009). http://pajamasmedia.com/phyllischesler/2009/01/19/there-is-no-such-thing-as-moderate-islam-continued-conversations-with-nonie-darwish/

99 Article entitled "Islamic Extremism" found at http://www.apsu.edu/oconnort/3400/34001ect04a.htm.

100 Stealth Jihad, op. cit. at 42.

101 Ibid at 38–39 (quoting from Brynjar Lia, "the Society of the Muslim Brothers in Egypt" (Ithaca, NY: Ithaca Press, 1998), 28).

102 "Roots of the Gaza Conflict" By Nonie Darwish, FrontPage Magazine (January 8, 2009)(quoting Sheikh Maolana Maududi).

103 http://www.geocities.com/nidham_al_islam/rfacts.htm

104 Mohamed Akram, "An Explanatory Memorandum on the General Strategic Goal for the Group in North America," May 22, 1991, Government Exhibit 003–0085, US v. HLF, et al. 7(21).

105 Muslim Brotherhood Movement Home Page. http://www.nefafoundation.org/miscellaneous/MB/ummahnet.pdf

106 http://www.islamicthinkers.com/index/index.php?option=com_content&task=view&id=208&Itemid=26

107 "Secularism vs. Islam" By Dr. Yusuf al-Qaradawi (excerpted from "How the Imported Solutions Disastrously Affected Our Ummah", Cairo: Maktabat Wahbah, 1977, pp 113–4). http://www.islamicweb.com/beliefs/cults/Secularism.htm

108 "The Muslim Brotherhood 'Project'" By Patrick Poole FrontPageMagazine.com (May 11, 2006) (quoting an English translation of S/5/100 report 1/12/1982 [December 1, 1982] entitled "Toward a worldwide strategy for

Islamic policy." Translation prepared by Scott Burgess and was first published in serial form by The Daily Ablution in December 2005).

109 http://www.think-israel.org/poole.muslimbrotherhood.html

110 Universal Declaration of Human Rights Adopted by UN General Assembly Resolution 217A (III) of 10 December 1948. http://www.un.org/cyberschoolbus/humanrights/resources/universal.asp

111 The Cairo Declaration on Human Rights in Islam Adopted and Issued at the Nineteenth Islamic Conference of Foreign Ministers in Cairo on August 5, 1990. http://www.religlaw.org/interdocs/docs/cairohrislam1990.htm

112 Universal Declaration, op. cit.

113 "Islam & human rights: Defending Universality at the United Nations," Center for Inquiry (September 2008).

114 "Universal Human Rights and 'Human Rights in Islam'" By David Littman, Islam Watch (January 13, 2008). http://www.islam-watch.org/Others/Universal-Human-Rights-and-Human-Rights-in-Islam'.htm

115 The Cairo Declaration, op. cit.

116 "Islam & human rights: Defending Universality at the United Nations," op. cit.

117 Text of Obama's speech in Cairo, New York Times (June 4, 2009). http://www.nytimes.com/2009/06/04/us/politics/040bama.text.html?_r=1

118 "If the mountain won't come to Muhammad, then Muhammad must come to the mountain."

119 For example, see United States General Assembly Resolution 56/47(December 7, 2001). *http://www.jewishvirtuallibrary.org/jsource/UN/unga56_47.html*
See also "Secretary-General Praises Partnership between UN, Organization of Islamic Conference in Promoting Tolerance, Equality, Development, in Message to Rabat Meeting," UN Information Service (July 12, 2006). http://www.unis.unvienna.org/unis/pressrels/2006/sgsm10560.html

120 "Universal Human Rights and 'Human Rights in Islam'" By David Littman, op. cit.

121 Ibid.

122 Ibid.

123 "A Table for Tyrants" By Vaclav Havel, New York Times Op-Ed page (May 11, 2009).

124 "US May Find Lonely Place on U.N. Human Rights Council" By Joseph Abrams, Fox News.com (May 11, 2009). http://www.foxnews.com/politics/2009/05/11/lonely-place-human-rights-council-1737855270/

125 The five regional groupings are the Western European and Others Group (WEOG), the Eastern European Group (now referred to as CEIT - countries with economies in transition), Latin American and Caribbean Group (GRULAC), the Asian Group and the African Group. EyeontheUN Web site. http://www.eyeontheun.org/view.asp?1 =11&p=55

126 "UN Human Rights Council Elections: How Human Rights Abusers Become Members" EyeontheUN Web site. http://www.eyeontheun.org/view.asp?1 =42&p=563

127 Ibid.

128 "How the Islamic states dominate the UN Human Rights Council," International Humanist and Ethical Union (April 2, 2007). See also "US on Human Rights Council" By Anne Bayefsky, Washington Times (May 14, 2009).

129 Islam & human rights: Defending Universality at the United Nations, op. cit.

130 Ibid.

131 "Islamic countries reject monitor for discrimination against women," EyeontheUN Alert (June 12, 2009).

132 Ibid.

133 The Organization of Islamic Conference created an Observatory on Islamophobia in 2006, which puts out yearly reports. http://www.muslimbridges.org/images/stories/pdfs/Islamophobia.pdf

    The OIC also publishes monthly listings of alleged incidents of Islamophobia. http://www.oic-oci.org/page_detail.asp?p_id=182

134 Statement by Ambassador Masood Khan, Pakistan's Permanent Representative to the United Nations, on behalf of the Organisation of the Islamic Conference, on the Universal Declaration of Human Rights, Geneva (December 10, 2007).

135 Report of the Special Rapporteur on contemporary forms of racism, racial discrimination, xenophobia and related intolerance, Doudou Diene, on the manifestations of defamation of religions and in particular on the serious implications of Islamophobia on the enjoyment of all rights, Human Rights Council (August 21, 2007). http://www.oic-oci.org/english/article/UNHRC-rep.pdf

136 Agora Web site. http://agora.blogsome.com/2006/03/22/translation-of-doudou-dienes-report/

See also "UN: Denmark Acted Irresponsibly in Cartoon Crisis" (March 19, 2006), http://www.todayszaman.com/tz-web/detaylar.do?load=detay&link=31079

137 http://www.un.org/News/Press/docs/2008/ga10801.doc.htm

138 Ibid.

139 Human Rights Council Press Release (March 19, 2009). http://www.unhchr.ch/huricane/huricane.nsf/view01/92A69A044F32BB22C12574110056DC1C?opendocument

140 "The Islamic-sponsored protocol to ban criticism of religion under international racism convention," UN Watch (March 21, 2009). http://unwatch.org/?p=278#more-278

141 Ibid.

142 "Islam & human rights: Defending Universality at the United Nations," op. cit.

143 "Iran's fatwa against Rushdie 'still stands'," ABC News (June 24, 2007). http://www.abc.net.au/news/stories/2007/06/24/1960389.htm

144 http://documents.scribd.com/docs/2imdqlyr10v881uzqeau.pdf See also "UN human rights body adopts resolution urging defamation of religion laws" By Andrew Gilmore, Jurist (March 26, 2009) and "Islamic States Push to Criminalize 'Defamation of Islam'" By Peter C Glover, American Thinker (March 25, 2009).

145 For example, the United Kingdom refused to allow Dutch politician Geert Wilders, an outspoken anti-Islamist, to enter the country. The reason was Wilders' controversial film Fitna which juxtaposes verses from the Koran with images of Islamic terrorist attacks. "Far-right Dutch MP Geert Wilders barred from UK over anti-Islam film" By Emily Gosden, Times Online (February 11, 2009). http://www.timesonline.co.uk/tol/news/uk/article5709892.ece

146 "U.N. to make ban on criticizing Islam mandatory? Expected proposal would criminalize such comments in US," World Net Daily (March 4, 2009).

147 http://www.un.org/News/Press/docs//2009/ga10826.doc.htm and http://geneva.usmission.gov/Press2009/June/0619UNHCR.html

See also "US wins UN rights council seat," Al Jazeera.net (May 12, 2009). http://english.aljazeera.net/news/americas/2009/05/2009512162847528412.html

148 "EyeontheUN: Human Rights Commission Stacked Against Israel" By Ezra HaLevi, Arutz Sheva (May 28, 2008).

Chapter Five

149 "The Muslim Brotherhood 'Project'" By Patrick Poole FrontPageMagazine. com, op. cit.

150 Organization of Islamic Conference - Vision for 2050 By Minhaj A. Qidwai (October 13, 2003). http://usa.mediamonitors.net/Headlines/ Organization-of-Islamic-Conference-Vision-for-2050

151 The Palestinian National Charter: Resolutions of the Palestine National Council, July 1–17, 1968. http://www.netaxs.com/~iris/plochart.htm

152 Speech by Yasser Arafat United Nations General Assembly, New York (November 13, 1974). http://www.weltpolitik.net/texte/policy/israel/Speecharafat_ 1974.pdf

153 UN General Assembly Resolution 3379 (November 10, 1975). http://www. zionism-israel.com/zionism_documents.htm

154 Speech by Yasser Arafat United Nations General Assembly, op. cit.

155 "Qaradawi lashes out at Arab unwillingness to fight Israel," Middle East Online (August 17, 2006). http://www.middle-east-online.com/english/ ?id=17281

156 http://www.acpr.org.il/resources/hamascharter.html

157 Ibid.

158 http://www.think-israel.org/poole.muslimbrotherhood.html

159 "OIC Resolution No. 1/2-Is: The Middle East And The Palestine Cause" (February 1974).

160 Ibid.

161 Letter dated 6 July 1977 from the Charge d'affaires a.i. of the Permanent Mission of the Libyan Arab Jamahiriya to the United Nations addressed to the Secretary-General, July 7, 1977, enclosing the text of the communiqué. http://unispal.un.org/pdfs/A32133.pdf

162 The so-called Non-Aligned Movement in the UN consists of 117 members, who constitute 61% of the UN's total membership of 192 members. The Organization of Islamic Conference is the largest single voting bloc within

the Non-Aligned Movement as well as within the bigger overlapping Group of 77 and China bloc, which has 132 member states. See the EyeontheUN Web site for statistics. http://www.eyeontheun.org/view.asp?1 =11&p=55

163 Final Communiqué on the Eighth Islamic Conference of Foreign Minis- ters Held in Tripoli, Socialist People's Libyan Arab Jamajiriya (May 16–22, 1977), p. 12. http://unispal.un.org/pdfs/A32133.pdf

164 Ibid., p. 13.

165 Ibid., p.14.

166 The Declarations and Programmes of Action adopted by the First (1978) World Conference to Combat Racism and Racial Discrimination. http:// www.racism.gov.za/substance/confdoc/declfirst.htm

167 Ibid.

168 Declaration and Programme of Action adopted by the Second (1983) World Conference to Combat Racism and Racial Discrimination http://www.rac- ism.gov.za/substance/confdoc/declfirst.htm

169 Third World Conference Against Racism, General Assembly Resolution 149, U.N. GAOR, 52nd Sess. (1997)

170 "Iran's OIC presidency boosted its int'l prestige: Khatami," IRNA (Janu- ary 6, 2001). http://former.president.ir/khatami/eng/cronicnews/1379/7910/ 791017/791017.htm

171 "OIC Summit In Qatar Highlights Importance Of Iran-Saudi Axis" By Safa Haeri, Iran Press Service (November 11, 2000). http://www.iran-press-ser- vice.com/articles_2000/nov_2000/oic_summit_111100i.htm

172 "Muslim Nations Bitterly Denounce Israel at Summit" By Susan Sachs, New York Times (November 13, 2000).

173 http://former.president.ir/khatami/eng/cronicnews/1379/7908/790822/ 790822.htm

174 "The Radioactive Republic of Iran By Michael Rubin,"Wall Street Journal (January 16, 2006).

175 Ibid.

176 "The Durban Debacle: An Insider's View of the World Racism Conference at Durban" By Tom Lantos, The Fletcher Forum of World Affairs (Winter/ Spring 2002),

177 "Durban II did not help the war against racism" By Henry Gombya, Daily Monitor (April 29, 2009).

178 "Durban Diary, day two: The outrage continues" By Anne Bayefsky, EyeontheUN (April 22, 2009). http://www.nydailynews.com/opinions/2009/04/22/2009–04–22_durban_diary_day_two_the_outrage_continues.html

179 "Durban II did not help the war against racism," op. cit.

180 Israel's UN Ambassador Gabriela Shalev, during a closed group discussion with her that I attended on May 7, 2009, revealed that this explanation was provided by Ban Ki-moon to Israeli President Shimon Peres the day before at a private meeting in which she had participated.

181 "EyeontheUN Web site: Human Rights Commission Stacked Against Israel" By Ezra HaLevi, Arutz Sheva (May 28, 2008).

182 "US on Human Rights Council" By Anne Bayefsky, Washington Times (May 14, 2009).

183 EyeontheUN Web site. http://www.eyeontheun.org/browse-un.asp?ua=1&sa=1&y=2008&tpa=1&search=1

184 Ibid.

185 Ibid.

186 Ibid.

187 "OIC Secretary General extols HRC's five resolutions condemning Israeli violations in the occupied territories," Relief Web (March 29, 2009). http://ocha-gwapps1.unog.ch/rw/rwb.nsf/db900sid/MWAI-7QM7ZT?OpenDocument&rc=3&cc=syr

188 "US insists on settlement freeze," AlJazeera.Net (May 29, 2009). http://english.aljazeera.net/news/americas/2009/05/200952902115543606.html

189 Barack Obama's speech in Cairo, New York Times (June 4, 2009). http://www.nytimes.com/2009/06/04/us/politics/04obama.text.html?_r=1

190 Secretary-General Kofi Annan's statement on International Day of Solidarity with the Palestinian People, delivered on his behalf by S. Iqbal Riza, Under-Secretary-General and Chef de Cabinet, New York, November 29, 2002.

191 "UN Urges Two-State Solution in Mideast," Wall Street Journal Digital Network (May 11, 2009). http://www.smartmoney.com/breaking-news/on/?story=ON-20090511–000506–1355

192 Full text of Khatami's Address at OIC Summit in Doha Doha, IRNA (November 12, 2000). http://former.president.ir/khatami/eng/cronicnews/1379/7908/790822/790822.htm

193 "Sami Gemayel, Lebanese MP and Son of Former Lebanese President Amin Gemayel: The Reason for All Lebanon's Catastrophes is the Front That Was Opened Against Israel—This Front Must Be Closed," MEMRI Special Dispatch No. 2386 (June 8, 2009).

194 http://former.president.ir/khatami/eng/cronicnews/1379/7908/790822/790822.htm, op. cit.

195 Ibid.

196 Ibid.

Chapter Six

197 See footnote 13. See also "Jihad Economics and Islamic Banking" By Dr. Rachel Ehrenfeld and Alyssa A. Lappen, Right Side News (July 28, 2008).

198 Ibid.

199 "Jihad Economics and Islamic Banking," op. cit.

200 "Islam and other economic systems," Salam Press (December 2008). http://salampress.wordpress.com/2008/10/12/islam-and-other-economic-systems/

201 Ibid.

202 "Economic Justice - Islam Versus Capitalism" By Dr. Mohammad Malkawi (March 28, 2002). http://www.internetmuslim.com/Economic_Justice.pdf

203 http://hdrstats.undp.org/indicators/145.html

204 "Hopes for the Future of Islamic Finance" By Dr. Abbas Mirakhor (Islamic Scholar and Executive Director International Monetary Fund), address to conference of Institute of Islamic Banking and Insurance (no date provided). http://www.islamic-banking.com/aom/ibanking/a_mirakhor.php

205 "Investing in Jihad: The perils of shari'a finance" By Alyssa A. Lappen, Front-Page Magazine (February 4, 2009) (quotes 11th century jurist Abul Hasan al Mawardi). Posted on The Terrorist Finance Blog: http://www.terrorfinance.org/the_terror_finance_blog/2009/02/investing-in-jihad-.html

206 UNDP Web site. http://www.undp.org.gy/index.php?option=com_content&view=article&id=61&Itemid=85

207 Ibid.

208 Ibid. at p.35.

209 Ibid.

210 Ibid.

211 Ibid.

212 "Programs to Help Poor Nations Criticized By Naomi Koppel," Associated Press (July 8, 2003).

213 UNDP Human Development Report (2005) at p.18.

214 Ibid. at p.32.

215 Ibid. at p.109.

216 Ibid. at p. 51.

217 http://www.undp.org/mdg/strategy.shtml

218 http://www.undp.org/mdg/tracking_donorcountryreports2.shtml

219 Ibid. See also "Obama's $845 billion U.N. plan forwarded to U.S. Senate floor" By Bob Unruh, WorldNetDaily (July 25, 2008). http://www.wnd.com/index.php?fa=PAGE.view&pageId=70308

220 http://content.undp.org/go/newsroom/2009/april/on-financial-crisis-melkert-warns-dont-let-rich-mans-worry-remain-poor-mans-plight.en?categoryID=593043&lang=en

221 "The UN Development Program Is Important For The Poor, It Therefore Must Be Made Transparent" By Matthew Russell Lee, Inner City Press (December 10, 2006). http://www.innercitypress.com/unhq121806.html

222 Ibid.

223 Ibid.

224 Ibid.

225 UNDP Web site. http://www.undp.org/execbrd/membership.shtml

226 "Jihad Economics and Islamic Banking," op. cit.

227 "Persian Gulf: Energy profile," Energy Publisher (July 6, 2007).

228 Ibid.

229 "Defeating the Oil Weapon" By R.J. Woolsey, Commentary (September 2002).

230 Iran Daily (January 31, 2008). http://www.iran-daily.com/1386/3052/html/economy.htm

231 Testimony by Anne Korin, Co-Director of the Institute for the Analysis of Global Security, to House Committee on Foreign Affairs (May 22, 2008).

232 Ibid.

233 See footnotes 95 through 97 and discussion of the jizya in the text.

234 "OPEC Revenues: Country Details," Energy Information Administration (June 2005). http://www.eia.doe.gov/emeu/cabs/orevcoun.html

235 "OPEC Revenues Fact Sheet," Energy Information Administration (May 2009).

236 "Al Qaeda, Other Terror Groups Swim in Global Sea of Saudi-Funded Wahhabi Institutions," Islam Daily (August 22, 2007).

237 Ibid.

238 "Jihad Economics and Islamic Banking," op. cit. See also "Saudi Wealth Fuels Global Jihadism" By Kenneth R. Timmerman, Insight (October 27, 2003).

239 Ibid.

240 See footnote 36.

241 RL32499 Saudi Arabia: Terrorist Financing Issues, CRS Report for Congress (September 14, 2007). http://www.fas.org/sgp/crs/terror/RL32499.pdf
     See also "Al Qaeda Money Trail Runs From Saudi Arabia to Spain" By Tim Golden and Judith Miller, New York Times (September 21, 2002).

242 "US Eyes Money Trails of Saudi-Backed Charities" By David B. Ottaway, Washington Post (August 19, 2004).

243 "RL32499 Saudi Arabia: Terrorist Financing Issues," op. cit.

244 "Bank of the Intifada to Join the U.N." By Anne Bayefsky, National Review (March 26, 2007). http://article.nationalreview.com/?q=Nzc2YjJlMWFiMzll ODE4NjY2YzVkNTc0YjcxMjc5MjM=

245 "UNDP-Islamic Development Bank collaboration pushes ahead," United Nations Development Programme press release (November 28, 2006). http://content.undp.org/go/newsroom/2006/november/undp-idb-20061128.en;jses sionid=aqvsIpbla3i9?categoryID=349525&lang=en

246 Ibid.

247 "Bank of the Intifada to Join the U.N.," op. cit.

248 "UNDP-Islamic Development Bank collaboration pushes ahead," op. cit.

249 Middle East North Africa Financial Network Web site (February 24, 2009). https://www.menafn.com/qn_news_story_s.asp?StoryId=1093235258

250 http://www.qcharity.org/english/Cooperations/index.html

251 http://www.who.is/whois/qcharity.org/

252 "Qatar Challenges Washington on Hamas" By Simon Henderson and Matthew Levitt, The Washington Institute for Near East Policy (February 2, 2009).

253 Ibid.

254 "Money Laundering Law & Legal Definition, USLegal Definitions," http://definitions.uslegal.com/m/money-laundering/
    Also see Written Testimony of David D. Aufhauser (General Counsel, Department of the Treasury)
    Before the Senate Judiciary Committee Subcommittee on Terrorism, Technology and Homeland Security (June 26, 2003).

255 Staff Report of the Permanent Subcommittee on Investigations, "United Nations Development Program: A Case Study of North Korea," United States Senate Committee on Homeland Security and Governmental Affairs, January 24, 2008. http://coburn.senate.gov/oversight/index.cfm?FuseAction=Files. View&FileStore_id=f8b55ce4–4139–4e60-af20–6fd5632e236f

256 Ibid.

257 "Bank of the Intifada to Join the U.N.," op. cit.

258 "Submission by Saudi Arabia: Fulfillment of the Bali Action Plan" (February 6, 2008). http://unfccc.int/files/kyoto_protocol/application/pdf/saudiarabia020209.pdf

259 "U.N. climate talks threaten our survival: Saudi Arabia" By Gerard Wynn, Reuters (April 8, 2009).

260 Ibid.

261 "OPEC States Want to Be Paid if Pollution Curbs Cut Oil Sales" By Andrew C. Revkin, New York Times (September 16, 2000).

262 "Submission by Saudi Arabia," op. cit.

263 See footnote 162.

264 "Levy on international air travel could fund climate change fight" By John Vidal, Guardian.co.uk (June 7, 2009). http://www.guardian.co.uk/environment/2009/jun/07/international-flight-levy-un-climate-change

265 Ibid.

266 Ibid.

267 "Jihad Economics and Islamic Banking," op. cit.

268 Koran: 9:60.

269 IslamiCity Web site. http://www.islamicity.com/mosque/Zakat/

270 "Jihad Economics and Islamic Banking," op. cit.

271 Ibid.

272 Ibid.

273 Ibid

274 Ibid.

275 "What Is Sharia Finance? Don't Ask the Treasury" By Alex Alexic   man Events (November 12, 2008).

276 Jihad Economics and Islamic Banking, op. cit.

277 "Plans to Establish World Fund for Zakah" By Galal Fakkar, Arab News (October 26, 2006) http://www.arabnews.com/?page=4&section=0&article=87233&d=26&m=10&y=2006
      See also "Islamic Finance, it's a Whole New World" (August 26, 2007). www.hindujagruti.org/news/3048.html

278 "Islamic Finance, it's a Whole New World," op.cit.

279 Text of Obama's speech in Cairo, New York Times (June 4, 2009). http://www.nytimes.com/2009/06/04/us/politics/040bama.text.html?_r=1

280 "Tithing for Terrorists Financing jihad." By Rachel Ehrenfeld & Alyssa A. Lappen, National Review (October 12, 2007) at The Terror Finance Blog Web site. http://www.terrorfinance.org/the_terror_finance_blog/2007/10/the-muslim-brot.html

281 "UNICEF signs an agreement with the International Islamic Relief Organization," UNICEF press release (June 9, 2008). http://www.unicef.org/media/media_44413.html

282 Ibid.

283 http://www.ustreas.gov/offices/enforcement/key-issues/protecting/charities_execorder_13224-i.shtml

284 "Consolidated list" of "Entities and other groups and undertakings associated with Al-Qaida" (last updated on April 20, 2009). http://www.un.org/sc/committees/1267/consolidatedlist.htm

285 "The Muslim Brotherhood 'Project'" By Patrick Poole FrontPageMagazine.com (May 11, 2006) (quoting an English translation of S/5/100 report

1/12/1982 [December 1, 1982] entitled "Toward a worldwide strategy for Islamic policy." Translation prepared by Scott Burgess and was first published in serial form by The Daily Ablution in December 2005). http://www.front-pagemag.com/readArticle.aspx?ARTID=4476

286 "Tithing for Terrorists Financing jihad" at The Terror Finance Blog Web site, op. cit.

287 Independent Inquiry Committee into the United Nations Oil-for-Food Program(October 27, 2005). See also "U.N. corruption cited in Iraq oil-food scandal" By Betsy Pisik, Washington Times (September 8, 2005).

288 "Saddam Hussein: The Blundering Dictator," AINA (January 11, 2007). *http://www.aina.org/news/20070110182245.jsp*
See also "Who is Taking Credit for Attacks on the US Army in Western Iraq? Al-Jama'a al-Salafiya al-Mujahida," By Lt. Col. Jonathan D. Halevi, Jerusalem Center for Public affairs (August 5, 2003).

289 "Middle East: Interview with top Saudi UN official on humanitarian aid," IRIN (January 2, 2008).

290 Ibid. For the data source, see UN Office for the Coordination of Humanitarian Affairs (OCHA) Global Humanitarian Contributions in 2009: Totals by Donor as of 16-September-2009 http://ocha.unog.ch/fts/reports/daily/ocha_R18_Y2009___0909160205.pdf

291 Islamic Republic of Iran United Nations Development Assistance Framework 2005–2009 (September 15, 2004) ("UN Iran Development Assistance Framework") at p.30.

292 UNDP Website. http://www.undp.org/execbrd/membership.shtml

293 UNDP Iran Web site. http://www.undp.org.ir/WhoWeAre.aspx

294 Country Programme Action Plan 2005–2009, sec. 6.2. http://www.undp.org. ir/reports/npd/CPAP.pdf

295 UN Iran Development Assistance Framework, op. cit.

296 Ibid.

297 Iran Watch Web site. http://www.iranwatch.org/suspect/records/iranian-research-organization-for-science-and-technology-(irost).html

298 Ibid.

299 Ibid.

300 UN Iran Development Assistance Framework, op.cit.

301 Ibid.

302 Ibid.

303 Ibid.

304 "Iran Khodro Eligible for UNDP Assistance," Iran Daily (March 6, 2005). http://iran-daily.com/1383/2230/html/economy.htm#49323

305 "Iran Khodro annual car production to hit 650,000 by March 2007: executive," Payvand's Iran News (July 21, 2006)

306 Iran Watch Web site. http://www.iranwatch.org/suspect/records/iran-khodro-company.html

307 "Military Industries in the Islamic Republic of Iran: An Assessment of the Defense Industries Organization (DIO)," Prepared for the United States Air Force Wright-Patterson AFB, Ohio (May 1996). http://cns.miis.edu/pubs/reports/pdfs/9707iran.pdf

308 http://www.unmis.org/English/2007Docs/mmr-jan18.pdf

309 "Tehran seeks to buy banned carbon fibre," The News.com (March 13, 2009). http://www.thenews.com.pk/daily_detail.asp?id=166958

310 Ibid.

311 UN Iran Development Assistance Framework, op. cit.

312 "Jailed for Outing the Mullah Mafia" By Amir Taheri, New York Post (June 13, 2008).

313 "UN Pressing Arab States for More Aid to Palestinian Refugees," The Journal of Turkish Weekly (February 9, 2007). http://www.turkishweekly.net/news/42496/un-pressing-arab-states-for-more-aid-to-palestinian-refugees.html

314 Ibid.

315 See the text of 111th CONGRESS 1st Session H. CON. RES. 29 (Expressing the sense of Congress that the United Nations should take immediate steps to improve the transparency and accountability of the United Nations Relief and Works Agency for Palestinian Refugees [UNRWA] in the Near East to ensure that it is not providing funding, employment, or other support to terrorists). http://thomas.loc.gov/cgi-bin/query/z?c111:H.CON.RES.29:

316 Ibid. See also "US Foreign Assistance to the Middle East: Historical Background, Recent Trends, and the FY2010 Request," Congressional Research Service (July 17, 2009). http://fpc.state.gov/documents/organization/128331.pdf

317 Text of 111th CONGRESS 1st Session H. CON. RES. 29, op. cit.

318 "US Foreign Aid to the Palestinians," Congressional Research Service (May 1, 2009). https://www.policyarchive.org/bitstream/handle/10207/4316/RS22967_20090501.pdf?sequence=14

319 General Assembly Resolution 302 (IV) of 8 December 1949.

320 "Dilemmas of Prolonged Humanitarian Aid Operations: The Case of UNRWA (UN Relief and Work Agency for the Palestinian Refugees)" By Emanuel Marx and Nitza Nachmias (2004). http://www.jha.ac/articles/a135.htm#_ednref3

321 Ibid.

322 Ibid.

323 "UNRWA News, Karen Koning AbuZayd '63 : Interview by Commissioner-General's Alma Mater" (March 2009). http://www.un.org/unrwa/news/statements/2009/TigerHeart_mar09.html

324 Ibid.

325 "Canada looking at UN agency over Palestinian connection," CBC News (October 4, 2004).

326 See the text of 111th CONGRESS 1st Session H. CON. RES. 29 (Expressing the sense of Congress that the United Nations should take immediate steps to improve the transparency and accountability of the United Nations Relief and Works Agency for Palestinian Refugees [UNRWA] in the Near East to ensure that it is not providing funding, employment, or other support to terrorists). http://thomas.loc.gov/cgi-bin/query/z?c111:H.CON.RES.29:

327 "A Double-standard Policy Toward Palestine" By Rami Almeghari, International Middle East Media Center (April 25, 2006). http://www.imemc.org/article/18294

328 UN Press Conference on Situation in Gaza (December 29, 2008). http://www.un.org/News/briefings/docs/2008/081229_Gaza.doc.htm

329 "President al-Assad Is Briefed by AbuZayd on UNRWA Work and Difficulties Facing Entrance of Aid to Occupied Palestinian Territories," United Nations in Syria News (April 27, 2009). http://www.un.org.sy/forms/news/viewNews.php?idField=255

330 "UNRWA in Gaza & Terror Groups: The Connection," Monograph prepared for the European Union, The Center for Near East Policy Research Ltd. (March 24, 2009). http://www.israelbehindthenews.com/library/pdfs/

UNRWA%20in%20Gaza%20%20and%20Terrorist%20Organizations%20
A%20Cooperative%20Relationship.doc

See also "the Connection between UNRWA and the Palestinian Terror Organizations in the Gaza Strip" By Lt. Col. (res.) Jonathan D. Halevi,
Middle East Strategic Information (January 14, 2009). http://www.mesi.org.
uk/ViewBlog.aspx?ArticleId=46

331 Press Briefing By UNRWA Commissioner-General Karen Koning AbuZayd
at New York UN headquarters (September 18, 2009).

332 "Gaza: Hamas Sweeps UNRWA Union Elections" By Nissan Ratzlav-Katz,
IsraelNationalNews.com (March 26, 2009). http://www.israelnationalnews.
com/News/News.aspx/130637

See also "UNRWA: Overview and Policy Critique" By Arlene Kushner,
The Center for Near East Policy Research Ltd (November 2008) at p. 28 and
Appendix II.

333 "UNRWA: Overview and Policy Critique," op. cit.

334 Text of 111th CONGRESS 1st Session H. CON. RES. 29, op. cit. http://
thomas.loc.gov/cgi-bin/query/z?c111:H.CON.RES.29:

335 "Gaza Bedfellows UNRWA And Hamas" By Claudia Rosett, Forbes.com
(January 8, 2009). http://www.forbes.com/2009/01/07/gaza-hamas-unrwa-
oped-cx_cr_0108rosett.html

Chapter Seven

336 "IDB chief urges G-20 to assess Islamic finance," A1Saudi-
Arabia.com (March 27, 2009). http://www.a1saudiarabia.com/
IDB-chief-urges-G-20-to-assess-Islamic-finance/

337 See footnote 56 and the surrounding text

338 "The UN takes charge on world finances, and that's much needed" By Joseph
E. Stiglitz, The Daily Star (July 6, 2009).

339 http://www.islamicity.com/m/news_frame.asp?Frame=1&referenceID=45140

340 "The Economics of Islamic Finance and Securitization" By Andreas A. Jobst,
International Monetary Fund Working Paper (August 2007).

341 Ibid.

342 "Malaysian PM: Financial crisis a chance for Islamic banking to shine," posted By Suapi Shaffaii on Islamic Finance News Portal from Star.com (November 12, 2008).

343 "Islamic Finance System 'Can Replace Capitalism'" By Patrick Goodenough, CNSNews.com (October 13, 2008).

344 "Vatican Says Islamic Finance May Help Western Banks in Crisis" By Lorenzo Totaro, Bloomberg (March 4, 2009)(posted on Mujahideen Ryder Muslim blog site) http://www.mujahideenryder.net/2009/03/11/vatican-says-islamic-finance-may-help-western-banks-in-crisis/)

345 "Islamic Banks Surge, Thanks to Financial Crisis" By James Joyner, *Atlantic Council, op.cit.* http://www.acus.org/new_atlanticist/islamic-banks-surge-thanks-financial-crisis

346 Ibid.

347 Ibid.

348 "Islamic Finance 101" Department of Treasury, Washington D.C. (November 6, 2008). http://www.saneworks.us/uploads/news/applications/7.pdf

349 "Lawsuit: US Controls Unconstitutional AIG 'Islamic Finance' Unit" By David A. Patten, Newsmax.com (March 23, 2009). http://www.newsmax.com/Newsfront/shariah-finance-aig/2009/03/23/id/329005

350 Ibid. See also "Hugging Shari'a Finance At The Fed" By Alyssa A. Lappen, FrontPageMagazine (December 10, 2008). http://97.74.65.51/readArticle.aspx?ARTID=33321. Bi-monthly Newsletter of the U.S.–Saudi Arabian Business Council, Volume XIV, Number 4 (2009).

351 "Islamic Banks Surge, Thanks to Financial Crisis," op. cit. "Dubai Debt Tests Laws of Islamic Financing" By Heather Timmons, New York Times (December 1, 2009).

352 Cruel and Usual Punishment By Nonie Darwish, Thomas Nelson (2008), pp. 116–127.

353 "Muslim World education 'falling behind'," Khilafah.com (February 4, 2008). http://www.khilafah.com/index.php/the-khilafah/education/2019-muslim-world-education-falling-behind

354 Ibid.

355 "Appropriate IP System Touted For Local Science-Based Industry In Islamic Nations" By Wagdy Sawahel, Intellectual Property Watch (September 4,

2008). http://www.ip-watch.org/weblog/2008/09/04/appropriate-ip-system-touted-for-local-science-based-industry-in-islamic-nations/

356 Cruel and Usual Punishment By Nonie Darwish, op. cit., Chapter 3.

357 "Islam, allegedly, is the Solution" By Dr. Sami Alrabaa, Islam Watch (October 8, 2008). http://www.islam-watch.org/Sami/Islam-the-Solution.htm

358 "Islamic Finance And Structured Commodity Finance Techniques: Where The Twain Can Meet Study" prepared by the UNCTAD secretariat (May 29, 2006).

359 Ibid. See also "Shariah Compliant or Complaint?," Shariahfinancewatch (June 23, 2009). http://www.shariahfinancewatch.org/blog/2009/06/23/shariah-compliant-or-complaint/

360 "Our followers 'must live in peace until strong enough to wage jihad'" By Andrew Norfolk, Timesonline (September 8, 2007). http://www.timesonline.co.uk/tol/comment/faith/article2409833.ece

"Dow Jones Islamic Market Index marks 10th Anniversary," Shariah Finance Watch (February 19, 2009). http://www.shariahfinancewatch.org/blog/2009/02/19/dow-jones-islamic-market-index-marks-10th-anniversary/

361 Ibid.

362 Ibid.

363 Statement by 30 Prominent Pakistani Islamic Scholars: "The Taliban Are Not Terrorists; Do Not Look Through American Eyes at [Those You Call] 'Terrorists'", MEMRI (from the London edition of the Urdu-language Pakistani newspaper Roznama Jang)(February 19, 2008). http://memri.org/bin/latestnews.cgi?ID=SD184608

364 Ibid.

365 "35 Pakistani Clerics Urge OIC to Declare Economic Boycott of Denmark," MEMRI, Special Dispatch - No. 1909 (from text of the letter as posted on the Web site of the Pakistani daily Roznama Jang (April 24, 2008).

366 "Our followers 'must live in peace until strong enough to wage jihad,'" op. cit.

367 http://www.albalagh.net/qa/0115.shtml

368 http://tyo.ca/islambank.community/modules.php?op=modload&name=News&file=article&sid=1572

369 "Jihad Comes to Wall Street By Alex Alexiev, NationalReview online (April 3, 2008). http://article.nationalreview.com/?q=ZjBhMTM5MTlmN2YzNzE0MmFkOTg20GYxNWM2MGNiNTQ

370 The Origins of Islamic Finance: A Response" By Chibli Mallat, Opinio Juris (January 29, 2008). http://opiniojuris.org/2008/01/29/the-origins-of-islamic-finance-a-response/

371 http://www.islamic-banking.com/shariah/sr_murabaha.php

372 Ibid.

373 "Islamic Finance And Structured Commodity Finance Techniques: Where The Twain Can Meet Study" prepared by the UNCTAD secretariat (May 29, 2006).

374 Ibid.

375 Ibid.

376 http://www.iibu.com/buy_home/murabahahow.htm

377 http://www.islamic-banking.com/shariah/sr_murabaha.php

378 Ibid.

379 Ibid.

380 Ibid.

381 "Islam, allegedly, is the Solution" By Dr. Sami Alrabaa, op. cit.

Chapter Eight

382 "Understanding Taqiyya Islamic Principle of Lying for the Sake of Allah" By Warner MacKenzie, Islam Watch (April 30, 2007). http://www.islam-watch.org/Warner/Taqiyya-Islamic-Principle-Lying-for-Allah.htm

383 Ibid.

384 Ibid.

385 Text of Obama's speech in Cairo, New York Times (June 4, 2009). http://www.nytimes.com/2009/06/04/us/politics/040bama.text.html?_r=1

386 Alliance of Civilizations Web site. http://www.unaoc.org/content/view/62/80/lang,english/

387 "The U.N.'s 'Alliance of Civilizations'"By Claudia Rosett, Forbes.com (March 26, 2009). http://www.forbes.com/2009/03/25/alliance-of-civilizations-opinions-columnists-obama-un.html

388 See footnote 172 and accompanying text.

389 See footnote 195 and accompanying text.

390 Turkish Press Review (April 6, 2009). http://www.byegm.gov.tr/yayinlarimiz/chr/ing2009/04/09x04x06.htm

391 Text of Obama's speech in Cairo, New York Times (June 4, 2009). http://www.nytimes.com/2009/06/04/us/politics/040bama.text.html?_r=1

392 United Nations Alliance of Civilizations, Report of the High-level Group (November 13, 2006), p. 11. http://www.unaoc.org/repository/HLG_Report.pdf

393 Text of Obama's speech in Cairo, op.cit.

394 United Nations Alliance of Civilizations, Report of the High-level Group, op. cit., p. 11.

395 Text of Obama's speech in Cairo, op.cit.

396 Ibid.

397 Ibid.

398 United Nations Alliance of Civilizations, Report of the High-level Group, op. cit., pp. 11–12.

399 Ibid., p. 12.

400 Text of Obama's speech in Cairo, op.cit.

401 United Nations Alliance of Civilizations Report of the High-level Group, op. cit., p.13.

402 "Criticism and Conciliation - Obama's Cairo speech: An NRO Symposium, Remarks of Bat Ye'or" (June 4, 2009). http://article.nationalreview.com/?q=Mzk4ZTgyNDI5MzFkMDU50WRiNjU5Njk2MjA40DA1MWE=&w=Mw==

403 Cruel and Usual Punishment: The terrifying global implications of Islamic Law By Nonie Darwish, op. cit. p. xxix.

404 Ibid., p. 25.

405 Ibid., p. x.

406 Ibid., p. 23.

407 Ibid., p. 35. Koran 4:24.

408 Ibid., pp. 31–34.

409 Ibid., p. 40. For biographical background on al-Ghazali, see http://www.ummah.com/forum/showthread.php?t=136450

410 Ibid., p. 35.

411 Ibid., pp. 48–50. Koran 4:128 and 4:34.

412 Ibid., pp. 41–43.

413 Ibid., p. 43.

414 Ibid., p. 56.

415 Ibid., p. 57.

416 Ibid., p. 57.

417 See footnote 131 and surrounding text.

418 Text of Obama's speech in Cairo, New York Times (June 4, 2009). http://
www.nytimes.com/2009/06/04/us/politics/04obama.text.html?_r=1

419 Jihad   Watch   (November   3,   2003).   http://www.jihadwatch.org/
archives/000043.php

420 "Al Qaradawi in Al Azhar" By Ayman Hamed, Asharq Alawasat (July 17,
2008). http://www.asharq-e.com/news.asp?section=3&id=13430

421 "In Friday Sermon, Sheikh Al-Qaradhawi Responds to Obama's Cairo
Speech," MEMRI, Special Dispatch | No. 2401 (June 14, 2009). http://www.
memri.org/bin/latestnews.cgi?ID=SD240109

422 "The Story of M A Gabriel, the former professor of Islamic history at Al-
Azhar University, Cairo, Egypt,Disillusioned at Al-Azhar," Arabic Bible
Outreach Ministry. http://www.arabicbible.com/testimonies/gabriel.htm
     See also http://www.faithfreedom.org/forum/viewtopic.php?t=17499

423 Ibid.

424 Ibid.

425 Ibid.

426 Ibid.

427 Ibid.

428 Ibid.

429 Ibid.

430 Ibid. See also "Islam Expert Answers Challenges" By Dr. Mark A. Gabriel,
author of "Islam and Terrorism." http://bibleprobe.com/MarkGarbriel-Intro-
duction.htm

431 http://www.freekareem.org/kareem-faq/

432 Ibid.

433 "UN experts: Egyptian blogger 'arbitrarily detained'" By Alexandra Sandels, Menassat (March 28, 2009). *http://www.menassat.com/?q=en/news-articles/6274-un-experts-egyptian-blogger-arbitrarily-detained*

434 http://www.freekareem.org/kareem-faq/

435 Ibid.

436 "UN experts: Egyptian blogger 'arbitrarily detained'" By Alexandra Sandels, op. cit.

437 Ibid.

438 http://www.freekareem.org/kareem-faq/

439 http://www.freekareem.org/kareem-faq/

440 "UN experts: Egyptian blogger 'arbitrarily detained'" By Alexandra Sandels, op. cit.

441 http://www.freekareem.org/kareem-faq/

442 "Cooperation Between The United Nations and the Organization of the Islamic Conference," Report of the Secretary-General to the General Assembly (October 17, 1995). http://www.un.org/documents/ga/docs/50/plenary/a50–573.htm

443 http://www.answers.com/topic/amadou-mahtar-m-bow

444 Address by Amadou-Mahtar M'Bow, Director-General of UNESCO at the opening of the International Seminar on Islam (December 4, 1980). http://unesdoc.unesco.org/images/0004/000425/042579eb.pdf

445 Ibid.

446 Records of the General Conference Fourth Extraordinary Paris (November 23, 1982 to December 3, 1982, p. 62. http://unesdoc.unesco.org/images/0005/000539/053978e.pdf

447 Ibid., p. 49.

448 http://www.answers.com/topic/amadou-mahtar-m-bow

449 Ibid.

450 "On the Topic of the US Returning to UNESCO, Summary of Dr. Hattori's interview on NHK radio program" (September 22, 2003). http://www.unesco.jp/meguro/shortnews/201/e201–2.htm

451 Ibid.

452 UN Elections.org. (March 3, 2009). http://www.unelections.org/?q=node/1096

453 "Farouk Hosni Is Tying Himself in Knots" By Bernard-Henri Lévy, Huffington Post (June 2, 2009). http://www.huffingtonpost.com/bernardhenri-levy/will-unesco-allow-a-man-t_b_210571.html

454 Ibid.

455 "Two Votes Switch, and Bulgarian is Elected UNESCO Chief, in a Setback for Egypt" By Steven Erlanger, New York Times (September 23, 2009).

456 "UNESCO`s Mission is to Fight Ignorance" By Eiji Hattori (2006). http://www.meguro-unesco.org/whats-new/e-whats-new.html

457 "Muslims and Islam in European History Textbooks: Seeking Security Through Culture" By Dalia Yusuf IslamOnline.net (January 25, 2005). http://www.islamonline.net/servlet/Satellite?c=Article_C&cid=11586583416 71&pagename=Zone-English-ArtCulture%2FACELayout##4

458 "Rewriting the text books" By Dina Ezzat, Weekly.Ahram.org.eg (December 2004). http://weekly.ahram.org.eg/2004/721/eg9.htm

459 Ibid.

460 "Muslims and Islam in European History Textbooks: Seeking Security Through Culture," op. cit.

461 "Revising Image of Islam in the French School Books" By Muhammad Dunia, Islamonline (December 29, 2005). http://www.islamonline.net/servlet/Satellite?c=Article_C&cid=1162385829992&pagename=Zone-English-Euro_Muslims%2FEMELayout

462 Ibid.

463 "The Rabat Commitment Conclusions and Recommendations of the Rabat Conference on Dialogue among Cultures and Civilizations through Concrete and Sustained Initiatives Rabat, Morocco (June 14–16, 2005). "

464 "This is a Saudi textbook. (After the intolerance was removed.)" By Nina Shea, Washington Post (May 21, 2006).

465 "Report: Saudi Textbooks Still Teaching Hatred of Jews, Non-Muslims - Berkley, Weiner, Crowley Call on President to Urge Saudis to Address Hate-Filled Texts" (June 3, 2009). http://www.lasvegasgleaner.com/berkley.release.pdf

466 Richard Landes, The Augean Stables.com and The Second Draft.org weblog.

467 "Children in Islam Their Care, Development and Protection" (2005). http://www.unicef.org/egypt/Egy-homepage-Childreninislamengsum(1).pdf

468 Ibid.

469 "Muslim Palestinians teach children to hate in cartoons," MEMRI TV Project http://www.youtube.com/watch?v=aV9M3mmqOII

470 Cruel and Usual Punishment: The terrifying global implications of Islamic Law, op. cit., p. 57.

471 Ibid., pp. 25–26, Chapter 3.

472 Ibid., PP. 43–45. See also "Unfree Under Islam" By Ayan Hirsi Ali, Wall Street Journal (August 16, 2005). http://www.opinionjournal.com/editorial/feature.html?id=110007112

Chapter Nine

473 Concluding observations of the Committee on the Elimination of Racial Discrimination: UNITED STATES OF AMERICA (February 2008). http://www2.0hchr.org/english/bodies/cerd/docs/co/CERD-C-USA-CO-6.p
      See also "U.N. Revisits US Policies on Racial Profiling" By Haider Rizvi, IPS (July 1, 2009).

474 Ibid.

475 http://en.wikipedia.org/wiki/Doudou_Di%C3%A8ne

476 "Racism and racial discrimination on rise around the world, UN expert warns," UN News Centre (March 7, 2006). http://www.un.org/apps/news/story.asp?NewsID=17718&Cr=racis&Cr1

477 Ibid.

478 "Freedom of Expression and the advocacy of religious hatred," International Humanist and Ethical Union Web site (October 6, 2008). http://www.iheu.org/node/3294

479 Statement by Ms. Tehmina Janjua, Acting Permanent Representative of Pakistan, on behalf of the OIC, under agenda item 9 Racism, Racial Discrimination, Xenophobia and related forms of intolerance, follow-up to and implementation of the Durban Declaration and Programme of Action, Geneva (September 19, 2008). http://missions.itu.int/~pakistan/2005_Statements/CHR/sthrcdurban_19sep08.htm

480 "Report of the Special Rapporteur on contemporary forms of racism, racial-discrimination, xenophobia and related intolerance, Addendum: Mission to

the United States Of America" By Doudou Diène, Appendix, p. 30 (List of Official Meetings) (April 28, 2009)

481 See, for example, Knight v. Florida, 528 US 990, 993–999 (1999) (Breyer, J. dissenting from denial of certiorari in a case involving the death sentences of long-term death row inmates who had stayed on death row for so long because they kept filing frivolous appeals). In his dissent, Justice Breyer cited foreign law, including the Supreme court of Zimbabwe—one of the most repressive regimes in the world—for the proposition that "lengthy delay in administering a lawful death penalty renders ultimate execution inhuman, degrading, or unusually cruel" (Emphasis in the original). Justice Breyer also cited Jamaica and the European Court of Human Rights.

482 http://ahmedbedier.blogspot.com/2008/06/fl-muslim-leaders-testify-at-united.html

483 Ibid.

484 Ibid.

485 Ibid.

486 Stealth Jihad By Robert Spencer, op. cit., pp 108–109.

487 "CAIR's Ahmed Bedier stops by Jihad Watch to tell me no one is reading Jihad Watch," Jihad Watch (November 6, 2006). http://www.jihadwatch.org/archives/013937.php

488 Stealth Jihad By Robert Spencer, op. cit., p. 70.

489 "U.N. Rapporteur Turns to Usual Suspects on 'Islamophobia'", The Investigative Project on Terrorism (June 13, 2008). http://www.investigativeproject.org/687/un-rapporteur-turns-to-usual-suspects-on-islamophobia

490 "Holy Land Foundation Defendants Guilty On All Counts," National Terror Alert (November 25, 2008). http://www.nationalterroralert.com/updates/2008/11/25/holy-land-foundation-defendants-guilty-on-all-counts/

491 "Muzzamil Siddiqui at Jerusalem Rally," The Investigative Project on Terrorism (October 28, 2000). http://www.investigativeproject.org/249/muzzamil-siddiqui-at-jerusalem-rally. See also ACT! for America web site, http://www.stopshariahnow.org/index.php?option=com_content&view=article&id=459&Itemid=157

492 "The Future of the Muslim Community in America" By Dr. Muzammil Siddiqui (May 31, 2000) Islamonline.net. http://www.islamonline.net/livedialogue/english/Browse.asp?hGuestID=04wWNv

493 http://www.cairchicago.org/ournews.php?file=on_unitednationshearing 05272008

494 Ibid.

495 "U.N. Revisits US Policies on Racial Profiling" By Haider Rizvi, op. cit.

496 "Report of the Special Rapporteur on contemporary forms of racism, racial discrimination, xenophobia and related intolerance, Addendum: Mission to the United States Of America" By Doudou Diène, p. 24 (April 28, 2009). http://www2.0hchr.org/english/bodies/hrcouncil/docs/11session/A. HRC.11.36.Add.3.pdf

497 Ibid., p. 24.

498 Ibid., p. 22

499 Ibid., p. 17.

500 Ibid., p. 16.

501 Ibid., p.28.

502 "Report by Mr. Doudou Diène, Special Rapporteur on contemporary forms of racism, racial discrimination, xenophobia and related intolerance : addendum : mission to Mauritania" (March 16, 2009), p. 5. http://www.unhcr.org/refworld/country,,UNHRC,,MRT,456d621e2,49fafcc82,0.html

503 Ibid. p.18.

504 Ibid., p. 15.

505 "Slavery: Mauritania's best kept secret" By Pascale Harter, BBC News (December 13, 2004).

506 "Report by Mr. Doudou Diène: addendum : mission to Mauritania," op. cit., pp. 17–19.

507 "Slavery on World Bank projects in Mauritania" By Pieter Smit, human rights counsultant (November 27, 2002). http://www.xs4all.nl/~pietersm/wp5eng.doc and http://www.xs4all.nl/~pietersm/

508 Ibid.

509 "Taming a Neo-Qutubite Fanatic Part I," SalafiPublications.com (undated), p. 24. http://www.salafipublications.com/sps/downloads/pdf/GRV070005. pdf See also "Author of Saudi Curriculums Advocates Slavery" By Ali Al-Ahmed, Saudi Information Agency (November 7, 2003).

510 Ibid.

511 Saleh Al-Fawzan, Wikipedia. http://en.wikipedia.org/wiki/Saleh_Al-Fawzan

512 "Slavery in Islam," Islamoscope (April 27, 2008). http://islamoscope.word-press.com/2008/04/27/slavery-in-islam/

513 See footnotes 496 and 497 and accompanying text.

514 "UN: Denmark Acted Irresponsibly in Cartoon Crisis," Today's Zaman (March 19, 2006). http://www.todayszaman.com/tz-web/detaylar.do?load=detay&link=31079

515 "City Limits A mosque in Rome? Sure. A non-Muslim in Mecca? No." By Jonathan V. Last, Wall Street Journal (August 29, 2003).

516 Ibid. (quoting from the Makkah Hilton's Web site)

517 Who Are We: The Challenge to American National Identity By Samuel Huntington, Simon & Schuster (2004). See also "Global Governance vs. the Liberal Democratic Nation-State: What Is the Best Regime?" By John Fonte, op. cit., which discusses Samuel Huntington's thesis extensively.

518 Ibid.

519 "Liberal Democracy vs. Transnational Progressivism: The Future of the Ideological Civil War Within the West" By John Fonte, Orbis (Summer 2002).

520 Ibid.

521 Ibid.

522 "Global Governance vs. the Liberal Democratic Nation-State: What Is the Best Regime?" By John Fonte, op. cit.

523 Ibid., pp. 6–7.

524 See footnote 70 and the surrounding text.

525 "Anderson Cooper 360 Degrees, Interview With President Barack Obama," CNN.com (February 3, 2009). http://transcripts.cnn.com/TRANSCRIPTS/0902/03/acd.01.html

526 "White House: 'War on terrorism' is over: 'Jihadists' and 'global war' no longer acceptable terms" By Jon Ward and Eli Lake, Washington Times (August 6, 2009). United Nations Alliance of Civilizations, Report of the High-level Group (November 13, 2006), op. cit. at p. 15.

527 "The Study of Political Islam" By Jamie Glazov, Interview with Bill Warner, the director of the Center for the Study of Political Islam, FrontPage Magazine (February 5, 2007). http://www.frontpagemag.com/readArticle.aspx?ARTID=297

528 "The real secret to defeating radical Islam" By David Kupelian, WorldNet-Daily (November 21, 2005). http://www.wnd.com/index.php?pageId=33474

529 Barack Obama's speech in Cairo, New York Times (June 4, 2009). http://www.nytimes.com/2009/06/04/us/politics/040bama.text.html?_r=1

530 "President Obama in Ghana: What He Refused To Say in Cairo: Stroking Muslim and Arab nations has become the hallmark of Obama's foreign policy" By Anne Bayefsky, EyeontheUN Web site posting of her Forbes article (July 12, 2009).

531 Ibid.

532 See footnotes 403 through 417 and surrounding text.

533 See footnotes 267 through 279 and surrounding text.

534 Koran, 9:5: "When the sacred forbidden months for fighting are past, fight and kill the disbelievers wherever you find them, take them captive, torture them, and lie in wait and ambush them using every stratagem of war."

535 Susan Rice Confirmation Hearing, Opening Remarks of Senator Kerry Before Senate Foreign Relations Committee. http://foreign.senate.gov/testimony/2009/KerryStatement090115p.pdf

536 "Ambassador Rice Holds A Media Availability," Highbeam.com (January 26, 2009). http://www.highbeam.com/doc/1P3-1632852911.html

537 "Breyer: Nat'l Legal Systems Are Finding Common Ground" By James Podgers, ABA Journal (August 11, 2007). http://abajournal.com/news/breyer_natl_legal_systems_are_finding_common_ground/

Chapter Ten

538 Statement attributable to the Spokesperson for the Secretary-General on US President Obama's speech in Cairo (June 4, 2009). http://www.un.org/apps/sg/sgstats.asp?nid=3899

539 Discoverthenetworks.org summary of Saul Alinsky's life and philosophy, and quoting from Saul Alinsky, *Reveille for Radicals* (New York: Vintage Books), 1989 (Original publication was in 1946) and from Saul Alinsky, *Rules for Radicals* (New York: Vintage Books), March 1972 edition (Original publication was in 1971). http://www.discoverthenetworks.org/individualProfile.asp?indid=2314#_edn65

540 Ibid., quoting from Saul Alinsky, *Rules for Radicals, p.26.*

541 Ibid., quoting from Saul Alinsky, *Rules for Radicals*, p. 145.

542 Ibid., quoting from Saul Alinsky, *Reveille for Radicals*, pp. 133–134.

543 "An American Muslim Journal" Posted By Junaid Afeef (August 26, 2008). http://americanmuslimjournal.typepad.com/an_american_muslim_journa/2008/08/index.html

544 "Some Tentative Thoughts On SNCC, Black Power & Black Nationalism" By Mike Miller (April 2007). http://www.crmvet.org/comm/bkpower.htm

545 Ibid.

546 "Know Thine Enemy" By Noam Cohen, New York Times (August 22, 2009).
       "Democrats' Platform for Revolution" By John Perazzo, Front-Page Magazine (May 5, 2008). http://www.frontpagemag.com/Printable.aspx?ArtId=30778

547 Ibid., quoting from Saul Alinsky, *Rules for Radicals, p.3.*

548 "Smears against Obama energized Muslim voters: experts" By Michael Conlon, Reuters (November 7, 2008). http://goatmilk.wordpress.com/2008/11/07/smears-against-obama-energized-muslim-voters-experts/
       Text of Obama's speech in Cairo, op.cit.

549 Discoverthenetworks.org summary of Saul Alinsky's life and philosophy, op. cit., quoting from Saul Alinsky, *Rules for Radicals*, p. 130.

550 "Obama to NAACP: Progress made but much still to accomplish," CNN (July 16, 2009). http://www.cnn.com/2009/POLITICS/07/16/obama.naacp/index.html?iref=newssearch

551 "The Next Phase of Islamist Lawfare" By Brooke Goldstein and Aaron Eitan Meyer, Newsweek.WashingtonPost.com (May 19, 2009). http://www.legal-project.org/article/325

552 "Democratic Realism An American Foreign Policy for a Unipolar World" By Charles Krauthammer 2004 Irving Kristol Lecture, AEI Annual Dinner (Washington). http://democraticpeace.wordpress.com/2008/12/17/democratic-realism-an-american-foreign-policy-for-a-unipolar-world/

553 Ibid.

554 http://en.wikipedia.org/wiki/My_Lai_Massacre

555 "The Struggle For Iraq: Treatment Of Prisoners; G.I.'s Are Accused of Abusing Iraqi Captives" By James Risen, New York Times (April 29, 2004).

556 "The Myth of Moral Equivalence" By Jeane Kirkpatrick, Imprimis (January 1986). https://www.hillsdale.edu/news/imprimis/archive/issue.asp?year=1986&month=01

557 Ibid.

558 "Joseph Stalin and H. G. Wells, Marxism VS. Liberalism: An Interview," New Century Publishers (September 1937; reprinted October 1950). http://www.rationalrevolution.net/special/library/cc835_44.htm

559 For disturbing examples of how Marxism and other forms of radical indoctrination have been packaged as courses offered to students on American college campuses over the past generation, see One-Party Classroom: How Radical Professors at America's Top Colleges Indoctrinate Students and Undermine our Democracy By David Horowitz and Jacob Laksin, Crown Forum (2009).

560 "At UN, Suicide Bombers Called Sane, High Vodka Prices Praised, Assisted Suicide Assessed" By Matthew Russell Lee, Inner City Press (September 10, 2009). http://www.innercitypress.com/un1suicide091009.html

561 Stealth Jihad By Robert Spencer, op. cit., p. 228.

562 Ibid., p. 237.

563 "Columbia U. Releases Edward Said Chair Donors: Names Arab Government" Campus Watch.org (March 19, 2004). http://www.campus-watch.org/article/id/1076

564 Stealth Jihad, op. cit., p 246.

565 "Allies of Palestinians see a friend in Obama" By Peter Wallsten, Los Angeles Times (April 10, 2008) http://articles.latimes.com/2008/apr/10/nation/na-obamamideast10
See also Stealth Jihad, op. cit., p. 247.

566 "Confronting Anti-Israel Attitudes on Contemporary College Campuses" By Robert David (KC) Johnson, Midstream, Campus Watch (November/December 2004). http://www.campus-watch.org/article/id/1494

567 Ibid.

568 "Imperial mementos" By Joseph Massad, AL-AHRAM, Issue No. 691 (May 20–26, 2004).

569 Stealth Jihad, op. cit. ., pp. 228–229.

570 One-Party Classroom: How Radical Professors at America's Top Colleges Indoctrinate Students and Undermine our Democracy, op. cit., p. 266.

571 Ibid., pp. 144–145.

572 "The Campus War Against Israel and the Jews" By John Perazzo, Frontpage Magazine (August 11, 2009). http://www.frontpagemag.com/readArticle. aspx?ARTID=35890

573 "Harvard President Sees Rise In Anti-Semitism on Campus" By Karen W. Arenson, New York Times (September 21, 2002).

574 Quotation from Harvard Muslim chaplain Taha Abdul-Basser as it appears on the Talk Islam Web site (April 3, 2009).

575 Ibid.

576 Ibid.

577 Ibid.

578 http://www.freerepublic.com/focus/f-news/1145998/posts

579 "Indian Commandos Storm Jewish Center" By Somini Sengupta and Keith Bradsher, New York Times (November 27, 2008). http://www.nytimes. com/2008/11/28/world/asia/28mumbai.html

580 "Terrorism Beyond Islam" By Nicholas D. Kristof, New York Times (January 8, 2002). http://www.nytimes.com/2002/01/08/opinion/terrorism-beyond-islam.html

581 Ibid.

582 "Symposium: The Death of Multiculturalism?" By: Jamie Glazov, FrontPage Magazine (September 08, 2006). http://www.frontpagemag.com/readArticle. aspx?ARTID=2695

583 Ibid.

584 Stealth Jihad By Robert Spencer, op. cit., pp. 207–221.

585 Ibid., pp. 26–27, 149, 217–221.

586 "Jihad In Schools?" Investors' Business Daily (July 9, 2007). See also http:// ibloga.blogspot.com/2006/05/california-uphold-islamic.html

587 Ibid. The case was Eklund v. Byron Union School District, 2005 WL 3086580 (9th Cir. Nov. 17, 2005).

588 "High court refuses 3 more First Amendment appeals" By First Amendment Center Online staff, Associated Press, (October 3, 2006). http://www.firstamendmentcenter.org/news.aspx?id=17473

589 Ibid.

590 Ibid.

591 Nurre v. Whitehead, No. 07–35867, (9th Cir. September 8, 2009). http://www.ca9.uscourts.gov/datastore/opinions/2009/09/08/07–35867.pdf

592 Stealth Jihad, op. cit., pp. 139–140.

593 "EEOC: Swift acted with bias: Muslims were discriminated against by the meatpacker, the federal panel determines" By David Migoya, Denver Post (September 1, 2009). http://www.denverpost.com/search/ci_13242457
     See also "Muslim advocates: EEOC letter says Neb. plant must do more for Muslim workers' prayer needs" (August 29, 2009). http://blog.taragana.com/n/muslim-advocates-eeoc-letter-says-neb-plant-must-do-more-for-muslim-workers-prayer-needs-153077/

594 Stealth Jihad By Robert Spencer, op. cit., pp. 173–174.

595 "Yale Press Bans Images of Muhammad in New Book" By Patricia Cohen, New York Times (August 13, 2009).

596 Ibid.

597 Ibid.

598 "Churches Destroyed In Islamic Violence in Nigeria" By Michelle A Vu, Christian Post (July 31, 2009). http://waltjr.wordpress.com/2009/07/31/churches-destroyed-in-islamic-violence-in-nigeria/

599 "Yale Press Bans Images of Muhammad in New Book" By Patricia Cohen, op. cit.

600 "The Myth of Moral Equivalence" By Jeane Kirkpatrick, op.cit.

601 Ibid.

602 "Obama Bows to Saudi King, Supports Saudi Initiative" By Maayana Miskin, Arutz Sheva (April 3, 2009). http://www.israelnationalnews.com/News/News.aspx/130746

603 Text of Obama's speech in Cairo, op.cit.

604 Ibid.

605 "Obama's State Department Submits to Islam" By Pamela Geller, American Thinker (August 18, 2009). http://www.americanthinker.com/2009/08/obamas_state_department_submit.html
     http://www.america.gov/ramadan.html

606 Ibid.

607 "Georgetown Says It Covered Over Name of Jesus to Comply With White House Request" By Edwin Mora, CNSNews.com (April 15, 2009). http://www.cnsnews.com/PUBLIC/Content/Article.aspx?rsrcid=46667

608 "Guest list for Obama's White House Ramadan dinner," Los Angeles Times (September 1, 2009). http://latimesblogs.latimes.com/washington/2009/09/obama-ramadan-dinner-white-house.html

609 Ibid.

610 "Second Circuit Overturns Muslim Scholar Visa Denial [on Tariq Ramadan]" By Jaclyn Belczyk, JURIST Legal News and Research (July 17, 2009). http://www.campus-watch.org/article/id/7801
"US revokes visa for Muslim scholar" By Tom Coyne, Associated Press (August 24, 2004). http://www.campus-watch.org/article/id/1250

611 "Transparency Interview: Jameel Jaffer The ACLU lawyer who helped uncover the detainee memos says there are more documents to come" By Clint Hendler, Columbia Journalism Review (May 4, 2009). http://www.cjr.org/campaign_desk/transparency_interview_jameel.php?page=3

612 Ibid.

613 Tariq Ramadan Web site http://www.tariqramadan.com/spip.php?article731
"The ACLU continues to go to court to protect your basic rights and freedom," American Chronicle (July 31, 2009). http://www.americanchronicle.com/articles/view/112413

614 "Ramadan's visa ban lifted" By Sheldon Chad, guardian.co.uk (January 23, 2010). http://www.guardian.co.uk/commentisfree/belief/2010/jan/23/tariq-ramadan-clinton-visa See also "Intellectuals Welcome Tariq Ramadan To Cooper Union" By Fern Sidman, Muslims Against Sharia (April 9, 2010). http://muslimsagainstsharia.blogspot.com/2010/04/intellectuals-welcome-tariq-ramadan-to.html

615 http://www.aclu.org/natsec/gen/38798res20090224.html

616 "Report: Detainees Shown CIA Officers' Photos Justice Department is investigating whether Guantanamo Bay detainees charged with roles in the Sept. 11 attacks were improperly given photos of CIA officers," Associated Press, Posted on FoxNews.com (August 20, 2009). http://www.foxnews.com/politics/2009/08/20/guantanamo-detainees-shown-cia-officers-photos/

617 Petitioners' Memorandum of Law in support of their Motion for Equitable Relief From the Government's Public Naming of Them as Unindicted Co-Conspirators, Case 3:04-cr-00240-P Document 1061 Filed 06/18/2008

http://www.nefafoundation.org/miscellaneous/FeaturedDocs/US_v_HLF_NaitIsnamotion.pdf

618 "Blocking Faith, Freezing Charity: Chilling Muslim Charitable Giving in the War On Terrorism Financing,'" American Civil Liberties Union (June 2009). http://www.aclu.org/pdfs/humanrights/blockingfaith.pdf

619 Ibid. at p. 134.

620 "Beyond Tolerance: a national conference on racism, Message from the United Nations High Commissioner for Human Rights," Mary Robinson, Australian Human Rights Commission (March 2002). http://www.hreoc. gov.au/racial_discrimination/conferences/beyond_tolerance/mary_robinson. htm

621 "US President awards America's highest civilian honor to staunch critic of Israel's human rights record," Middle East Online (August 5, 2009). http://www.middle-east-online.com/ENGLISH/?id=33563

622 Newsletter of the International Conference on Engaging Communities (August 15, 2005).

623 "Report of The Eminent Jurists Panel on Terrorism, Counter-Terrorism And Human Rights, Assessing Damage, Urging Action," International Commission of Jurists (February 2009), p. V

624 Ibid., p. 49.

625 Ibid., pp. 49, 165–166.

626 Ibid., p. 166.

627 Ibid., p. 165.

628 http://ejp.icj.org/hearing2.php3?id_article=167

Chapter Eleven

629 "US vows to embrace UN in break with Bush-era policy" By Louis Charbonneau, Reuters (August 13, 2009). http://www.alertnet.org/thenews/newsdesk/N12189461.htm

630 Statement by Ambassador Susan E. Rice, US Permanent Representative, on Respect for International Humanitarian Law, in the Security Council, USUN Press Release # 020(09) (January 29, 2009). http://www.amicc.org/

docs/USUN%20PRESS%20RELEASE%20IHL%20SC%20January%20
29%202009.pdf

631 "Democratic Realism An American Foreign Policy for a Unipolar World" By
Charles Krauthammer, op. cit.

632 Ibid.

633 "Tactical Hudna and Islamist Intolerance" By Denis MacEoin, Middle East
Quarterly (Summer 2008).

634 "Obama Bombs American History 101 Sorry, Barack, But There Were No
Muslims On The Mayflower" By Paul L. Williams, Ph.D., op. cit. See also
"When the Founding Fathers Faced Islamists" By Michael Weiss, posted on
PajamasMedia Web site (May 27, 2008). http://pajamasmedia.com/blog/
when-the-founding-fathers-faced-islamists/

635 "Closing Guantanamo" By Greg Bruno, Council on Foreign Relations Back-
grounder (February 12, 2009). http://www.cfr.org/publication/18525/clos-
ing_guantanamo.html

636 "US decision to close Guantánamo Bay detention centre hailed by UN rights
chief," UN News Centre (January 22, 2009). http://www.un.org/apps/news/
story.asp?NewsID=29627&Cr=united+states&Cr1=human+rights

637 "Freed by the US, Saudi Becomes a Qaeda Chief" By Robert F. Worth, New
York Times (January 22, 2009). http://www.nytimes.com/2009/01/23/world/
middleeast/23yemen.html?_r=1

638 Ibid.

639 "Gitmo closure: A welcome decision, but late" By Donna Abu-Nasr,
Associated Press Writer (January 23, 2009). http://article.joins.com/article/
ap/article.asp?Total_ID=3468798

640 "Background: President Obama signs Executive Orders on Detention and
Interrogation Policy," White House Press Office (January 22, 2009). http://
www.whitehouse.gov/the_press_office/BACKGROUNDPresidentObama-
signsExecutiveOrdersonDetentionandInterrogationPolicy/

641 FM 2–22.3 (FM 34–52) Human Intelligence Collector Operations, Headquarters, Department of the Army (September 2006).

642 Ibid., Appendix M.

643 Ibid.

644 Ibid.

645 Ibid.

646 Ibid., 5–21.

647 Ibid., 8–25.

648 "Torture is still a frequent or even standard practice in many countries, warns UN expert," UN Press Release (October 24, 2008). http://www.unhchr.ch/huricane/huricane.nsf/0/B41633C8FCEA240AC12574EC0034096F?opendocument

649 "UN Special Rapporteur Calls on American Psychological Association to Withdraw Psychologists from Guantanamo" By Stephen Soldz, OpEdNews.com (August 12, 2009). http://www.opednews.com/populum/page.php?a=95320&p=1

650 "Obama's U.N. State of Mind" By Anne Bayefsky, National Review (February 11, 2010). http://article.nationalreview.com/424651/obamas-un-state-of-mind/anne-bayefsky?page=1

651 "Prosecutor to Probe CIA Interrogations" By Carrie Johnson, Washington Post (August 25, 2009).

652 "Ex-CIA Chiefs Ask Obama to Halt Probe" By Pamela Hess, Associated Press (September 19, 2009). http://news.aol.com/article/ex-cia-directors-ask-obama-to-halt/637010

653 "UN human rights chief welcomes US investigation into alleged CIA abuses," UN News Centre (August 25, 2009). http://www.un.org/apps/news/story.asp?NewsID=31846&Cr=torture&Cr1

654 "The Geneva Conventions: the core of international humanitarian law," Web site of The International Committee of the Red Cross. http://www.icrc.org/Web/Eng/siteeng0.nsf/htmlall/genevaconventions

655 Ibid.

656 Convention (III) relative to the Treatment of Prisoners of War. Geneva, 12 August 1949.

657 FM 2–22.3 (FM 34–52) Human Intelligence Collector Operations, op. cit.

658 "Transcript: Interview with U.N. torture official Manfred Novak," Salon.com (April 25, 2009). http://www.salon.com/opinion/greenwald/2009/04/25/nowak/

659 "What to do about torture? Manfred Nowak interviewed" By Kanishk Tharoor, Open Democracy (January 15, 2007). http://www.opendemocracy.net/conflict-terrorism/nowak_4249.jsp%20%20

660 "The Geneva Conventions: the core of international humanitarian law," Web site of The International Committee of the Red Cross, op. cit.

661 Hamdan v. Rumsfeld, 548 US 557 (2006).

662 Ibid.

663 Amicus Curiae Brief Of 271 United Kingdom And European Parliamentarians In Support Of Petitioner (December 2, 2004). http://www.law.georgetown.edu/faculty/nkk/documents/britedusct.pdf

664 Ibid.

665 http://www.un.org/documents/ga/res/39/a39r046.htm

666 http://www4.1aw.cornell.edu/uscode/18/usc_sec_18_00002340——000-.html

667 Second Periodic Report of the United States of America to the Committee Against Torture (May 6, 2005).

668 "Transcript: Interview with U.N. torture official Manfred Novak," Salon.com, op.cit

669 "UN Rapporteur: Initiate criminal proceedings against Bush and Rumsfeld now" By Scott Horton, Harpers' Magazine (January 21, 2009). http://www.harpers.org/archive/2009/01/hbc-90004250

670 "Transcript: Interview with U.N. torture official Manfred Novak," Salon.com, op. cit.

671 The episodes of waterboarding following 9/11 were for very short periods of time and involved cellophane or a cloth placed over the mouth and nose so that no water entered the terrorist's lungs, nose, or mouth. There was never any possibility, much less an imminent threat, of drowning. Under the Senate's standard discussed in the text, there was no "prolonged mental harm" resulting from such causes as "the intentional infliction or threatened infliction of severe physical pain or suffering or the threat of imminent death."

672 "General Hayden's Remarks at the Council on Foreign Relations, Transcript of Remarks by Central Intelligence Agency Director Gen. Michael V. Hayden" at the Council on Foreign Relations (September 7, 2007). https://www.cia.gov/news-information/speeches-testimony/2007/general-haydens-remarks-at-the-council-on-foreign-relations.html

673 Congressional Record (Senate), Page S10243-S10274 (September 27, 2006). http://fas.org/irp/congress/2006_cr/s092706.html

674 House Report 111–189 - Resolution Of Inquiry Requesting That The President And Directing That The Attorney General Transmit To The House Of Representatives All Information In Their Possession Relating To Specific Communications Regarding Detainees And Foreign Persons Suspected Of Terrorism. http://www.fas.org/irp/congress/2009_rpt/hrpt111–189.html

675 "UN Special Rapporteur on Torture Speaks at Columbia Law School" Human Rights Institute (October 28, 2008). http://www.law.columbia.edu/media_inquiries/news_events/2008/october2008/nowak

676 "Gitmo closure: A welcome decision, but late" By Donna Abu-Nasr, op. cit.

677 Brief Of Amicus Curiae United Nations High Commissioner For Human Rights In Support Of Petitioners Lakhdar Boumediene, Et Al. to the US Supreme Court (August 24, 2007). http://ccrjustice.org/files/Brief%200f%20Amicus%20Curiae%20United%20Nations%20High%20Commissioner%20for%20Human%20Rights%20In%20Support%200f%20Petitioners.pdf?phpMyAdmin=563c49a5adf3t4ddbf89b

678 Ibid. at p. 3.

679 http://www.fas.org/irp/congress/2009_rpt/hrpt111–189.html, op. cit.

680 "Ruthless yet Humane - Why Obama cited Churchill on torture." By Christopher Hitchens, Slate (May 4, 2009).

681 "Winston Churchill On Islamism" By Adrian Morgan, Islam Watch (April 10, 2007). http://www.islam-watch.org/AdrianMorgan/Winston-Churchill-Islamism.htm

682 Ibid.

683 Ibid.

684 "Winston Churchill and the Sinews of Peace Address: The Sinews Of Peace" (March 5, 1946).

685 Remarks of President Barack Obama to the United Nations General Assembly (September 23, 2009). http://www.america.gov/st/texttrans-english/2009/September/20090923110705eaifas0.3711664.html

686 "Analysis-Struggling at home, Obama to get warm UN welcome" By Louis Charbonneau, Reuters (September 19, 2009). http://alertnet.org/thenews/newsdesk/N18262277.htm

687 "US, Israel on collision course over settlements" By Matt Spetalnick, Reuters (September 4, 2009). http://www.newsdaily.com/stories/tre5831e1-us-palestinians-israel/

688 "UN Fact Finding Mission finds strong evidence of war crimes and crimes against humanity committed during the Gaza conflict; calls for end to impunity," United Nations Press Release (September 15, 2009). http://www.unhchr.ch/huricane/huricane.nsf/view01/9B63490FFCBE44E5C12576320 04EA67B?opendocument

689 "Double Standard Watch: Goldstone investigation undercuts human rights," Posted by Alan M. Dershowitz, Jerusalem Post (September 17, 2009). http://cgis.jpost.com/Blogs/dershowitz/entry/goldstone_investigation_undercuts_human_rights?

690 Ibid.

691 Ibid.

692 Remarks by Ambassador Susan E. Rice, US Permanent Representative to the United Nations, on Somalia, the Middle East and the 2009 H1N1 influenza pandemic, at the Security Council Stakeout (September 17, 2009). http://usun.state.gov/briefing/statements/2009/september/129303.htm

693 Ibid.

694 Statement of Ms. Navanethem Pillay United Nations High Commissioner for Human Rights at the 12th session of the Human Rights Council (September 15, 2009). http://www.unhchr.ch/huricane/huricane.nsf/view01/2DD 5A4BD46C13CEFC1257631002D5B6B?opendocument

695 "U.N. Human Rights Council bars Honduras ambassador," Reuters (September 15, 2009). http://uk.reuters.com/article/idUKLF403533

696 "US denies Honduras' Micheletti visa," Al Jazeera (September 13, 2009). http://english.aljazeera.net/news/americas/2009/09/2009912212840716902.html

697 "US Would Consider A New Iranian Nuclear Proposal" By David Gollust, State Department, Voice of America (September 2, 2009). http://www.voanews.com/english/2009-09-01-voa20.cfm

698 "Mahmoud Ahmadinejad's renewed attack on Israel hastens walkout" By Ewen MacAskill, The Guardian, (September 24, 2009). http://www.guardian.co.uk/world/2009/sep/24/mahmoud-ahmadinejad-un-speech-criticised

699 Ibid.

700 "UN Secretary-General Ban Ki-moon congratulated and invited Ahmadinejad to UN assembly on Sept. 22," Translated by Payvand.com from Mehr News Agency Persian service (August 12, 2009). http://www.payvand.com/news/09/aug/1098.html

"Ahmadinejad Plans U.N. Visit" By Thomas Erdbrink, Washinton Post (September 1, 2009).

701 "UN Secretary-General Ban Ki-moon congratulated and invited Ahmadinejad," Mehr News Agency Persian service, op. cit.

702 Daily Press Briefing by the Offices of the Spokesperson for the Secretary-General (September 25, 2009). http://www.un.org/News/briefings/docs/2009/db090925.doc.htm

703 UN Secretary General Ban Ki-Moon Press Conference (September 17, 2009). http://www.un.org/apps/sg/offthecuff.asp

704 Ibid.

705 State Department Daily Press Briefing (September 14, 2009). http://www.state.gov/r/pa/prs/dpb/2009/sept/129185.htm

706 "Obama Failed Iran: Leading Iranian Dissident 'I'm Disappointed in President Obama'", posted on Atlas Shrugs (September 16, 2009). http://atlasshrugs2000.typepad.com/atlas_shrugs/2009/09/obama-failed-iran-leading-iranian-dissident-im-disappointed-in-president-obama.html

707 "Iran counters U.N. on uranium plan" By Glenn Kessler and Thomas Erdbrink, Washington Post (October 30, 2009).

708 "Obama calls for 'world without' nukes" By Jonathan Martin and David S. Cloud, Politico (April 5, 2009). http://www.politico.com/news/stories/0409/20901.html

709 "President Truman's diary regarding June 18, 1945 meeting" from Truman Library Web site, http://www.trumanlibrary.org/whistlestop/study_collections/bomb/large/documents/fulltext.php?fulltextid=10

710 "Chronology regarding Truman and the A-bomb from August 2–10, 1945," from Truman Library Web site http://trumanlibrary.org/whistlestop/study_collections/bomb/large/documents/fulltext.php?fulltextid=21

711 "Another spring, another step forward in Prague ..." By David Rothkopf, The New ForeignPolicy.com (April 6, 2009). http://rothkopf.foreignpolicy.com/posts/2009/04/06/another_spring_another_step_forward_in_prague

712 "Politics: Obama to Bolster Nuclear Disarmament at U.N." By Thalif Deen, IPS (August 12, 2009). http://ipsnews.net/news.asp?idnews=48056

713 Remarks by Ambassador Susan E. Rice, outlining the Security Council's September Program of Work, in the UN Press Briefing Room (September 2, 2009). http://usun.state.gov/briefing/statements/2009/september/128596.htm

714 Ibid.

715 "Security Council calls for world free of nuclear weapons during historic summit," UN News Centre (September 24, 2009). http://www.un.org/apps/news/story.asp?NewsID=32223&Cr=disarmament&Cr1=
   Remarks by President Obama at the United Nations Security Council Summit on Nuclear Non-Proliferation and Nuclear Disarmament (September 24, 2009).

716 "Sarkozy Mocks Obama at UN Security Council: Hello, Big Media?" By Maura Flynn, Big Government (September 25, 2009). http://biggovernment.com/2009/09/25/sarkozy-mocks-obama-at-un-security-council-hello-big-media/#more-8762

717 "RPT-US drafts UN resolution urging nuclear disarmament" By Louis Charbonneau, Reuters (September 11, 2009). http://www.reuters.com/article/latestCrisis/idUSB731605

718 "Security Council calls for world free of nuclear weapons during historic summit," UN News Centre, op. cit.

719 Security Council resolution 1887 (2009) [on nuclear non-proliferation and nuclear disarmament]. http://www.unhcr.org/refworld/docid/4abcd4792.html

720 "Bush Calls on UN to Curb WMD Proliferation, The 'greatest threat before humanity today.'" By Robert Longley, Transcript of Bush's Radio Address as posted on About.com (February 14, 2004). http://usgovinfo.about.com/cs/thepresident/a/radi0021404.htm

721 "Obama's UN Gambit: King of the Universe and the Polls" By Anne Bayefsky, National Review (September 5, 2009). http://article.nationalreview.com/?q=MWNkMWViY2YyZjU50TY5ZDcyNDQ1MzIwY2NkNWUyOTU=

722 "'Global disarmament cannot be postponed any longer,' Ban says," UN News Centre (July 31, 2009). http://www.un.org/apps/news/story.asp?NewsID=31648&Cr=nuclear+disarmament&Cr1

723 "Renewed Multilateral Cooperation Needed to Address 'Unacceptable' Situation, Disarmament Commission Told, General Assembly DC/3062" (April 9, 2007). http://www.un.org/News/Press/docs/2007/dc3062.doc.htm

724 Ibid.

725 Remarks of President Obama to the United Nations General Assembly (September 23, 2009). http://www.america.gov/st/texttrans-english/2009/September/20090923110705eaifas0.3711664.html

726 Ibid.

727 "Ros-Lehtinen Comments on Reports of IAEA Cover-up of Iranian Nuclear Activities," Office of the ranking Republican member of the House Foreign Services Committee press release (August 19, 2009). http://foreignaffairs. republicans.house.gov/apps/list/press/foreignaffairs_rep/081909IAEAiran. shtml

728 Ibid.

729 http://newcitizenship.blogspot.com/2008/01/mohamed-elbaradei-useful-idiot-or.html

730 Ibid.

731 Barack Obama's speech in Cairo, New York Times (June 4, 2009). http:// www.nytimes.com/2009/06/04/us/politics/040bama.text.html?_r=1

732 "US and Allies Press Iran Over Nuclear Plant 'Deception'" By David E. Sanger and William J. Broad, New York Times (September 26, 2009).

733 "Obama's UN Gambit: King of the Universe and the Polls" By Anne Bayefsky, op. cit.

Chapter Twelve

734 "Obama's Prize, Wilson's Legacy" By John Milton Cooper, New York Times (October 11, 2009).

735 "AP Newsbreak: Nobel jury defends Obama decision" By Ian Macdougall and Karl Ritter, CBS News (October 13, 2009). http://www.cbsnews.com/ stories/2009/10/13/ap/world/main5381672.shtml

736 http://www.whitehouse.gov/the_press_office/remarks-by-the-president-to-the-united-nations-general-assembly/

737 EyeontheUN Web site, http://www.eyeontheun.org/facts.asp?1=1&p=16

738 http://www.whitehouse.gov/the_press_office/remarks-by-the-president-to-the-united-nations-general-assembly/

739 Declaration of Independence (July 4, 1776). http://www.archives.gov/exhibits/charters/declaration_transcript.html

740 Washington's Farewell Address (1796). http://avalon.law.yale.edu/18th_century/washing.asp

741 "Obama Says US Could Be Seen as a Muslim Country, Too" By Jeff Zeleny, New York Times (June 2, 2009). http://thecaucus.blogs.nytimes.com/2009/06/02/obama-signals-themes-of-mideast-speech/?hp

742 "US deficit hits record $1.42 trillion," Associated Press (October 16, 2009). http://www.suntimes.com/news/nation/1829297,us-deficit-record-trillion0101609.article

743 Hamdan v. Rumsfeld, 548 US 557 (2006) and Boumediene v. Bush, 553 US ___ (2008).

744 US Internal Revenue Code, 26 USC. Section 501(c)(3).

745 http://www.newsmax.com/headlines/gingrich_2010_palin/2009/11/23/289975.html?s=al&promo_code=91D8-1

746 "The Case for a Federalism Amendment - How the Tea Partiers can make Washington pay attention" By Randy E. Barnett, Wall Street Journal (April 23, 2009). http://online.wsj.com/article/SB124044199838345461.html

747 Ibid.

748 "Dangers of a Constitutional Convention" By Larry Greenley, New American (June 23, 2009). http://www.thenewamerican.com/index.php/usnews/constitution/1241 See also http://oregonvotes.org/nov596/voters.guide/MEASURES/MEAS48/M48AO.HTM

749 The Gettysburg Address, Gettysburg, Pennsylvania (November 19, 1863).